I

MAINE POLITICS AND GOVERNMENT, SECOND EDITION

*Politics and Governments
of the American States*

Founding Editor

Daniel J. Elazar

Published by the University of
Nebraska Press in association
with the Center for the Study
of Federalism at the Robert B.
and Helen S. Meyner Center
for the Study of State and Local
Government, Lafayette College

KENNETH T. PALMER, G. THOMAS TAYLOR,
MARCUS A. LIBRIZZI, AND JEAN E. LAVIGNE

Maine Politics and Government

SECOND EDITION

UNIVERSITY OF NEBRASKA PRESS
LINCOLN AND LONDON

Chapter 5, "The Constitutional Tradition," is
a revision of Kenneth Palmer and Marcus A.
LiBrizzi, "Development of the Maine Constitution: The Long Tradition, 1819–1988," *Maine
Historical Society Quarterly* 28 (Winter 1988–
89):126–45, and is published here by permission
of the Maine Historical Society.

Chapter 15 is a revision of Kenneth T. Palmer
and Edward B. Laverty, "Maine Documents and
Sources," NEWS for Teachers of Political Science
34 (Summer 1982):17–19, and is published here
by permission of the American Political Science
Association.

Library of Congress Cataloging-in-Publication
Data
Maine politics and government /
Kenneth T. Palmer . . . [et al.].—2nd ed.
p.   cm.—(Politics and governments of the
American states)
Prev. ed. entered under: Palmer, Kenneth T.
Includes bibliographical references and index.
ISBN 978-0-8032-8785-3 (pbk.: alk. paper)
1. Maine—Politics and government. 2. Local
government—Maine. I. Palmer, Kenneth T.
II. Palmer, Kenneth T. Maine politics & govern-
ment.
JK2816.P35   2009
320.4741—dc22
2009022515

Set in Times by Bob Reitz.
Designed by Mikah Tacha.

CONTENTS

TABLES AND MAPS

TABLES

MAPS

Authors' Preface to Second Edition

The authors wish to thank several persons who assisted us with the second edition of the book. We especially appreciate the work of Cindy D'Angelo, who guided the technical preparation of the manuscript. Several persons in Maine government provided assistance to specific areas: Lynn Randall, formerly head librarian of Maine's law and legislative reference library, helped us locate research materials; Jane Lincoln, chief of staff to Gov. John Baldacci, described the work of the executive branch; Daniel Wathen, former Chief Justice of the Maine Supreme Judicial Court, discussed recent developments in the Maine courts; and Michael Johnson, communications director for the majority party in the Maine Senate, provided insights on the legislative process.

Peter Crichton, Cumberland County Administrator, and environmentalist Sally Jacobs were both very helpful in reviewing parts of our manuscript. Research assistants Debbie Ellingwood and Ken Savary (University of Maine) and Nate Walton (Bates College) were helpful in assisting the authors during this four-year project.

Additionally, several persons listed on the preface to the first edition also aided us in this version, and we are pleased to thank them again for their assistance.

Authors' Preface to First Edition

This volume seeks to provide a systematic overview of Maine politics and government. The emphasis is on primary themes that seem to be reflected in the state's political life. In some ways, Maine is best known for accomplishments remote from the realm of government and politics: its marvelous scenery, its quaint villages, and its native population about whom a substantial folklore has evolved over the years. But government has always been important in the Pine Tree State. We try to show government's significance in transmitting the values of the state's political culture into the work-a-day world of the political system. Accordingly, we spend some time on the evolution of Maine politics as a basis for exploring the institutions and policies of the present.

We are indebted to many people who contributed in important ways to the production of the book. Daniel J. Elazar provided the initial direction, and showed us how we could improve the first draft of the manuscript. John Kincaid reviewed the material as it neared completion and provided much helpful editorial assistance. John N. Diamond, former majority leader of the Maine House of Representatives, read the manuscript from the vantage point of a political practitioner and gave us useful suggestions as well as alerting us to potential errors. In carrying out the research, we had valuable help from several University of Maine students, including Michael Donovan, Paula Ashton, Steven York, Angela Vigue, Todd Jarrell, Andrew Robinson, Connie Massingill, Darlene Shores, Patrick Maxcy, and Danielle Tetreau. Muriel Sanford of the Special Collections Department of the Fogler Library, University of Maine in Orono, and Laura Goss and Robert Michaud of the Maine State Law Library in Augusta were unfailingly helpful in guiding us to appropriate sources.

Several administrators, legislators, and faculty colleagues took time from their busy schedules to help us with specific problems and to read individual chapters. We are particularly grateful to Stephen M. Bost and N. Paul Gauvreau, members of the Maine Senate; to William Buker of the State Budget Office; to James Clair, Kevin Madigan, and John Wakefield of the Legislative Office of Fiscal and Program Review; to Sarah C. Tubbesing, executive director of the Legislative Council; to James Chute, chief clerk of the Maine Supreme Judicial Court; to Willis Lyford, press secretary to Gov. John. R. McKernan Jr.; to Robert Miller, former city solicitor for Bangor; and to Professors C. Stewart Doty, Richard W. Judd, and Eugene A. Mawhinney of the University of Maine. Finally, we give our special thanks to Julie A. O'Connor, Eva M. McLaughlin, and June W. Kittridge, who know much more about computers than the authors and who provided fine technical assistance in preparing the manuscript.

MAINE POLITICS AND GOVERNMENT, SECOND EDITION

CHAPTER ONE

State of the State

Significant changes have taken place in Maine during the past two decades. Its population and economy have become much more diversified, and its public policies far more complex. The state government is rapidly becoming professionalized, a process that is contributing to a growing centralization of state functions. Despite these alterations, the political attitudes of Maine's people show a remarkable degree of stability. As this chapter will illustrate, some essential traits of Maine politics and government are being confirmed even as they are being challenged.

CURRENT TENSIONS

Change has accelerated so much in recent decades, especially when compared to the very slow development of Maine in the past, that it is sometimes easy to disregard the past and to focus only on contemporary events. To do this, however, would be to arrive at a distorted picture of the present. Maine's past is a vital part of its present. The state's constitution testifies to this fact. Not only does Maine operate under its original 1819 constitution, but the many amendments added over the years have largely maintained the original constitutional structure while making it more relevant to changing circumstances. The past is also helpful in understanding current events when they seem to diverge from tradition. Recently, Maine has been challenged by tension between its different regions. This phenomenon has deeper consequences in Maine than it might in another state because Maine has long enjoyed politics based on consensus.

Maine's political heritage originated in town meeting–style politics that still exists, and that underscores the central role of local politics in Maine's history. The town-meeting tradition has helped foster a strong impression of the state as a community of like-minded individuals. This social and political unity has been threatened by uneven economic development in the state. When Joseph Brennan was governor (1979–87), the State Planning Office spoke of "two Maines" to explain the state's changing conditions. The idea was that the state has two key regions: a southern region undergoing rapid urbanization and a northern region largely bypassed by development. It is a fair estimate that the idea repulsed most Maine politicians, especially those who aspired to the governorship. Every Maine chief executive who followed Brennan (John McKernan, 1987–95, Angus King 1995–2003, and John Baldacci, 2003–) explicitly rejected the "two Maines" notion. In office, each man tried to fashion policies to diminish economic disparities among the state's regions. The objection the "two Maines" idea presents is its challenge to the state's historic cultural and political consensus. The view that there are now different "Maines" presupposes the idea that there was once only one.

GOVERNMENT PROFESSIONALISM

If state development is creating fragmentation, it is also producing new forms of political coordination and unification. A growing trend of state centralization exists, even while local governments retain much autonomy. The rather sudden appearance of a potent state bureaucracy owes its existence to many factors, including the rise of the Democratic Party, innovative social policies, and the availability of progressive revenue sources. Another factor is diversification in the state's economy, population, and intergovernmental relations. The state government is no longer dominated by a few powerful economic interest groups, as it was in the past. Instead, many different coalitions, such as those representing women, workers, and the environment, are influential. Maine has developed some of the most generous social programs in the country. A strong state government is necessary to implement these programs because citizens are sparsely scattered over a large terrain.

The growth of bureaucracy poses a special challenge to the state's political heritage. Although professionalization of government is required by the current complexity of issues, it conflicts with the participatory politics of the town meeting. That tradition is premised on citizen involvement in government, and the idea that government should always be accessible. The state's citizen legislature, composed mostly of amateur legislators, has been a cherished symbol of Maine politics. A major clash between the two values occurred in 1993, when state voters overwhelmingly endorsed a proposal placing term limits on Maine legislators. After more than two decades of becoming a more professional body with long-serving leaders and an enhanced staff, the legislature provoked the ire of its citizens, who decided to restore the value of participation. Similar tensions exist in the state judiciary where centralization and professionalization have already attenuated the close relations that citizens once had with their courts. Citizen judges have become a thing of the past.

Maine politicians are struggling to resist some of these trends. Members of the state legislature and the congressional delegation devote a substantial portion of their time to one-on-one relations with their constituents, which requires extensive travel throughout the state. Perhaps the strongest force keeping citizens in touch with their government is a commonality of values in Maine. Public officials and citizens tend to agree on most public questions. The legislature generally seems to enact the wishes of the citizenry, which brings about a high degree of congruence between public opinion and public policy.[1]

DIVERSITY AND MODERATION

Maine's style is generally moderate in political discussions and in governmental arrangements. Unlike neighboring New Hampshire, which is very conservative and decentralized in its governmental operations, and Vermont, which is quite centralized and liberal, Maine tends to stay in the middle of the road. Personalities of candidates and specific issues have always received more attention during elections in Maine than ideology. Candidates, even incumbents, who are identified with the ideological left or right have been consistently defeated. This kind of moderation seems to extend the town-meeting qualities of compromise and consensus-building to state politics.

Until recently, Maine's tendency to settle difficult issues through compromise permitted the state government to work effectively even though, during much of the post–World War II era, one party had control of the governorship and the other party held majorities in the legislature. In the 1991 legislative session, however, a major shortfall in revenues created a budget crisis in Augusta that received national attention. Republican governor John McKernan and the Democratic legislature could not come to terms on a 1991–93 budget (the passage of which the governor insisted on linking to reform of the workmen's compensation system) until mid-July, more than two weeks into the new fiscal year. The consequence was that during that period, most state services were sharply curtailed and most state workers were laid off. The persistence of serious financial problems is likely to continue to affect the moderate tendencies of state government.

Likewise, recent demographic changes have confirmed the state's participatory culture, even as they challenge it. New voices are heard in state and local politics from the in-migrants from southern New England and other states. Even more important, the rise of a two-party system in Maine helped widen the political forum. In keeping with the state's governmental emphasis on representation and shared values, Maine's most prominent politicians reflect the new demographic diversity. In the past, political leadership was dominated by Protestant, Republican, upper-class males. In 1948 Margaret Chase Smith, who came from modest origins, defeated former governors Horace Hildreth and Sumner Sewall in the primary for the Republican nomination for the U.S. Senate. In 1954 Democrat Edmund S. Muskie, of Polish immigrant parentage, overcame a Republican Party that had ruled for a century, and was elected governor.

Maine's present congressional delegation reflects a broadly representative background compared to earlier decades. For example, the state's senior U.S. senator, Olympia J. Snow (nee Bouchles), is one of a handful of members of Congress of Greek ancestry and was the second woman elected to Congress from Maine when she ran for the House of Representatives in 1978 (she was elected to the Senate in 1994). Michael Michaud, who became Maine's Second District representative (northern part of the state) in 2003, is one of the few blue collar workers serving in the U.S. House. He was a long-time employee of the Great Northern Paper Company in Millinocket. Senator Susan Collins, the state's junior senator, is from a family long involved in public service. Her parents both served terms as mayors of Caribou (near the Canadian border), and her uncle was a justice on the Maine Supreme Judicial Court. One leading example of the greater diversity of Maine's politicians is the increase in the numbers of women in public office. Maine is one of only two states whose two U.S. Senators are women. From the 1940s to the late 1990s, the state legislature changed from having almost no women to one of the top five legislatures in the country in its portion of women members.[2] Both chambers have elected women presiding officers in recent years.

While social diversity has seemed to strengthen Maine's participatory culture, it has threatened it in other respects. Urbanization is altering the population distribution in the state and, consequently, is challenging some traditional political values. Maine's political culture evolved from very small communities where interests were shared and politics was conducted on a neighbor-like basis. Throughout its history, the state's patterns of

settlement have reinforced this form of politics. Population has been distributed among nearly five hundred small towns. Despite considerable growth,
in 2000 about two-thirds of Maine's population resided in towns having
fewer than 10,000 persons. Even the remaining one-third was scattered over
a relatively large number of communities; the combined population of the
state's three largest cities—Portland, Lewiston, and Bangor—made up just
slightly over 10 percent of the state's total population in 2000. However, as
Maine experiences urbanization, the town-meeting tradition of governance
becomes harder to maintain. In larger communities, town-meeting governance has given way to city councils and career politicians, whose relations
with citizens have become more formalized, and sometimes even distant.

A PLACE APART

Maine's identity has always been connected to its geographic separateness.
On a map of the United States, its relative isolation is apparent. Maine is the
only continental state to border on only one other state (New Hampshire).
Geographic isolation was intensified after the Civil War when a long period of economic decline set in. Much as occurred in Appalachia, Maine's
poverty helped isolate the state from the national mainstream. As part of
rural New England, Maine was part of "the first agricultural region to grow
old."[3] The sense of separateness has shaped the state's political culture in
important ways. By identifying with the distinctiveness of their state, Mainers have sometimes been able to transcend demographic, economic, and
partisan barriers, and to see their state as an autonomous community. Current anxiety over regional divisions in the state can be partly attributed to
the importance that Maine has long placed on its cultural and political unity.
That sense of oneness, in turn, has been greatly reinforced by the idea that
the state is "a place apart."

Where does a state's distinctiveness come from? Sociologist Wendy Griswold believes three factors or situations are involved.[4] One is that the state
is on the national periphery. Regional identity is strongest when an area
sees itself as separate from, or even in opposition to, the national culture.
Additionally, the state is widely visited by well-educated tourists, who support local crafts, native cuisine, and artists. A third factor is that the state
has what Griswold calls "a strong book culture," meaning the area fosters
an extensive literature that expresses its unique qualities. Maine seems to fit
all three situations. It is on the geographical periphery of the country, but it
is still close to major population centers in the northeastern United States, as
well as many leading education institutions. Its tourists generally have both

education and a reasonable amount of money to spend. Maine's strong book culture (the state ranks third in library book volume per capita) has been reinforced by the state's recent popularity as a setting for many films.

Efforts to preserve the state's distinctiveness are noticeable in the actions of its public officials, as evidenced by their efforts to maintain close ties with citizens. Another example is the state's generous social programs, which reflect a communitarian attitude of "taking care of one's own." A third example is the great concern that Maine shows toward the protection of its natural environment. More than three-quarters of the respondents in one poll agreed that "the natural beauty of Maine should be preserved even if it means spending more public money or interfering with private investment decisions."[5]

Although New England was settled early, Maine has always remained something of a frontier. It has considered itself rather different from the rest of New England for this reason. The state has a landmass nearly equal to that of the remaining New England states. Even today, almost 90 percent of the land is wooded. Although Maine's frontier character contributes to the state's sense of separateness, in another sense that quality seems to connect the state to the rest of the country. The American frontier has played an important role in shaping the nation's values, especially the ideas of optimism and the possibilities of social betterment. The twentieth century has witnessed the drastic exploitation of the natural environment through industrialization and urbanization. That process, in turn, has given rise to a growing awareness that the natural environment must be protected. Although the challenges that Maine faces are unique, they also represent the same dilemma facing all American states: the need to preserve what is cherished in an age of rapid change.

That problem is central in this study of Maine politics and government. We describe the various institutions and processes that comprise the way Maine's citizens are governed. But the primary aim is not to provide extensive detail. Instead, our concern is to explore the role of government in a period that may be a watershed in state affairs. We are interested in how some traditional and important features of Maine—citizen government, political moderation, and a sense of separateness—are faring under challenges from some newer factors: government professionalization, economic development, population mobility, and budgetary crises. While the focus is on Maine, we keep in mind that similar clashes can be found in most other states. Indeed, this exploration of Maine politics may give some support to the saying that "as Maine goes, so goes the nation."

CHAPTER TWO

Maine's Political Culture: The New England Frontier

Many of Maine's most distinctive features suggest a form of separateness. These include its geographic location, its decades of economic decline at a time of national growth, and its place as a northeastern frontier. Yet culturally, Maine has much in common with its New England neighbors. In fact, the "Downeast Yankee" is often said to be the embodiment of old New England. A tension has always existed in the state between belonging and not belonging. Maine's political culture has originated and developed out of this tension. In some ways, the state's culture is unique; in others, it is representative of the political culture of its region.

A political culture is an orientation that a large number of people share toward politics. It includes the expectations citizens have of their government, and of their own involvement with that government. Geography, economy, and patterns of settlement are some of the major elements that shape a political culture. Daniel J. Elazar has identified three basic types of political culture in the American states: the moralistic, the traditionalistic, and the individualistic.[1]

Although the moralistic culture originated in the Puritan towns of New England, it should not be associated primarily with ethics. The moralistic culture is community-oriented. It stresses the idea of the state as a commonwealth, and the government as citizen-run. The traditionalistic culture, unlike the moralistic, is little concerned with popular participation. Associated with parts of the South, the traditionalistic culture tends to accept a self-perpetuating political elite, often drawn from a small number of families. The individualistic culture, on the other hand, grows out of an urban setting. It sees politics almost as a form of business run by professionals. As development continues in Maine, the individualistic culture may become more widespread. Right now, the state strongly retains its moralistic political culture. Maine shares this culture with New Hampshire and Vermont, as well as with other states in the northern parts of the United States, but Maine has some special variations, which are products of its history.

SETTLEMENT, 1700–1820

Separateness marked Maine in the early colonial period because it was an outpost between two historic enemies, the French and the English. Maine also was isolated from the rest of the Massachusetts Bay Colony because of the Indian strength present in the region. Unlike the Native Americans in the southern parts of the Massachusetts Bay Colony, Maine Native Americans (Abenakis and Etchemins, members of the Algonquin nation) were not as quickly hit by plagues. Disease wiped out whole tribes in southern Massachusetts and made settlement for Puritans around Boston much easier, both politically and economically, than it was beyond the Kennebec River in central Maine.

Even if they were not notorious for their military prowess, Maine's Native Americans could successfully attack the English townships scattered throughout the remote territory. Between 1675 and 1760 more than one thousand English settlers were killed and hundreds more captured.[2] Early on, this constant threat reinforced the importance of the local community—an importance that persists in present-day Maine. Localities depended on themselves for protection, rather than on the colonial government in Boston. The houses still huddled together in the oldest coastal towns attest both to communities' insecurity and to their self-reliance.

The hostility of the Maine Native Americans was sometimes incited by the French during the seventy-year period of the French and Indian Wars, which ended in 1759, the year England gained control of Quebec. By this time, sickness and warfare had reduced the many Indian tribes to two, the Penobscots and Passamaquoddies, which signed treaties with the Commonwealth of Massachusetts (treaties that Maine assumed when it became a state). With peace after 1759, both the English population and its prosperity rose dramatically. From 1780 to 1790 the year of the first U.S. census, Maine's population doubled from 50,000 to 97,000. By the end of the century, the population exceeded 150,000.

Apart from renewing English prejudices—and, possibly, naming the state after a province in France—the French did not extend great influence over colonial Maine at the time. Creating permanent settlements was usually not the primary goal of most coureurs de bois (traders and trappers), missionaries, and explorers, whose families had often been left behind in Europe. The French who did attempt to settle the land had either emigrated during the chaos before 1759, or were later forcefully dispersed among the thirteen colonies and Europe, as were the French Acadians by Col. Charles Lawrence of Massachusetts in 1755.

Because wide-scale settlement occurred during the latter part of the eighteenth century, the primary goal for most settlers was to carve out a livelihood, not to escape religious intolerance like their Puritan forebears. Pragmatism, therefore, had as much a basis in the settlement of Maine as idealism had in Massachusetts, in which Maine had been a district. The moralistic, participatory culture inherited by Maine was confirmed among its Yankees because settlement occurred heavily during the years of the American Revolution, and because statehood came in 1820 at a time of growing democratization. By removing voting restrictions against Catholics and Jews, Maine's constitution provided more representation than the 1780 Massachusetts Constitution, much of which Maine otherwise copied wholesale into its own charter.

The moralistic political culture was also reinforced by the rapid establishment of agriculture, which came to define the character of the state and its people. Reliance on the weather, especially in a climate as harsh and unpredictable as Maine's, placed great cultural importance on the relationship between the individual and his or her community. The town meeting—the staple of the moralistic culture—encourages a similar relationship. An individual freely participates, but usually in ways geared toward reaching agreements with fellow participants. The importance of the town and its political forum was established by the distribution of population over a large number of small communities. Those towns that became cities, such as Portland and Bangor, never had populations large enough to dominate the state.

Instead of being diminished, Maine's frontier character was enhanced by settlement. Not only was the state settled later than the rest of New England, but it was settled in a manner similar to some western states. To encourage settlers, Massachusetts offered free one hundred-acre plots to out-of-staters willing to turn the wilderness into pastures or fields. When Maine finally gained statehood, it was during a time of westward expansion. In fact, Maine was formed under the Missouri Compromise, whereby the balance between free states and slave states was maintained by adding one of each (Maine and Missouri) to the Union. Frontierism makes an important contribution to the moralistic culture by reinforcing the relationship between the individual and the local community. However, the civic emphasis of the moralistic culture is sometimes compromised by a kind of frontier individualism. In isolated parts of Maine, there is still an attitude that people can—and sometimes will—do whatever they want on their own land.

STATEHOOD, 1820–60

A new kind of separateness came to characterize Maine during the first years of statehood, summed up in one historian's statement that "Maine was being singled out as a place with a marvelous destiny, a place clearly of the future."[3] The attractiveness of Maine was entwined with all the frontier had historically held for America—the promise of economic and social progress. In the mid-1800s, Gov. Joshua Chamberlain told the Maine Legislature that the state reminded him "more of the western states than the rest of New England . . . [she has] virgin soil, undeveloped powers, vast forests, and vigorous men."[4]

The state's resources were being developed at a spectacular rate. Maine dominated national ship construction, which was not surprising considering the state's vast forests and 3,500 miles of coastline. By 1820 Bangor had become the world's largest lumber-shipping port. Quarrying and ice harvesting were expanding, along with the textile mills that were beginning to spread into the state from Massachusetts. The large-scale construction of railroads in the 1840s connected Maine's industries to a national market, while the construction of dams on several Maine rivers rendered them suitable for mill sites. Population growth responded to the prosperity, doubling to 300,000 from 1800 to 1820, the year of statehood, and doubling again to 600,000 by 1860.

The moralistic, participatory culture of Maine seems to have contributed to this success. Citizens strove to realize their vision of a government responsible for the direction of its society. In 1830 ethical opposition to state lotteries led to their discontinuation. The harnessing of politics to social reform was sometimes a response to the environment. Maine could seem like a kind of Wild West in the middle of pristine New England. It has been said of the state that "'there was little law or respect for law' in the early days; 'rum was the common beverage, and spirits were consumed on all occasions.'"[5] Exchange Street in Bangor was the setting for fabled brawls between sailors and log drivers.

In response to the problems associated with alcohol, the state was home to the world's first Total Abstinence Society. During the next decades, many more temperance groups sprung into existence.[6] These were effectively organized on a statewide basis by Neal Dow, a Portland businessman. In 1851 the temperance movement had enough power to enact a prohibition law widely referred to as the "Maine Law" because it was copied by many other states. This law, which would later become an amendment to the Maine Constitution, was enforced until the mid-1930s when prohibition ended nationally.

The state's occasional frontier lawlessness did not always bring about ethical responses from representatives of the moralistic culture. The arrival of the Irish during this period, following the 1842 potato blight in Ireland, incited the natives to occasional acts of violence. One way to understand these acts is to see them as negative extremes of the state's culture. The town-meeting philosophy of consensus and participation, and the desire to shape the direction of society were all present, but in perverted forms. The basis of hostility was often economic, with natives believing that immigrants were flooding the job market and lowering wages. However, natives also seemed to fear their identity would be jeopardized by large-scale immigration. Natives objected to the Catholicism of the Irish more than anything else.

Maine's anti-Catholic violence paled in comparison with that of some other states, such as Massachusetts, New York, and Pennsylvania. Nonetheless, such demonstrations represented a severe compromise in the ideals of the state's political culture. In the 1850s, Catholic churches were burned in Lewiston and Bath. Ellsworth was the setting for a Bible controversy centering on public education. The Catholics, mostly Irish, resented the fact that their taxes supported a school system that required its students to read the Protestant Bible. When one citizen chose to educate his children himself and then billed the state for the costs, the Protestant majority in Ellsworth literally rose up in arms.[7] At one point, the local Catholic priest was tarred, feathered, and run out of town.[8]

The issue was finally settled by the Maine Supreme Judicial Court, which overrode all Catholic objections in a ruling that was fairly typical for the time.[9] For the most part, however, the state government was not openly nativist. The U.S. nativist political party, known as the Know-Nothing party (since it was originally a secret society) achieved statewide recognition in Maine only in 1854, when Anson Morrill ran successfully for the governorship on a fusion ticket of Maine Law and Know-Nothing parties. In nearby Massachusetts, the government was overrun by Know-Nothing politicians.

Any fears of the natives that their identity might be endangered proved unfounded. In general, the Irish assimilated rapidly into the state. The expanding economy easily accommodated them, and they were employed in large numbers to build canals and dams, and to work in the textile mills. Their experience with eviction in Ireland propelled many, even at great sacrifice, to become property owners. This, along with the fact that many served during the Civil War, earned the Irish in Maine social and political influence rather quickly. They began to aggressively enter politics and filled the ranks of the Democratic Party in Maine, as well as in other states where the party was more powerful. They also dominated the Catholic church hierarchy.

Because of immigration, as well as the dynamic economy, Maine's population grew more rapidly in the 1830–60 period than that of any other New England state. During this period, "Downeast" Washington County (the easternmost county in the United States) enjoyed a larger population than it would a century later.

TRANSITION, 1860–1900

After the Civil War, Maine experienced a more challenging form of separateness: economic and population decline. Major technological innovations rendered several key industries obsolete. The demand for wood was quickly surpassed by demands for iron, oil, and coal. Ships were operated by steam, not sails. While the shipyards at Bath would be able to make the transition, many others in the state were eventually abandoned. In growing numbers, farmers left the thin, rocky soil of New England for the rich lands opening up in the West, prompting grange leaders, such as D. H. Thing of Mount Vernon, to plead with young men to stick with farming in Maine.[10]

At first, it was not apparent that the state was drifting into economic backwaters. If the bounty of the fisheries had begun to decline, the hotels in Portland, Rockland, and Bar Harbor were reaping the benefits of an emerging tourist industry. Even if shipbuilding had taken a serious blow, the post–Civil War boom in textiles seemed to make up for this. The new industrialization lured a mass migration of French Canadians from Canada's St. Lawrence valley, which was undergoing an agrarian depression in the 1860s.

From 1865 until the turn of the century, thousands of French Canadians migrated to New England. Besides New Hampshire, Maine would come to have the highest percentage of first- and second-generation Franco-Americans, accounting for nearly one-sixth of the state's population.[11] The distribution of the immigrants was uneven, with some towns receiving virtually none, and others, such as Lewiston, becoming more than 80 percent Franco-American. In general, settlement of French Canadians was heaviest in the industrial centers, such as Auburn, Biddeford, Brunswick, Rumford, and Waterville, in addition to Lewiston. The Franco-Americans occupied the unskilled manufacturing positions which the Irish had held, as well as new positions created by the expanding textile industry.

Perhaps because the Franco-Americans kept to themselves and lived in the few urban centers, nativist reactions were mild compared to the past. The state was more settled at the time, and seems to have expressed its prejudices in its laws, rather than in lawlessness. In 1893 the Twenty-ninth

Amendment to the Maine Constitution was perceived as nativist by Franco-Americans. This measure required that voters be able to read the constitution in English as well as write their names. Already enrolled voters were exempt.

Assimilation was slower for Franco-Americans, who stood out from the general population until the 1960s. This was partly because of the language barrier, but also because of the close proximity to Canada, allowing old ties to continue. Another force was the nationalistic campaign known as *la survivance*. While dependent on French newspapers and societies, *la survivance* centered on the Catholic churches and their parochial schools, which until the 1960s actively preserved the cultural heritage through bilingual masses and curricula. The overall equation behind *la survivance* seems to have been a fusion of ethnic and religious norms, whereby a "loss of language meant a loss of faith, and a loss of faith meant a loss of identity."[12]

Perhaps another impediment to assimilation was that the political culture of the Franco-Americans differed from that of the Yankees and Irish. Coming from a highly conservative agricultural society in the St. Lawrence Valley, with antecedents in the feudal society of France, the Franco-Americans possessed what may be called a traditionalistic political culture. This culture accepts a political oligarchy drawn from a self-perpetuating elite, which in the case of the French-Canadians was the Catholic clergy. The lack of experience in political action that characterized the French Canadians of this period was perpetuated when the Catholic Church and the British government came to a "working agreement" after 1759. In return for religious freedom, the church prescribed submission to the British crown.[13]

Partly because of their political culture and partly because many considered their stay in the United States temporary, the Franco-Americans never used their numerical power to its full potential beyond local politics. Franco-Americans did not even consistently vote for Franco-Americans, as in the case of the 1956 congressional primary, when Franco-Americans voted for Yankee Frank M. Coffin over a Franco-American candidate.[14] The Irish dominance of the Catholic hierarchy in Maine early on instigated the only Franco-American statewide action. Beginning in the last decades of the nineteenth century, they fought for control over their own parishes.

Under the Catholic law known as "Corporation Sole," the bishop of Portland, a position that tended to be held by someone Irish, exercised almost complete control over all Catholic parishes in the state. This circumstance was particularly troublesome to the Franco-Americans because the Irish leaders actively fought for the assimilation of all Catholics, which was in direct opposition to *la survivance*. In 1908 the Franco-American Le Comite

Permanent de la Cause Nationale du Maine commissioned a private census of the state to prove their numerical superiority (and, hence, their right to greater influence in the diocese). A compromise in representation was eventually worked out through the creation of a bishop's advisory council.

Franco-American political power was felt more effectively and consistently in local government. In other states, such as Massachusetts, Franco-Americans sometimes avoided the Democratic Party principally because it was associated with the Irish. Democrats there also seemed to oppose Franco-American conservatism. The weakness of the Democratic Party in Maine, and the nativism among Maine Republicanism, helped impel the Franco-Americans to the Democratic Party in that state. A similar process took place in Vermont.[15] Communities in Maine with large Franco-American populations soon revealed the power of those groups in local elections. In Waterville, Lewiston, Biddeford, Sanford, and other manufacturing communities, Franco-Americans began consistently serving as mayors, city councilors, aldermen, and selectmen in the early twentieth century.

Growing out of an urban environment, Franco-American local politics was sometimes characterized by an individualistic culture. In this culture, politics tended to be seen as a form of business in which some corruption was considered inevitable. Lewiston, in particular, came to possess a Democratic machine.[16] Political scandals in the 1930s led voters to adopt a new city charter, but the machine continued in power. Perhaps, despite apparent differences, the traditionalistic culture of the Franco-Americans prepared them for the individualistic culture. Both cultures, at any rate, tend to take for granted a political elite.

If it had not been for Maine's immigrants, particularly its Franco-Americans, the state's population might have declined sharply after 1860. Instead, from 1860 to 1870, the state's population did drop slightly, by 1,364. Between 1870 and 1900 the population increased from 627,000 to only 694,000, while the population of the rest of the country was doubling. By 1900, some 93,000 persons living in Maine—14 percent of the state's population—were foreign born.[17]

ENTRENCHMENT, 1900–1960

With the onset of the twentieth century, Maine's separateness from an industrialized and urban society became increasingly more visible. For various reasons, native traits and attitudes seem to have been strengthened, sometimes even exaggerated, during this period, which in turn reinforced the state's aloofness. One factor was the cultural isolation produced by economic and population declines. In much the same way as occurred in Appalachia, Maine society began to seem inward-looking and even autonomous from the national mainstream.

Another factor seems to have been that social traits are products of many different forces. Pride, independence, and a sense of belonging to "a place apart," which were fostered by the state's one-time prosperity, were also supported by the frontier lifestyle that is still retained to some extent. No doubt defensiveness also played a part in the retention of these traits. One historian has written that a central theme in Maine history has been an "ambivalence—toward Boston, toward cities, toward the west, and toward governments."[18] This ambivalence, in turn, has been viewed as having contributed to "a sort of inferiority complex which manifests itself by bragging about itself in relation to others, [and] in attempting to find fault with others."[19]

The nativism that flared up for a last time during this period seems to support some of these ideas. The nineteenth century closed with a serious economic depression. At this time, the permanence of the Franco-American presence became unequivocal, and Yankee families who had not moved out of the mill towns earlier now took their cue. The rise of the pulp and paper industry (when pulp replaced rag) lured some new immigrants from southern and eastern Europe, who supplemented the steady inflow of Franco-Americans.

During the 1920s, Maine became a stronghold for the Ku Klux Klan, whose membership at its peak in 1924 was about 40,000—slightly more than 5 percent of the state's population.[20] The Klan's campaign to put Bibles back in schools, fill the Protestant churches, and replace corrupt politicians with "100 percent Americans" read much like a Know-Nothing Party platform from the 1840s. The Klan's supporters included rural farmers and prominent civic leaders, such as Owen Brewster, who would serve as governor and U.S. Senator. As in the 1840s, hostility was focused on Catholicism. For the Franco-Americans, as well as the Irish, Italians, and Poles, Catholicism was not only a church but an important foundation of group identity.

Although surface appearances might suggest otherwise, the 1900–1960 period was a time when Maine's population became more homogeneous. The static economy, and the isolation it imposed on the state, restricted change and gave the population a chance to develop a distinctive character. In the interval from 1900 to 1940, the population grew by only about 150,000. While agriculture was generally successful during this time, it declined as a way of life for many people as family farms were consolidated into larger commercial units. The rise of the pulp and paper industry coincided with the decline of textiles, as the South became the center of that industry. It seems to be a pattern in Maine that one major industry regularly replaces another. This allows the state to avoid a crisis, but it also prevents it from making substantial progress. The phenomenon has contributed to the seeming timelessness that has sometimes characterized the state and, in particular, this period.

With a static economy paired with the onset of the Great Depression, immigration into Maine during this period never occurred on the same scale as during earlier decades. Although Maine had enough advantages to attract some immigrants, the mid-Atlantic states, southern New England, and the western states possessed far more resources, and new settlements tended to grow in those areas. The Italians, Poles, Greeks, and Albanians who came to Maine, together with other nationalities, were numerically too small to significantly change the character of the state. Maine continues to be a state whose population is divided between a mostly Anglo-Saxon/Scotch-Irish native stock and a large French-Canadian minority.

Even as the Franco-Americans kept to themselves, there was a slow process of integration into the dominant Yankee culture. The majority of the Franco-Americans were becoming bilingual. Studies also have shown that they minimized their cultural differences with the Yankees, believing that language was the primary basis of differentiation.[21] Both groups shared a strong work ethic and valued civic responsibility. Despite their affiliation with the Democratic Party, Maine Franco-Americans were deeply conservative, especially on social issues. Each group also sought to preserve its society in the face of a materialistic, mainstream culture often perceived as antagonistic. Perhaps the most important factor binding the people of Maine was the sense of belonging to a place apart. Despite their demographic differences, citizens seemed united in perceiving a gulf between them and residents of other states. The state's sense of its separateness as a polity made its people Mainers in addition to being Yankees or Franco-Americans or Protestants or Catholics.

Toward the close of the 1900–1960 period, Maine's moderate style of politics, which continues to characterize the state, became more manifest. Governor John McKeman ascribed the moderation to the pragmatism of Maine people, although it undoubtedly grows from other causes, too, such as the cautiousness of a people who sometimes seem to have had the role of observers rather than participants in social, economic, and political trends in the United States.[22] Moderation has also been encouraged by social and political diversity.

Starting in the late 1950s, a two-party system of politics slowly evolved on a statewide basis. Many progressive policies, such as those concerning the environment, welfare, and education, began about this time. With Republicans and Democrats waging more competitive battles, issues were discussed more publicly. The governor and legislature had to seek compromises more often. Moderation became the practical expression of the state's moralistic political culture, which expects the consensus of the people to set the tenor of government.

DEVELOPMENT, 1960–2010

Maine's separateness has been challenged since the 1950s. Rapid development attests to the fact that Maine is no longer an outpost. Instead, people seek it out almost as they did in the very early days of statehood. Motorists traveling north on Interstate 95, shortly after they cross the bridge over the Piscataquis River, which separates Maine from New Hampshire, encounter a sign reading, "Maine: The Way Life Should Be." During the past five decades, the idea of Maine as a place where one can enjoy a slower and perhaps more traditional lifestyle than is possible in the metropolitan centers of the Northeast has attracted new residents. The changes of this period, propelled by a generally dynamic state economy, have done more than increase population statistics and alter the appearance of the land. The cultural unity of the state, including its moralistic orientation, has begun to be challenged by new and sometimes opposing forces.

For the Franco-Americans, Maine's modernization has encouraged greater assimilation. After nearly a century of *la survivance*, ethnicity broke down in less than a decade. This change was partly based on economic development. Service industries grew so rapidly that by the early 1970s, they were among the most important sources of employment. They included government and professional services as well as wholesale and retail trades. In cities such as Lewiston, many of the employees in the service industry were Franco-Americans who were forced to seek new employment when the textile mills shut down in the 1950s. This occupational change has been seen as contributing to the rapid assimilation of the Franco-Americans.[23]

Other factors also contributed. After World War II, the Franco-Americans developed a large middle class of their own. Under new economic conditions, many families left the tenement areas in the mill towns for residential districts, breaking up the ethnic communities.[24] New employment opportunities, a growth in the number of mixed marriages—associated with a growing middle class—and the decline of the parochial school system (which was part of a national trend during the 1960s) stimulated assimilation. In 1971 Lewiston elected a non-French mayor for the first time in forty years.

Despite their economic assimilation, Maine's Franco-Americans in the current decade have demonstrated a renewed interest in emphasizing their language and culture. Starting in 2002 the state legislature has held an annual Franco-American Day, with legislative business and the Pledge of Alliance recited in French. Lewiston has opened a new Franco-American Center. The French language, once discouraged, is taught in "reacquisition" classes in several parts of the state. A popular French immersion program operates in L'Ecole Francoise in the Town of South Freeport. Approximately five percent of Mainers speak French at home—the highest portion of any state.

At the same time Franco-Americans were receding as a distinctive ethnic group, Maine's Native Americans were consciously and politically differentiating themselves from the general population. As in the case of the Franco-Americans, however, the cultural change was in response to national and international trends emphasizing native heritages. Long in decline, the number of Maine Native Americans, estimated at 36,000 in 1615, had shrunk to about 7,000 in 2000.

During the 1970s, two Native American tribes—the Passamaquoddies and the Penobscots—filed suit against the state for the restitution of 12.5 million acres, which they alleged the state had taken from them illegally. Tribal consciousness coalesced in a new and assertive way during these proceedings. In the 1970 gubernatorial election, the Passamaquoddies gained publicity for their claims by their persistence in obtaining an opinion from each of the candidates prior to election and by bargaining their political support. Earlier that same year, a group of Native Americans in full tribal regalia went to Augusta and demanded the payment of livestock, produce, textiles, and silver as guaranteed in an old treaty assumed by Maine when it became a state. The most effective spotlight on their claims was the Maine Municipal Bond Bank's withdrawal of a $27 million bond because of uncertainty in property titles in over half the state. Eventually, in 1980, the federal government agreed to pay the two tribes more than $80 million.

Despite the land claims settlement, tensions have persisted between the tribes and the state government. As in many other states, Maine's Native Americans have pursued gambling ventures as a means of improving their economic condition. In Maine, those activities require the approval of the state legislature. In 2002 the legislature put to referendum a proposal supported by the Native Americans to construct a large casino in the town of Sanford, near the New Hampshire border, which proponents claimed would create 10,000 jobs in the relatively depressed area. After a hard-fought campaign, the proposal was defeated by a nearly 2 to 1 margin, though in the same referendum racino (slot-machine) gambling was authorized in a few areas of the state. The state has encouraged Native Americans to take advantage of the state's higher education facilities by providing scholarships for students who are members of a state or federally recognized tribe. About five hundred students take part in the program in the University of Maine system.

Demographically, Maine remains one of the least diverse of the American states. The 2000 census found that while one of three U.S. residents was non-white or Hispanic, only one Maine resident in 29 was, making the state the whitest in the country. A major cause of difference is that about half the national population growth in recent decades—and most of the immigration—has comprised persons entering the United States from nations in Asia and in Latin and South American. Located on the country's northeastern border, Maine has gained relatively little new population from those areas.

Nonetheless, some minorities have recently settled in the state, and have begun to affect its politics despite their small numbers. The leading example is the city of Lewiston, where approximately three thousand immigrants from Somalia have settled since 2000, composing about 10 percent of the city's population. The group had originally located in larger metropolitan areas, but discouraged by high rates of crime, moved to Maine. Despite some friction, the Somalias have generally gained acceptance. An estimated ten thousand refugees live in the Portland area, drawn from dozens of counties, mostly in Africa and Eastern Europe. Unemployment is a persistent problem among the new immigrants, usually due to a combination of their difficulty with English and a lack of sufficient education to compete for better-paying jobs. The state government has recently tried to address the concerns of minority communities. In 2007 Governor Baldacci named a task force to design a Diversity Employment and Business Resource Center to be located within the state university system. In another move, the state judiciary has issued guidelines—and has begun to train court clerks and judges—in determining the eligibility for court-appointed interpretation and translation services for individuals involved with court business.

Beginning in the 1960s, Maine reversed a century-long trend where more people left the state each year than entered.[25] The number of in-migrants now annually exceeds the total of out-migrants, a trend that has accelerated since 2000. The state's population grew slightly more than 4 percent in the 1990s, but between 2000 and 2005 it showed an annual increase of about 1 percent. The new growth moved Maine from 45th to 26th among the states in its level of population increase, the biggest jump of any state in 2000–2005. The preferred destinations of the new residents have been heavily in the two southwestern counties of York and Cumberland. Other counties bordering the state's long coastline (with the single exception of easternmost Washington County) have also witnessed major growth. Those seven counties increased their populations in the 1980s and 1990s at levels of between 40 and 90 percent. Newcomers have included business and professional people who still commute to workplaces in New Hampshire and eastern Massachusetts. The tighter link between southern Maine and the rest of New England was documented in the 2000 census, which placed several towns in York County in the Boston Metropolitan Statistical Area. All coastal counties have benefited from an influx of retirees, who have come primarily from southern New England and the Middle Atlantic states. In that regard, Maine has joined a trend that Vermont and New Hampshire—geographically closer to those large states—have experienced for several decades.

This trend, which was again nationwide, saw large cities lose some of their population to neighboring rural or semi-rural areas. Studies showed that the prime motivation for migration to rural areas was a quality-of-life factor that included such rural characteristics as natural scenery, a low crime rate, a low cost of living, and a supposedly simpler style of life.[26] With its vast tracts of forest and hundreds of abandoned farms, Maine was an attractive place for reversed migration, even while the state was experiencing traditional migration, especially to the Portland region in the south. To the new Maine in-migrants, the state was once again a frontier with a "marvelous destiny." Its geographic separateness, once preserved by a stagnant economy, was sought by back-to-nature artisans, suburbanites, and retirees, all of whom were anxious to "get away" from a more urban lifestyle.

Within Maine, population change has also been a mostly urban-to-rural migration. About 95 percent of the growth since 1960 has taken place outside of urban areas, that is, among the roughly 450 towns the census defines as rural. The fastest growing communities are ones 20 to 30 miles from cities (or "service centers"), and are commonly home to commuters living in two-income households with workplaces in two different locations. More than three-quarters of Mainers living in rural areas commute to jobs outside of their town of residence. That settlement pattern has contributed to sprawl, and in turn, to the relatively high cost of local government. For instance, between 1975 and 1995, Maine spent $330 million on new school construction, mostly in rural areas, even though the state's overall elementary and secondary school population dropped by almost 30,000 students.[27]

Maine's new residents fall into certain age groups. They are mostly over age 35, with a substantial number 65-plus. Despite its population's more rapid growth after 2000, Maine continued to have a net out-migration of people in the 25–34 age group—a trend it experienced during most of the twentieth century. Between 1960 and 2000 the U.S. median age rose by six years, but in Maine it grew by ten years. An aging population increases the number of single-person households and contributes to sprawl.

The regional impact of population change has been significant. In contrast to rapid growth in York and Cumberland counties on the southern coast, Aroostook County in the far north sustained a 30 percent decline in population between 1990 and 2000, although since 2000 it has, along with all other Maine counties, experienced modest growth. The idea of "two Maines"— that is, two regions divided by the Kennebec River, which travels from the northern forests through the middle of the state to the Atlantic Ocean—continues to be important in political discussions. The state's two congressional districts have long been drawn roughly to correspond to the north and south regions. After the 2000 census, the district lines had to be moved southward because the southern First District had, over the preceding decade, gained about fifty thousand more people than the Second District. It is clear that levels of poverty and unemployment, as well as population loss, are higher in northern Maine. However, a more precise term favored by the media is "rim" country, which better separates geographically the wealthier and poorer areas of the state. The reference is to non-coastal counties that border New Hampshire and Canada. Rim counties long shared a dependence on the exploitation of natural resources, and have undergone the most difficult adjustments to the emerging service economy. For instance, they encompass the southern Maine county of Oxford, bordering New Hampshire, which unlike its neighbors showed little population change in 1980–2000.

In one respect, events in the past two decades have diminished the importance of geography in maintaining Maine's sense of being "a place apart," separate from the national mainstream. Some towns in southern Maine are now considered part of the greater Boston metropolitan area. More will likely be added in the 2010 census. Importantly, the numbers of tourists have dramatically risen, from 4 million in 1974 to 26 million in 2003.[28] While the portion of Maine's high school graduates attending college is rising, more of them are attending out-of-state institutions.

On the other hand, attitude may be supplanting geography in sustaining Maine's critical sense of place. The state's newcomers, like its longtime residents, are settling heavily in small towns outside urban areas, and generally favoring rural lifestyles. While the new residents stem from large population centers where the individualistic political culture predominates, the smaller towns in which they settle are strongholds of the historic participatory culture. Those communities may have more effect on the political habits of new residents than the residents do on their adopted surroundings. A 2006 report by the Brookings Institution underscored the idea of place, asserting that "Maine has—in its vivid small towns and waterfronts, its lakes and fields and rocky coastline—exactly the sort of authenticity and quality of place that can set a place apart. Maine is unforgettable and distinctive, and that matters."[29] In 2007 Gov. John Baldacci established the Council on Maine's Quality of Place to work with the State Planning Office in determining ways in which the idea might fit into future community and economic development.

CONCLUSION

While Maine has a history of ethnic diversity, it has a population that is still remarkably homogeneous in certain ways. Perhaps the most important factor that unites Maine residents is their sense of belonging to "a place apart." The state's geographic location and its economic history have instilled a tradition of separateness among its citizens. The frontier-like natural environment, much of which remains largely untouched, encourages people to identify with the physical beauty of their state, particularly as development escalates elsewhere in New England.

Maine shares a moralistic political culture with the other northern New England states, but Maine has some noticeable differences. Its tendency toward moderation, its history as a frontier, and its sense of separateness make Maine's political culture distinct from that of Vermont and New Hampshire. Many of the forces that have contributed to Maine's uniqueness have also nurtured its participatory politics. The expansive geography and harsh climate have demanded both the independence of the individual and the closeness of the community. The stagnant economy of 1900–1960 postponed a confrontation between the moralistic culture and the individualistic culture associated with an urban society. How that clash played out in subsequent decades has been primarily influenced by developments in the state's politics.

CHAPTER THREE

Maine's Traditional Politics and Its Transformation

In 1954 a revolution took place in Maine politics. The Republican Party, which had run the state almost without interruption for one hundred years, was defeated in a gubernatorial election by a young Democratic legislator of Polish immigrant parents, Edmund S. Muskie. In a landslide victory, Muskie became governor, ending Maine's one-party, Republican rule. Today Maine is known as "one of the nation's most intensely competitive states in partisan politics."[1] Many factors have contributed to the transformation of Maine's traditional political system in recent decades, including the political culture of the state, the nature of federal party patronage, and the strategies used by the Democratic and Republican parties.

REPUBLICAN HEGEMONY

Except for Vermont, Maine was probably the most thoroughly Republican state in the nation until the mid-1950s. The two states, in fact, proved their loyalty to the GOP in 1936 when they became what one writer has called a "lonely two-state coalition," after they voted for Alfred Landon for president over Franklin D. Roosevelt.[2] Today, with Maine's two-party politics well established, it is difficult to envision how monolithic the Republican Party was until the early 1950s. During the previous one hundred years, it seemed like a part of the landscape.

The daily newspapers normally represented only varying shades of Republican ideology. When young people came to register to vote in primaries, they might be shown only the Republican candidate lists. If they insisted on seeing the lists of Democratic candidates, they might even be asked if their fathers knew what they were doing.[3] There is a story sometimes attributed to Maine, sometimes to Vermont, in which an election warden is counting out the votes and is shocked when he suddenly comes upon one Democratic vote. A short while later, he finds a second Democratic vote, at which time he promptly tears up both of the votes, saying. "They are illegal. The Democrat, whoever he is, voted twice!"

Part of the Republican Party's strength in Maine came from the circumstances of the party's formation. The Maine Republican Party was formed in July 1854, soon after the formation of the national Republican Party, and just one hundred years before Edmund Muskie won the governorship. As in other states, Maine Republicans were made up of a fusion of many different forces: antislavery and independent Democrats, Whigs, Prohibitionists, and Know-Nothings. What brought together these diverse parties was their opposition to the spread of slavery. This opposition was encapsulated in the condemnation of the Kansas-Nebraska Act.

That measure, passed by the Congress in 1854, repealed the Missouri Compromise of 1820 by permitting slavery in the territories of Kansas and Nebraska, where it had been prohibited prior to 1854. Maine, which gained its statehood under the Missouri Compromise, had many citizens who had a personal interest in repudiating the Kansas-Nebraska Act. When the Civil War broke out, Maine's contribution was steep. The number of men from Maine who enlisted in the Union forces, for example, represented more than 10 percent of the state's total population.[4] The Republican Party's influence was greatly extended, and by the same token, the Democratic Party was discredited because it had taken a pro-slavery compromise stance in its nomination of James Buchanan for president in 1856. Years after the Civil War, state Republican leaders like William Pierce Frye and James Gillespie Blaine fanned the memories by rhetorically waving the "bloody shirt of the rebellion" and repeating the campaign cry, "vote as you shot." For many years a Democrat in Maine was something of a synonym for a renegade. Through its origins, the Republican Party in Maine became a representative of the state's moralistic political culture, which envisions a government responsible for the direction of society. This was a period of great exuberance in Maine, when economic development triggered efforts to reform society. In the 1850s, the temperance movement in Maine was strong enough to enact a prohibition law that was enforced for approximately eighty years.

The Republican Party's formidable strength in Maine was based on ideology as well as origins. By making prohibition a plank in its platform, the Republican Party in Maine made the party even more compatible with Maine's moralistic political culture. The Republican stance that saw government controls as something to be suspected, if not restricted, dovetailed neatly with some of the other important cultural aspects of the state. The frontier character of Maine in its early days emphasized the independence of the individual, particularly on his or her own land. The Maine electorate was historically suspicious of a government removed from its people, which was one of the reasons Maine separated from Massachusetts in 1820. The suspicion of distant government controls was also a product of the state's participatory political culture. The Maine electorate seems to have considered its Republican representatives as "watchdogs" in Augusta and Washington.[5]

During the late nineteenth century, Maine voters could rest assured that their interests were represented in Washington. Because of its connections with the federal government during this period, Maine's Republican Party enjoyed a prestige that lasted for many years. The administration of President Benjamin Harrison (1888–92) has been referred to as "the Maine administration."[6] With Thomas Brackett Reed as Speaker of the House, James G. Blaine as Secretary of State, Eugene Hale as Senate majority leader, Nelson Dingley as House Chairman of the Ways and Means Committee, and Melville Fuller as the Chief Justice of the U.S. Supreme Court, the nation seemed mostly in the hands of Maine politicians. This kind of illustriousness of Maine's GOP had a precedent in the figure of Hannibal Hamlin, who made the famous declaration, "I am leaving the Democratic Party forever!" (after it had adopted a proslavery, compromise platform). Hamlin became Maine's first Republican governor before going on to become the vice president under Abraham Lincoln.

The power of the Republican Party in Maine was also increased by its connections with big business. In fact, Republicanism and corporate interests were often the same thing in Maine for two reasons: (1) the extractible nature of the state's resources virtually guaranteed the involvement of large corporations in state government; and (2) Maine was a one-party, Republican state. An alliance of lumber and paper, textile, and utility interests supported the Republican Party wholeheartedly in return for weak environmental policies, defense from rate cutters or competitors, and favorable tax policies. Until the 1970s, a clear indication of Maine's control by the extractive corporations was the existence of many loopholes in the state's water pollution laws, rendering them virtually ineffectual.[7]

Along with the nature of the state's resources, demographics helped maintain Republican control. Between 1850 and 1950 the state's population grew only slightly, in part because of the departure of the state's youth in search of economic opportunities not available in Maine. This exodus acted to increase the median age of the population, which helped to create more widespread conservatism and, hence, greater Republican strength.[8]

The state's legislative apportionment also reinforced conservative policies by favoring rural areas. What Democratic support existed was found largely among Franco-Americans and other minorities clustered in the state's industrial centers, such as Lewiston and Biddeford, which were slightly discriminated against in apportionment.

Even the state's custom of conducting state elections in September, instead of November like the rest of the nation, assisted the Republican Party. National Democratic victories helped to carry Democratic candidates in many other states during election years.[9] In Maine, this could hardly occur because state elections were held prior to national elections. This factor does not seem to have been overlooked by the Republicans in Maine, who were able to prevent November elections until 1957. At that time, a constitutional amendment was adopted to make Maine's election dates conform with the rest of the nation.

Important as these elements of strength were for the Republican Party, its approval by Maine voters was due more fundamentally to general voter satisfaction with the way in which it handled state affairs. Unlike one-party systems in some other states, the Maine Republican Party governed in a generally responsible fashion. If the Republican politicians were not seen as particularly progressive or imaginative, nor were they known for incompetence or corruption. They kept the state on a sound fiscal course during a time when it had a static population and ranked among the lowest in the country in per capita income. The success of the party could be seen in its ability to hold the Democrats at bay, even though the Democratic Party always had a solid foundation of supporters.

The hopelessness of Maine Democrats was exhibited strikingly in 1948 by the fact that Republican candidates in half of the legislative districts faced no opposition whatsoever.[10] Indeed, after 1932, most of the state's most promising Democrats were siphoned off to Washington where they benefited from federal patronage. One example was Dr. Clinton Clauson of Waterville, who preferred to continue his position as federal collector of revenue for the State of Maine rather than run for governor, although he was mentioned prominently as a candidate several times after 1946.[11]

REPUBLICAN FACTIONALISM

Since the party was supported by so many formidable forces, one may wonder how the Republican hold on Maine was ever dislodged. Ironically, the party's overwhelming strength in both Washington and Augusta was probably the biggest cause of its downfall. Internal cohesion tends to break down in parties that have had years to entrench themselves as the dominant party. Contests for power do not revolve around what party will rule; instead, they focus on which faction of the dominant party will rule. This became the case in Maine.[12]

Consistent with the state's participatory culture, Maine's Republican Party was not a very tight-knit organization. Republican primaries (which were tantamount to general elections) did not reveal a contest between "organization" and "anti-organization" forces, as was true in some other one-party states. Instead, the primaries tended to show a multifactional pattern with numerous candidates. The outcomes usually depended on personality considerations, which is still the case today. When President Roosevelt came into office in 1933, federal Republican patronage stopped, and many top-line Maine Republicans returned to their state. During the 1930s and 1940s, there were probably too many candidates available for elective and appointive office, and younger party members began to resent the secondary position in which they found themselves.[13]

As factionalism spread, several heated contests occurred. Governor Frederick Payne beat longtime U.S. Senator Owen Brewster in a hard-fought 1952 primary in which Brewster was seeking renomination. Four years earlier, Margaret Chase Smith had beaten Horace Hildreth and Sumner Sewall, both former governors, to win the Republican nomination for the U.S. Senate. When conservative politician Robert L. Jones challenged Smith in the 1954 Republican primary, he implied at one point that Smith supporters had tried to bribe him to leave the race. The charges were never proved, and Smith won the primary overwhelmingly, but such internecine conflict began to discredit the party.

Republican factionalism was encouraged by certain outside forces. Nationally, the Republican Party was ideologically divided during the years immediately following World War II. Republicans had once favored free enterprise at home and an isolationist foreign policy. After the Second World War, when the United States emerged as a world power with broadened responsibilities, Republicans began to question their beliefs. For a time, this led to splits in the national party as different factions attempted to define a new ideology—a process that naturally affected the party in Maine.

Republican factionalism and disenchantment grew during the governorship of Burton Cross (1953–55), especially during his unsuccessful reelection campaign in 1954. Cross, a florist by trade and something of a government reformer, made himself unpopular to both his constituents and party colleagues. By cutting the state budget, and trying to reform the state's Highway Commission and Liquor Commission, both of which had become corrupt, Cross made many political enemies. A lack of diplomacy hurt him with various groups of voters. His denunciation of the potato price-support program helped to get him into trouble with the Aroostook County potato farmers. A remark to the inhabitants of poverty-stricken Washington County that they should "lift up their own bootstraps" did more than enrage the county's citizens. The statement was eventually syndicated by the Soviet news agency Tass as an example of capitalism's disregard for the downtrodden.[14]

Normally in Maine, a Republican governor was routinely supported for reelection by his party. Cross's 1954 campaign for reelection, however, produced the dismal spectacle of members of his party abandoning him. Prominent Republican Neil Bishop led the formation of "Republicans for Muskie" clubs in the state. Obed Millet, a Republican legislator and agricultural leader, helped to put together "Farmers for Muskie" clubs.[15] The collapse of the automatic statewide Republican majority in Maine dates from the dramatic 1954 election, when Democrat Edmund S. Muskie upset Governor Cross.

DEMOCRATIC GROWTH

While the Republican Party was splintering, a group of young Maine politicians was assembling a new and dynamic Democratic organization. When Dwight D. Eisenhower became president in 1952, Democratic federal patronage stopped, and many Democrats, like Frank M. Coffin, returned to state affairs. Coffin, a Harvard Law School graduate and member of a family that had worked for the Maine Democratic Party for generations, was responsible for some successful strategies when he became chair of the Democratic Platform Committee in 1954. His approach stressed an "open" style of politics, new at the time, enlisting the support of schoolteachers, farmers, and textile workers. Citizen sentiment on a large variety of issues was sought through questionnaires circulated throughout the state. The result was widespread enthusiasm.

In Edmund Muskie, the Democratic Party had the charismatic leader the Republican Party lacked. His personal charm and candidness, as well as his message of economic growth through industrial development, earned him popular support early in the 1954 campaign. His relative youth became a political asset. He performed particularly well on television, which had come to the state only the year before. The Democrats' use of television in 1954 was also part of the party's "hands-on," accessible style of politics, which successfully tapped into the state's participatory tradition. A child of immigrant parents, Muskie represented the growing diversification of the state's population. Although Maine was not yet seeing the more diverse in-migration, which would occur during the 1970s, new groups in the elector-ate were becoming influential. Largely because of the Second World War, Maine's Democratic Franco-Americans developed a large middle class of their own, a factor that contributed to their assimilation and greater political involvement. These factors contributed to the breakdown of the century-long Republican consensus not only in Maine, but also in Vermont, which nearly elected a Democratic governor in 1954, and which would elect its first statewide Democratic official in 1958.

Muskie's campaign and personality helped overcome the rural electorate's idea of a Democrat as a "big city hack." Don Nicoll, who was an adviser to Muskie when he was a U.S. Senator, once explained how Muskie felt very much at home with Maine's Yankees: "He has their reticence, a low-key quality, a kind of flinty insistence on facts . . . [a] deliberate approach to life. Essentially, it's an unhurried rural quality."[16] Muskie also looked the part with his lanky frame and heavy, imposing jaw. As the underdog, Muskie came to personify the independence and individualism cherished in Maine. In the 1950s, Maine had fallen behind the economic development of other states, and nurtured its independence from the national mainstream, per-haps defensively. Muskie enjoyed popular support partly because his own campaign against the Republicans symbolized the odds that Maine was up against in a rapidly industrializing and wealthy society, and the need for competence and new ideas in government if progress was to be made.

The campaign had a kind of breathless exhilaration. Even though the Democratic Party could barely scrape together $15,000 for the entire gu-bernatorial campaign, Muskie covered the state. Pushing across the coun-tryside, he would stop in a town for ten or fifteen minutes, shake hands with citizens, and then head out for the next town. At night he would stay in the homes of party members. His campaign, rustic as it was, was very success-ful. He received huge margins in the Democratic mill towns, and he cut into the Republican strength in the countryside. The results were 135,673 votes for Muskie and 113,298 for Cross. Interestingly, when Vermont's Phillip Hoff became the first Democrat to win the governorship in that state in 1962, he revealed many of the same character traits as Muskie, such as youth, charisma, and role as an underdog.

The transformation of the state's political system could, in one sense, have been anticipated by the splintering of the Republican Party, and by the dissatisfaction with the party by groups that had once helped form the Republican coalition, such as working-class persons and ethnic minori-ties. The economic and cultural changes of the mid-twentieth century had brought about a more complex political environment in Maine, one that now gave rise to competing political parties, at least in statewide races. In another sense, though, the transformation of the state's political system was sudden and, at least in the beginning of the campaign, unexpected. During his 1968 campaign for vice president, Muskie recounted for a Texas crowd his feelings on the election night of 1954:

> I never had an experience like that. If I win elections from now until the year 2000—this election, if we win it, won't be nearly the exhilarating experience of that one. We won against hopeless odds. We won with almost no resources. We had to literally walk that state from one end to the other. We had to talk to Republicans who had never seen a live Democrat in their lives. We had to learn the political skills none of us had ever developed. We had to do it against . . . a political organization which had had a century to entrench itself.[17]

BIPARTISAN POLITICS

The rise of the Democratic Party in Maine is important mostly because it initiated the bipartisan politics in existence today. Bipartisan politics, and the political moderation it has encouraged, have become the practical realization of the state's participatory political culture. This is not to say that the years of one-party Republican rule deviated from that culture. The state's population was less diverse and more static in the period of one-party politics, and thus found itself adequately represented by only one party. Also, the loosely organized Republican Party, which emphasized the personalities and personal organizations of candidates, was in keeping with the participatory culture of the state. Although campaign strategies and federal party patronage have importantly influenced party development in Maine, changes in the state's economy and population have been equally influential.

As governor, Muskie implemented several important programs with the cooperation of the Republican majorities in the legislature. He created the Department of Industry and Commerce, which was very popular, especially after it enticed several new industries to the state.[18] His appointments, carefully cleared by the Republican-controlled Executive Council, minimized partisanship. As a party builder, Muskie has been compared with Hubert H. Humphrey in Minnesota, George McGovern in South Dakota, G. Mennen Williams in Michigan, and William Proxmire and Gaylord Nelson in Wisconsin.[19] In 1956 Muskie was reelected with a plurality that was approximately double his 1954 margin. At the same time, Frank Coffin won the first of two terms in the U.S. House of Representatives. Two years later, Muskie became Maine's first Democratic U.S. Senator in more than forty years, and Clinton Clausen, who was finally persuaded to run, was elected governor.

During the 1960s and early 1970s, a system of bipartisan politics was established. After Governor Clausen died suddenly in office in December 1959, Republican John Reed was elevated to the governorship from the position of president of the state senate. Although Reed was elected in 1960 and reelected in 1962, his margin in the latter year over Democratic candidate Maynard C. Dolloff was small. In 1966 Reed was defeated by Democrat Kenneth M. Curtis, a popular Maine secretary of state who would serve as the state's chief executive for two terms. Although at age thirty-six, Curtis was the youngest governor in the nation at the time of his election, he was successful in instituting innovative and important changes, such as the introduction of a governor's cabinet. The former plethora of boards and commissions that had made the state bureaucracy faceless and sometimes unaccountable was restructured into a handful of departments directly accountable to the governor. Governor Curtis also succeeded in winning passage, with Republican cooperation, of a state income tax in 1969.

Two-party politics in Maine has evolved mostly in a context of moderation. Intense partisan combat is rare. Politics had always been loosely run and moderate in the sense of pragmatic. However, conflicting concerns were balanced and compromises were sought more frequently than during the Republican past. Ideologically conservative Republicans have not won statewide elections since the early 1950s, when Senator Owen Brewster, once a member of the Ku Klux Klan, and Robert L. Jones, a supporter of Senator Joseph McCarthy, were defeated in Republican primaries. Senator Margaret Chase Smith, who won reelection in 1954, is perhaps best remembered for her "declaration of conscience" speech before the Senate in which she eloquently denounced McCarthyism. Environmental legislation, which had been virtually nonexistent, got underway with Muskie and was continued by his successors, Republicans and Democrats alike. By the mid-1970s, Maine was in the forefront of some environmental policies, such as waste-water treatment.

William S. Cohen, who won a seat in the U.S. House of Representatives in 1972 (and the Senate in 1978), cast consistently moderate-to-liberal votes. Other Republican leaders in the state, including Harrison Richardson and Kenneth MacLeod, have been considered progressive.[20] During the 1960s, Richardson was a house majority leader and MacLeod was senate president. Both men worked closely with Governor Curtis in the enactment of Maine's income tax in 1969. Likewise, the cautiousness and moderation that characterized Muskie's political style was perpetuated by the Democrats who succeeded him. During the 1972 Democratic state convention, liberal members of the party were unable to gather enough support to expand the platform to include equal rights for homosexuals and amnesty for Vietnam War draft resisters.

The moderation and lack of ideological emphasis gave Maine's government a strong continuity during a period of two-party competition. Although liberal preferences in the state grew faster than conservative ones, the overall effect was still an increase in moderation, especially in light of the fact that the state had been very conservative in the past. New organizations appeared to balance the old. Labor unions are one example. Their rise has been closely associated with the growth of the Democratic Party. Another group, environmentalists, became instrumental in Maine politics in the 1960s and has grown in strength. The number of registered Democrats more than doubled between 1954–74, moving from 99,386 to 212,175.[21] On the other hand, the number of registered Republicans declined, from 262,367 to 227,828, although they still held a slight majority of the registered electorate on the eve of James Longley's unexpected gubernatorial victory in 1974.

CONCLUSION

The century of almost uninterrupted Republican rule in Maine was replaced by a competitive, two-party system of politics in a relatively short period of time. Examined closely, the breakdown of the GOP was largely an outgrowth of its position as the undisputed party. Multifactionalism is encouraged in one-party politics. In Maine, this was especially the case because the Republican Party was never a tight-knit organization. During the 1932–52 period, when the U.S. presidency was filled by Democrats, federal Republican patronage stopped, and many of Maine's top-line Republicans returned to the state, which already possessed a surplus of candidates. Conversely, Maine's Democratic Party was strengthened when federal Democratic patronage stopped in 1952. The party, which needed to build itself from the bottom up, depended heavily on the expertise and leadership of such individuals as Frank Coffin, Clinton Clausen, and Edmund Muskie.

Maine's two-party politics evolved in a way that involved strong competition but loosely organized party structures. Campaigns tend to center on issues and the personalities of the candidates, rather than strong ideology. In general, power has been concentrated in the hands of moderate Democrats and liberal Republicans. These and other factors show that the

transformation of Maine's traditional political system has encouraged political stability. In general, the transformation of Maine politics in the 1950s
and 1960s reflected the overall development of the state during that period.
Maine's economic and demographic diversification was translated into a
broadening of its political system and its policy priorities.

CHAPTER FOUR

Contemporary Maine Politics

By 1974 Maine politics had evolved into a two-party system, similar to the systems of the other northeastern states since the end of World War II. Our concerns in this chapter are with the structure of the parties at the present time, and the place of interest groups in state politics.

THE PARTY BALANCE

The largest political grouping in Maine in 2006 was composed of independent (technically, "unenrolled") voters (see table 1).[1] They comprised some 38 percent of the electorate, with Democrats having 31 percent, Republicans 28 percent, and the Green Party 3 percent. The growth of independents was particularly noticeable during the 1970s and early 1980s, when their numbers approximately doubled. Although the increase in independents has slowed somewhat since the mid-1980s, their presence has had a major impact on Maine politics.

Unlike parties in some states, Democrats and Republicans in Maine have generally revealed little differences in per capita income. Maine parties show less division along class lines than they do according to cultural and ethnic factors. Republicans tend to be concentrated among college-educated voters, older citizens, and residents of small communities and suburbs.[2] Democrats show lower levels of formal education and more urban residential patterns. Independent voters tended to be fairly young, and to have lived in the state for shorter periods of time than Democrats and Republicans. Consistent with the state's moralistic political culture, voter turnout in all groups has been relatively high. Maine's level of turnout among registered voters consistently places it among the top five states in voter participation.

Table 1: Political party registration in selected years

Year	Democrats	Republicans	Independents (Unenrolled)	Greens
1990	272,089	246,277	306,292	
1994	311,491	274,271	349,373	
2006	309,525	279,641	375,235	29,347

Source: State of Maine, Office of Secretary of State.

THE ELECTORAL BATTLE

Independent voters have had an impact on gubernatorial elections. The national spotlight fell on Maine in 1974 when independent James Longley won a stunning gubernatorial victory. He campaigned on a platform calling for sharply reduced state government spending. Two decades later another independent candidate, Angus King, running on a somewhat different platform, won election as governor. King's victory followed a series of intense, highly publicized partisan battles in the state legislature. King pledged to work with members of both parties in seeking solutions to the state's problems, especially its financial woes.

A look of the Longley and King elections is revealing of the shifts in Maine politics in the period between 1974 and the end of the King administration in 2003. A wealthy insurance executive whom Gov. Kenneth Curtis had named to head a group of businesspeople who were to study ways to bring about reductions in government expenditures, Longley became a political activist when state officials appeared to ignore his group's recommendations. In the 1974 elections, which took place in the aftermath of the Watergate scandals, citizen politicians were unusually popular. In his campaign for governor, Longley was able to put together a large voting bloc from his home city of Lewiston, Maine's second largest city and normally a heavily Democratic city, with substantial statewide support from usually Republican voters, who were not swayed by the Republican gubernatorial nominee's uncommonly inept campaign. Longley won the three-man race by just under 40 percent of the vote.[3]

Following the very conservative (and controversial) Longley administration, like-minded conservative candidates mounted statewide campaigns as independents in three of the next four gubernatorial elections: Buddy Franklin, a Bangor minister, in 1978. John Menario, a Portland developer, in 1986, and Andrew Adam, a self-styled libertarian, in 1990. Adam's candidacy was largely ignored by the major party candidates; he obtained only

9 percent of the vote in a hard-fought race in which Gov. John McKernan narrowly won reelection over former governor Joseph Brennan. In contrast, Franklin and Menario each mounted strong independent campaigns in their years, and were widely covered by the media. They obtained 25 and 15 percent of the vote, respectively. In 1986 a second independent candidate, Sherry Huber, a former state legislator running on a platform stressing cultural liberalism and environmental issues, entered the race and also won 15 percent of the vote. (When Governor Brennan successfully sought reelection in 1982, he faced no independent challenge.) The independent candidates, particularly ones in 1978 and 1986, forced the major party candidates to address ideological issues more than they probably otherwise would have done. However, the presence of independents also seemed to shunt highly issue-oriented voters away from the parties. As a result, the parties were able to take fairly moderate positions on most issues. Such a pattern was especially noticeable in 1986, when independents Huber and Menario garnered most of the strongly liberal and the strongly conservative votes in a four-person race.

In 1994 Angus King, a well-known personality on Maine public television, entered the gubernatorial race as an independent. His candidacy adhered to the pattern set in 1978 and 1986 whereby a challenge from a strong independent took place in a contest with no incumbent. King's impact on Maine politics would be sharply different from that of James Longley. Far from being an ideologue, King was a self-styled moderate who maintained the state needed to emphasize bipartisan solutions to its problems. His campaign began the year after angry Maine voters had approved a referendum limiting legislators to four consecutive terms in the house or senate. A shutdown of state government in 1991—when Governor McKernan and house Speaker John Martin could not agree on a budget—had fueled resentment against "Augusta politicians." King favored term limits, and promised if elected to lower the level of party combat.

The 1994 party primaries had no shortage of candidates. Former governor Joseph Brennan defeated three rivals for the Democratic nomination, garnering more than half the vote. The Republican contest was closer, attracting seven contenders, most of whom were conservatives. Partly for that reason the winner was moderate Susan Collins, once a senior member of Senator Bill Cohen's Washington staff and, more recently, a cabinet member of the McKernan administration. In addition to Angus King, a second independent candidate, Jonathan Carter, joined the race, running as the candidate of the Green Party (though the party was not listed as such). As the contest unfolded it became clear that the race was between Brennan and

King. Both men focused their campaigns on the state's economy and on improving its business climate. Republican efforts in 1994 were concentrated on electing Congresswoman Olympia Snowe to the U.S. Senate, hampering the Collins' effort. The state media paid relatively little attention to Carter.

King beat Brennan 36 percent to 34 percent, paralleling Longley's win over Mitchell. Both in 1974 and in 1994 the independent benefited from the weakness of the Republican candidate. King ran well in Portland and Lewiston, won decisively in their suburbs, and carried the once strongly Republican coastal counties. He also benefited from Carter's candidacy, whose support (7 percent of the vote) appeared mostly drawn from Joseph Brennan. Despite clear similarities in the Longley and King electoral coalitions, there is little evidence of an identifiable "independent bloc" in Maine politics, one that persists from election to election. The 1992 presidential race offers an illustration. In that year, Independent Ross Perot won 30 percent of the state vote—the highest of any state. Perot ran best in the traditionally Republican towns and cities in northern Maine, a region that Susan Collins carried in the 1994 governor's race. In the southern Maine cities and suburbs—areas of King's greatest support in 1994—Perot ran far behind Bill Clinton.

In winning reelection in 1998 with 75 percent of the vote, Governor King set a state record. Only token candidates stood for the two major parties. King's success in working with the state legislature, and his message of making Maine friendlier to business and investment, resonated with voters. In 2002 with King constitutionally limited to two terms, the contest over the governorship returned to a two-party battle. The state's Second District Congressman, Democrat John Baldacci, defeated Republican Peter Chinchette by a margin of 48 percent to 42 percent. The remaining votes went to Green Party Candidate Jonathan Carter. Baldacci won reelection in 2006 over a conservative Republican state senator, Chandler Woodcock, by a similar margin, 38 percent to 30 percent. In that race, three independent candidates garnered one-third of the vote. Despite King's success and the persistent efforts of independent candidates, they have not replaced the parties. Independent victories show that voter identification with the two parties is shallow and especially unpredictable in gubernatorial contests, and thus subject to the vagaries of a specific campaign. Independents can win when the electorate believes the parties have failed to deal with pressing issues effectively.

As far as elections to the U.S. Congress are concerned, Maine has had a bipartisan delegation since 1960, when the state's seats in the U.S. House dropped from three to two. Independent candidates have played little role here, where the important aspect of races for house seats since the early

1970s has been the power of incumbency. In 1974 Democratic incumbent Peter Kyros was upset by Republican David Emery in the First District, in the southern part of the state. Since then, incumbent representatives have generally not faced serious challenges. At the same time, in races in which no incumbent has been running, the elections have tended to be close. David Emery was reelected with increasingly large margins in 1976, 1978, and 1980. In 1982 he gave up the seat to run unsuccessfully against George Mitchell for the U.S. Senate. His place was taken by Republican John McKernan, who won a narrow race in 1982, but who widened his margin in 1984. In 1986 when McKernan sought the governorship, outgoing Democratic Gov. Joseph Brennan entered the First District race, and won by a fairly close margin over Republican Rollin Ives. In 1990 when Brennan decided to challenge McKernan in the gubernatorial race, the seat was won by Democrat Tom Andrews, a Portland legislator. Andrews defeated David Emery, who sought to regain the position, by a lopsided margin. Andrews left the seat in 1994 to challenge unsuccessfully Olympia Snowe for the U.S. Senate. His successor was James Longley Jr., son of the former governor. A conservative Republican, Longley benefited from the national Republican tide in that year. In 1996 Democrat Tom Allen, a Portland city councilman, defeated Longley, who had had difficulty establishing himself in the district. Allen won reelection easily in races from 1998 to 2006. In 2008 he unsuccessfully challenged U.S. Sen. Susan Collins when she sought a third term. His seat was won by Chellie Pingree, a former Democratic majority leader in the state senate.

The Second District, which covers the northern two-thirds of the state, turned Republican in 1972. In that year, Democratic Congressman William Hathaway relinquished his seat to wage a successful campaign against veteran senator Margaret Chase Smith. Hathaway's place was taken by William Cohen, who defeated Elmer Violette, the Democratic floor leader in the state senate, by about 17,000 votes. Cohen faced only token opposition in subsequent races. He moved to the U.S. Senate in 1978, defeating Hathaway, who was trying for a second term. Cohen's successor, Olympia Snowe, a Republican state senator, was elected in a hard-fought contest over Mark Gartley, a Vietnam War veteran. Snowe's portion of the vote in 1978 was only 51 percent. It rose to more than 70 percent in her 1980 reelection and remained close to that level in most subsequent races. In 1994 after Snowe declared her candidacy for the U.S. Senate, John Baldacci, a popular Bangor city councilman, entered the House race, winning the seat handily over a conservative Republican. In the next three elections, Baldacci faced little opposition. After he joined the governor's contest, Democrats nominated Michael Michaud, a mill worker from the town of Millinocket—in northern Maine—and a veteran legislator who had served as president of the state senate. His Republican opponent, Kevin Raye, had long served on the staff of Senator Olympia Snowe. Michaud won by three percentage points in a hard-fought race. Labor unions organized voters in the hundreds of small communities in the district and were a key factor in his victory. Consistent with Maine's preference for incumbents, Michaud was reelected easily in 2004, 2006, and 2008.

Maine's U.S. Senate seats have also provided their occupants with considerable electoral safety, though not quite as much as its House members have enjoyed. William Hathaway won election to the Senate in 1972 by defeating Senator Smith, who had represented Maine in that chamber since 1948. Hathaway, in turn, was soundly beaten in 1978 by Congressman Cohen, who attacked Hathaway as being a doctrinaire liberal and insufficiently strong on defense issues. During much of 1981 and 1982 it appeared that Senator George Mitchell, who had been appointed to the Senate in 1980 after President Jimmy Carter named Senator Muskie as U.S. secretary of state, might encounter the same fate. However, because his opponent, Congressman David Emery, was seen as very ideologically conservative, Mitchell won in a landslide. After twelve years in the Senate—six as Democratic majority leader—Mitchell retired in 1994. Maine's two members of the U.S. House, Congressman Tom Andrews and Congresswoman Olympia Snowe, vied to replace him. The contest appeared to be close at the outset, but Snowe ran the more effective campaign and won by 60 percent. In 2000, she defeated Mark Lawrence, the outgoing president of the Maine Senate, by 69 percent to 31 percent, to gain reelection. Snowe won again in 2006 in a landslide against only token Democratic opposition. Senator William Cohen left the Senate in 1996, giving rise to a spirited contest between the two runners-up in the 1994 governor's race—Democrat Joseph Brennan and Republican Susan Collins. Collins' campaign was better organized than in 1994, and she had help from Cohen's strong political organization. She beat Brennan 52 percent to 48 percent. In 2002 she defeated former state senate majority leader, Chellie Pingree, by 58 percent to 42 percent, and in 2008 she beat Congressman Tom Allen by a margin of 61 percent to 39 percent.

Maine has historically elected as U.S. senators individuals who not only protect its interests in the national arena and try to "bring home the bacon," but develop as well a national stature in domestic and foreign policymaking. Several of its senators have been very distinguished figures; it is the only state to have had two Senate majority leaders in the post–World War II period. The importance the state places on the senatorial office has led to races that are rarely closely contested. Well in advance of an election, a politician is usually the acknowledged favorite by virtue of his or her familiarity to the voters and long experience in politics. Since 1972 in only one race—1996—has a winning candidate gained less than 58 percent of the vote, and in only one—1978—has an incumbent senator been defeated.

Turning to the legislature, the Democratic and Republican parties have been competitive since the early 1970s. Democrats have enjoyed solid, though not overwhelming, control of the house since 1975. They have held majorities in the senate since 1983, with the exception of 1992–94, when the Republicans had a 27 to 23 seat advantage, and 2000–02, when each party had 17 seats and an independent senator held the balance of power. Despite the Democrats' persistent advantage, a surprising amount of competition takes place in legislative races, reflecting the state's highly participatory culture. In 2004, for instance, the two parties had candidates competing in all but four of the state's 186 house and senate districts. Many races were very close. A significant portion (approximately 40 percent) of the successful candidates carried their districts by less than 55 percent. In a house district of about eight thousand people, that margin of victory indicated a contest settled by just a few hundred votes.

From a regional perspective, both parties compete throughout the state. Nearly all of Maine's 16 counties regularly send bi-partisan delegations to the house of representatives. The Democrats' persistent strength in the legislature is due, to a considerable degree, to their support in the state's largest communities. For instance, in 2005 the party held 25 of the 31 house seats located in or mostly in the eight largest cities (those with populations exceeding 20,000). Republicans won five seats, and one legislator (from Portland) was a member of the Green Party. Together, the eight localities constituted 20 percent of the state's population, but they elected one-third of the Democratic House caucus. Only Sanford, in southern Maine, elected a Republican delegation. It is interesting to note the imposition of legislative term limits in 1993 has had little effect on the Democrats' long-standing urban advantage. Looking back to the 1988 elections, for example, the Democratic Party held 35 of the 38 house seats situated in the nine towns and cities that, at the time, counted more than 20,000 people.

ORGANIZATIONAL DEVELOPMENT

When Maine was a one-party Republican state, Democratic strength was confined to a few larger towns and cities, such as Portland, Lewiston, Biddeford, and Waterville, which comprised about one-fifth of the population. Mostly these were cities with large concentrations of Franco-American voters. Power rested in those urban machines and with a few skilled statewide leaders, such as Edmund Muskie. The state party focused almost entirely on the statewide campaigns of its gubernatorial and senatorial candidates. In contrast, the Republican Party had a network of elected officials and party machinery in every corner of the state. The party's lopsided control of the state legislature and of executive officials elected by the legislature (such as the attorney general, the secretary of state, and the state treasurer) gave it less reason to focus on statewide races.

In the past four decades, as Democrats have gained majorities in the state legislature, the party's organizational styles have, to an extent, switched. Democrats devoted new attention to the tasks of party-building and candidate recruitment throughout the state, especially in areas where they had not traditionally contested elections. In the 1960s, the state committee established a state headquarters and hired an executive director. The party chairmanship was strengthened by the recruitment of ambitious politicians who would later hold major offices. Both William Hathaway (U.S. Senate, 1973–79) and George Mitchell (U.S. Senate, 1980–1995) served a term as state Democratic chairperson.

Facing a competitive Democratic Party, Republicans countered with efforts of their own. Their attempts to match the Democrats' organizational success were initially hampered by ideological divisions.[4] From the 1960s to the 1980s, the state committee was split into moderate and conservative factions. The conservatives—usually in the majority—prevailed in electing the state chairperson. On the other hand, conservative Republican candidates seeking statewide offices lost badly in general elections. The party was unable to elect a governor from 1966 to 1986. More seriously, local party structures eroded. In 1980 the party failed to nominate candidates in 38 of the 151 house districts. The few Republicans who were successful tended to be charismatic figures, such as Senator William Cohen, who pointedly ran their campaigns independently of the official state organization.

In 1982 the state's three Republican members of Congress, alarmed over the deteriorating condition of the party, pressed their allies on the state committee to overhaul the state machinery. Through their influence, Lloyal Sewall, a moderate who pledged to make the party structure more inclusive, was installed as state chairman. Sewall encouraged the participation of individuals with new viewpoints on state and county committees, and helped move the organization's position on controversial issues to a more centrist posture. His efforts contributed toward Republican's regaining the governorship in 1986. Subsequently, the party was able to take advantage of Democratic missteps in the legislature. It successfully supported the 1993 referendum imposing legislative term limits, the effect of which was to depose several leading house Democrats.

Maine's contrarian tendencies have led to tensions between the state and national parties. This has been true with the Republicans in regard to ideology. The growth of conservatism in the national party has proved hard for many middle-of-the-road Maine Republicans to accept. The state delegation strongly opposed the selection of Barry Goldwater at the 1964 national Republican convention. In 1980 it backed George Bush over Ronald Reagan for the Republican nomination. For several election cycles, the party has included a pro-choice plank in its state platform, in contrast to the pro-life position of the national party. Within the U.S. Senate, Olympia Snowe and Susan Collins were often at odds over policies with President George Bush and the Republican leadership. Despite those ideological differences, the national party has provided significant funding for state party activities and for the campaigns of Republican candidates for congressional offices.

Democrats in Maine have had few policy struggles with their national counterparts. Their program ideas have generally been in accord with Democratic parties in other northern states. They generally favor expanded government spending for education and social services, and greater reliance on progressive taxes to finance programs. Suggesting the general policy congruence between the Maine party and the national scene, Democrats in the U.S. Senate elected George Mitchell as their majority leader in 1988. On the other hand, Maine Democrats have fought with the national committee over certain operating practices. The Maine party has prided itself on local control, and has resisted national efforts to govern its activities. In 1980 state Democrats tried to prevent the national party from altering the way they selected delegates to the national convention. In 1984 the state party struggled with the national party over the date for holding party caucuses to choose delegates to its state convention. In both 1988 and 1992 the issue concerned voting procedures used in the Democratic state convention. The national committee ruled that the state could not send a delegate to the national convention pledged to a presidential candidate who had support of less than 15 percent of the state convention. Largely through the intervention of Senator Mitchell, Maine was able to resist the rule. Eventually with Mitchell out of office, the party accepted the national standard.

CURRENT PARTY ORGANIZATION

The organization of Maine's political parties involves a structure of party committees that is fairly typical among the states. The basic level is the town committee, which is selected by a town or municipal caucus, composed of all the members of the party in the community. The caucuses assemble every two years, usually in February or March, when they have traditionally selected delegates to the state conventions that meet during April or May, and elected their town committees for the next two years. Traditionally, the delegate-selection role meant that the town caucuses could influence the kind of delegation that the state convention put together, every four years, to attend the national presidential nominating conventions. That function sometimes causes a flurry of excitement at the time of the town caucuses, as presidential candidates invade the state to speak with party activists in as many communities as possible. However, attendance by local party members at the caucuses was so poor in 1988 (only about 5 percent of registered party members participated) that the legislature later that year approved a measure that authorized the parties to hold presidential nominating primaries if they choose. However, neither party exercised the option in 1992.

Both parties opted for primaries in 1996 and 2000, which were held in March. In 1996 Bob Dole won easily, and Bill Clinton had no competition. In 2000 tight races emerged in both parties. George Bush defeated John McCain 51 percent to 44 percent, which was his only primary victory in New England. Al Gore beat Bill Bradley by 54 percent to 41 percent. The state had hoped that the March date might enable Maine's primary to play a strategic role in the presidential nominating process. However, the results were enveloped by the returns from Super Tuesday primaries in many other states, and thus had little impact. A further problem was that the primary—as a substitute for a local party caucus—had the effect of weakening party activity in some small communities. In 2004 the state abolished the presidential primary.

In addition to town committees, both parties maintain county committees. The strength of the individual municipal and county committees varies widely. If a committee has strong leadership, it can be instrumental in a candidate's success in winning election to the legislature or to county office such as sheriff, probate judge, and county commissioner. In many cases, however, the committees are not active, and candidates are left on their own. Party organizations tend to be weak, especially in the smaller towns and sparsely populated counties.

Each party has a state committee and holds a state party convention every two years in the spring. The principal tasks are the writing of the party platform and the naming of delegates to the national party conventions every four years. State conventions are usually rather elaborate, two-day affairs held in a civic auditorium in Portland, Lewiston, Augusta, Bangor, or Presque Isle, with more than a thousand delegates in attendance. Candidates running for the Democratic or Republican nomination in the party primaries held in June for the U.S. House or Senate, or for governor, typically provide hospitality suites and campaign intensively for support among the delegates. Because Maine politics is highly personalized, though, the parties' state conventions, like the state and county committees they oversee, are of less significance in winning and holding office than the candidates' own organizations.

A major change in politics has occurred in the area of campaign finance. Historically, Maine politicians could undertake campaigns for the state legislature and even for statewide office for relatively little cost. In 1954, Edmund Muskie and his allies spent approximately $10,000 in his successful bid for the governorship. Candidate costs for the Maine house rarely exceeded a few hundred dollars. Beginning in the 1980s, the amount of money involved in statewide campaigns began to soar. During the 1982, 1986, and 1990 gubernatorial elections, average spending per candidate climbed from $500,000 to $1 million to $1.5 million. In 1989 voters rejected a referendum proposal to provide public financing for governor's races. Despite that defeat, interest in public funding for elections grew. Attention was focused on legislative races, where financial constraints were starting to limit the pool of people available to run for a seat in Maine's traditional "citizen" assembly. Some campaigns for the state senate during the early 1990s revealed candidate expenditures of more than $50,000.

Finally, in 1996, voters approved in a referendum "The Maine Clean Election Law" (MCEL), which provides public financing to the campaigns of state legislative candidates. In 2002 gubernatorial aspirants were brought under its arrangements. The purpose of the law is to reduce the role of money in campaigns and to level the playing field among candidates. Under MCEL, funds are made available to candidates who demonstrate a required level of financial support.[5] To qualify in 2006 a house candidate needed to collect at least $5 from a minimum of 50 registered voters in electoral district. Senate candidates had to raise $5 from at least 150 registered voters. For gubernatorial aspirants, the threshold was $5 from 2,500 voters. Persons seeking office could accept a limited amount of money from individuals to start their campaigns—$500 for house candidates, $1,500 for senate candidates, $50,000 for gubernatorial candidates.

Separate allocations are provided for primary elections and general elections. In each instance, the sums vary according to whether a candidate had an opponent. In 2006 a house candidate with primary opposition received $1,504; if he or she had an opponent in the general election, the amount was $4,362. The comparable figures for senate races were $7,746 and $20,082, respectively. The number of candidates taking part in the program has risen steadily. During the 2000 election cycle, about one-third of all general election candidates took part; that portion increased to 62 percent in 2002; in 2004 some 79 percent of legislative candidates were involved, and a slightly higher figure (81 percent) participated in 2006. More Democrats have taken part than Republicans, but the margin of difference has not been large. The 2006 state legislative races cost about $3.3 million in public funds.

The only gubernatorial candidate to use the Clean Election Law in 2002 was the Green Party's nominee, Jonathan Carter, whose campaign received about $1.2 million. In 2006 two Republican candidates used Clean Election funds in their party primary, including the primary winner, Chandler Woodcock. In the general election Woodcock and two independent candidates obtained financing through the program, which contributed a total of $3.5 million to gubernatorial aspirants that year. Some wealthy candidates understandably remain outside the MCEL. A leading example was John Linnehan, a car dealer and financier in eastern Maine, who spent $200,000 in a losing effort to win a state senate seat in 2004.[6]

The Clean Election Law has not eliminated the role of Political Action Committees (PACS) in legislative campaigns. Although candidates who run "clean" must adhere to strict rules on accepting outside funds for their own campaign, they may raise PAC money for other candidates who choose not to take public funding. As a result, PACS organized by legislative leaders, or prospective legislative leaders, are a factor in elections. In 2002 such PACS provided nearly $1 million to candidates.[7] Overall, however, MCEL has reduced the influence of PACS in legislative races. Since the mid-1990s, the state party committees and their staffs have expanded, and party-building activities have taken on increased importance across the state.

INTEREST GROUPS IN MAINE

Like other rural states whose economies have depended heavily on extractive industries, Maine has a history of powerful interest groups. When Duane Lockard wrote *New England State Politics* in 1959, he identified pulp and paper companies, utilities, and manufacturing concerns as the "big three" economic interests, and argued that they did more than influence Maine politics. As he phrased it, "'control' is probably a more accurate term."[8] The interests were based, of course, on the state's abundant resources of timber and water power. Executives of the companies that exploited the natural resources worked closely with the leaders of the dominant Republican Party in formulating public policy.

The "big three" economic interests tended to focus most of their attention on the legislature. Their influence with legislators in the 1940s and 1950s was enhanced by the importance they had as employers of members of the legislature during and after their legislative service, as well as being employers of legislators' constituents. Furthermore, the nearly total absence of legislative staff meant that lobbyists often served as unofficial aides to legislators and to the legislative committees.

Over the past half century, the place of interest groups has much changed. A national survey in 2007 held that Maine interest groups existed in a "complementary" relationship to the political parties and that their impact on policymaking was weaker than in many other states.[9] The difference from earlier periods is related to the rise of a more diverse economy and to the development of two-party system. Those factors have caused both the number and types of interest groups to grow. Asked in a survey to nominate the "most influential" groups, state legislators identified the following seven organizations: environmentalists, the Maine Teachers Association, labor unions, paper companies, the Maine Municipal Association, utility companies, and state executive departments.[10] Labor unions are closely associated with the growth of the Democratic Party. Environmentalists became active in the 1960s and have remained a force ever since. Government at all levels is a much greater force in Maine than in past decades. The paper companies and the utilities remain major players but in a much larger field.

For a development as fundamental as the emergence of pluralism among Maine's interest groups, it took place with surprisingly little political fireworks. The primary reason seems to be that the business organizations that had been so powerful in the immediate post–World War II years were "simply no longer interested in paying the price to influence Maine's political landscape."[11] The changes that we have already described—the growth in political activity of minority groups, the arrival in the state of new residents, the emergence of a competitive Democratic Party, and the rise of career politicians in the legislature—all contributed to making the process of influencing the formation of public policy more complex. One scholar maintains that, at present, Maine businesses "will not actively recruit citizen legislators . . . " and "will not cooperate . . . in meaningful ways to alter the makeup of the Legislature. They are not interested in the struggle or the hassle."[12] It should be noted that the Maine Clean Election Act of 1996 has accelerated this process by helping to reduce the role of interest groups generally in legislative elections.

Maine interest groups are, then, a good deal more diverse than in the past. Moreover, alterations in their power and influence constitute only one of the important changes that have occurred in Maine politics. Related shifts have taken place in the way in which interest organizations work with the political parties, and also with each other. Additionally, the state now has a substantial number of idea- oriented or issue- oriented groups to compete with the more established economic groups. We look at these developments in turn.

In the 1980s, state Senator (now Governor) John Baldacci, a Bangor Democrat and co-chair of the legislature's Public Utilities Committee, initiated a widely publicized investigation of the opinion-polling activities of utility companies. Baldacci and some other Democrats believed that the utilities were aiding Republican candidates by quietly sharing polling data with them.[13] To the substantial embarrassment of Baldacci's group, its investigation revealed that utilities had actually provided polling data to Democratic Gov. Joseph Brennan during Brennan's reelection campaign in 1982. The companies sometime later supplied the same information to Brennan's Republican opponent, Charles Cragin. In the 1950s, Baldacci's suspicions that the utilities were helping only the Republicans might well have been correct. By the 1980s, even very conservative business organizations had accepted the reality of Maine's two-party politics and, accordingly, tried to maintain friendly relations with both parties.

As policymaking has become more sophisticated, think tanks and similar organizations have emerged as important actors in the world of interest groups. An example is the Maine Heritage Policy Center which was founded by Bill Becker, finance director for Republican Peter Cianchette's unsuccessful campaign for governor in 2002.[14] With five staff members, the Center promotes various conservative public policies. It has focused particular attention on the state's high tax burden. It is often opposed by the Maine Center for Economic Policies, which stakes out liberal positions on most issues. Another important group is the Maine's Women's Lobby, founded in 1978.[15] It currently has about five hundred members. The group claimed credit for passage in 2003 of measures to make part-time workers eligible for unemployment compensation and to permit judges to take guns away from certain suspected abusers. A conservative voice on social issues is the Maine Christian Civic League. In recent years the League has figured prominently in several state referendum battles over legislation extending equal rights to gay persons, reflecting a rise in interest group activity in popular lawmaking.

In recent legislative sessions, health insurance, gambling issues and education have attracted unusual interest group attention. Governor John Baldacci made creation of a new health-insurance system for small businesses ("Dirigo Maine") a major administration program in 2003. The issue prompted the highest expenditure by organized interests, including Eli Lilly, Anthem Blue Cross and Blue Shield, and the Maine Hospital Association, of any bill in that session—approximately $370,000. Gaming issues were a major source of contention in 2004. In 2002 when the state—at the behest of two Native American tribes—held a referendum that would have permitted the building of a casino in southern Maine, voters rejected the proposal, but they approved the use of slot machines (racino gambling) at certain racetracks. Estimates of future gross revenues at one racetrack in Bangor ran to $100 million per year. After Governor Baldacci submitted legislation to regulate the activity, lobbyists descended on Augusta. In January 2004 the *Portland Press Herald* reported that twenty-one lobbyists representing ten racino interests were paid more than $90,000 to work on the governor's bill. One of them called the measure "a full-employment program for lobbyists."[16] The issue creating the most fireworks in the 2007 session centered around a proposal, strongly pressed by Governor Baldacci, to consolidate Maine's approximately 290 school districts into about 80 districts, and to reduce accordingly the number of school superintendants. The most involved interest group, the Maine School Management Association, spent slightly over $100,000 in helping to shape the final legislation.

While interest groups generally operate "behind the scenes" in Augusta, their battles sometimes erupt into public view. In 2004 the leaders of a group called Citizens for Fair Bear Hunting (CFBH) sought passage of a bill to ban the use of bait, traps, and dogs to hunt bear. CFBH claimed that about 70 percent of Maine voters supported the ban. In an unusual move, CFBH refused to testify in behalf of its bill, asserting that the standing legislative committee handling it—Inland Fisheries and Wildlife—had "been bought and sold on this issue by cronyism and political payoffs from the Sportman's Alliance of Maine."[17] An organization of about fourteen thousand members, the Sportman's Alliance (SAM) is regarded as very influential in the legislature, and often decisive on issues specifically affecting hunters. The chairperson of the Inland Fisheries and Wildlife Committee vehemently rebutted CFBH's charges on the house floor, and received a standing ovation from his colleagues. After the legislature rejected the bill, CFBH acquired sufficient signatures to put the proposal to referendum, but the voters affirmed the legislature's decision by narrowly defeating it.

LOBBYISTS AT WORK

In 2007 the Maine Ethics Commission, which regulates lobbying activities, reported that 306 lobbyists were registered in that year. They represented about 450 employers. The power and influence of individual lobbyists and their organizations vary tremendously, of course. A longstanding practice in Maine is that the most influential groups tend to use law firms to represent them. The law firms most heavily involved in state politics usually have as partners or associates several political figures, sometimes recently retired from office.

One firm is Preti, Flaherty, Beliveau, and Pachios, located in Portland. It was one of the first to establish an office in Augusta, a recognition of the growing impact of state government on its clients. The firm's political coloration is Democratic. Peter Flaherty was a member of Gov. Joseph Brennan's (1978–86) executive staff. Severin M. Beliveau attempted to succeed Brennan, but failed to win the Democratic nomination in the 1986 primary. Beliveau is widely regarded as the dean of Maine lobbyists and perhaps the most influential. He has held numerous political and governmental positions—member of the Democratic National Committee, state Democratic chair, state legislator, and member of the University of Maine System's Board of Trustees. He comes from a prominent legal family; his father served on the Maine Supreme Judicial Court, and his grandfather and uncle were trial judges. One legislator described his influence this way: "When Beliveau is here (in the Capitol), you say 'What the hell is going on today'?"[18] He represents a rotating group of clients. In 2004 they ranged from the Bath Iron Work Corporation to Catholic Charities of Maine to the Ski Maine Association.

The rise of the Preti, Flaherty, Beliveau, and Pachios firm has to some extent come at the expense of Verrill and Dana, still a very influential (and Republican-leaning) law firm located in Portland. Its ties to the Maine Republican Party go well back into the nineteenth century. One of its early partners was Thomas Brackett Reed, Speaker of the U.S. House of Representatives in the 1890s. Before his election to the governorship, John McKernan was a partner in Verrill and Dana. Still other partners have included Charles Cragin, the unsuccessful Republican candidate for governor in 1982; Howard Dana, who managed President Ronald Reagan's 1980 campaign in the state and became a member of the Maine Supreme Judicial Court; and Loyall Sewall, who chaired the Republican State Committee in the mid-1980s.

Of course, not all lobbyists work in prestigious law firms. The presence of term limits has accelerated the movement of former legislators into the lobbying community. In 2004 former Rep. Charles Fisher (D.-Brewer), who represented the town of Brewer, was forced to sit out a term before running again for his seat. As a lobbyist, he represented a restaurant in his area pressing for off-track betting facilities to install slot machines.[19] Another group of interests, including Maine Funeral Directors and Philip Morris USA, employed in that year former Rep. Edward Pineau, who has relinquished a district in western Maine to join the lobbying community. Some lobbyists are veterans of the executive branch. The head of the state personnel department under Gov. Joseph Brennan, Jadine O'Brien, found employment as a lobbyist for Blue Cross and Blue Shield after she left office. She explained why she found the arrangement a good one: "They thought they could teach me the basics, and I brought them a knowledge of state government. It was a perfect match."[20] In other instances, lobbyists translate into state officials. Gov. Angus King hired Kay Rand, formerly chief lobbyist for the Maine Municipal Association, as one of his three senior policy advisors. In the Baldacci administration, Commissioner of Labor Lynda Fortman had earlier been chief spokesperson for the Maine Women's Lobby.

What has been the impact of legislative term limits on lobbying activities? When Maine adopted term limits in 1993 some observers worried that interest group influence would grow, perhaps even bring back the period when economic interests ruled the legislature. A 1999 survey of members of the house and senate found little support for that idea.[21] Most legislators believed that the impact of lobbyists on their activities was only slightly greater as a consequence of term limits. The major obstacle lobbyists faced was dealing with the constant influx of new members. Lobbyists had to devote much time to becoming acquainted with new legislators, and informing them about their positions on legislation and explaining the legislative process. The long-time ties with senior members evaporated as legislators were termed out. That change particularly affected solo lobbyists. Law firms with several legislative representatives were more able to deal with the altered environment.

Consistent with its participatory political culture, Maine has fairly tough lobby-registration laws. Any person who engages in lobbying in excess of eight hours in any calendar month must register with the State Ethics Commission, and pay a $200 registration fee. They must disclose on a monthly basis detailed financial information connected to lobbying, such as any expenditures of more than $25 spent in behalf of a legislator or the legislator's immediate family. Where a lobbyist's compensation exceeds $1,000 for a particular bill or legislative action, the legislative documents must be recorded in their reports. Still, reflecting the friendly nature of Maine politics, the legislature permits a lobbying desk to operate in the corridor between the senate and house chambers. It serves about twenty clients. The person staffing the desk keeps lobbyists in contact both with their offices and with legislators.

POPULAR LAWMAKING

A final topic in this survey of contemporary politics involves the initiative and the referendum. Maine's participatory culture and the growth in the complexity of state policies have combined to bring about increasing use of these devices for popular lawmaking. Under the Maine Constitution, a state-wide referendum must take place to approve bond issues and constitutional amendments, after the measures are first proposed by the legislature. These proposals have traditionally enjoyed a high rate of success. Voters have approved about 90 percent of the amendments and bond proposals that have appeared as ballot questions in the past several decades. In contrast, referendums that have taken place in response to an initiative have tended to be more controversial. An initiative gets under way in Maine when the number of voters equivalent to 10 percent of the total vote in the last gubernatorial election signs petitions seeking either to repeal a law already enacted, or to establish a new law. Under the constitution, an initiated measure must first be considered by the legislature. If the legislature fails to accept the proposal as it is set out in the initiative, a referendum is called.

Between 1911 (when the initiative and referendum were first used) and 1970 only seven initiated statures were considered. In the shorter period between 1971 and 2007, however, a total of forty-three measures were voted upon, and about one-third won approval. Initiatives designed to repeal laws already on the books have generally failed. They have included efforts to end the hunting season on moose (1983), to terminate the forced deposit on bottles initiated to encourage their return (1979), and to abolish the Maine income tax (1971). On the other hand, in 1998, voters rejected a gay-rights measure that had been passed by the legislature (the bill would eventually be reenacted, and would withstand a referendum to repeal it.)

Most successful initiatives have set policy in areas where the state government had not spoken. In several cases, the policy changes have significantly altered the operation of state government. Voters approved a term-limit measure in 1993, established public funding of political campaigns in 1996 and in 2005 forced the state to raise its level of financial support of local schools to 55 percent. Other examples of new policies included the establishment of flat-rate telephone service for local calls (1986), legalizing the medicinal use of marijuana (1999), indexing the state's income tax to allow the schedules to shift according to rates of inflation (1982), and allowing large stores to sell merchandise on Sundays (1990).

The referenda campaigns that imposed legislative term limits and enhanced financial support of local schools came about because the legislature had noticeably failed to address two issues Maine citizens strongly believed needed attention. In other instances, the legislature probably turned an initiated measure over to the voters because of its importance to the state, not because the legislature opposed the policy idea. The question of public funding of political campaigns seemed to be an example. With the growth of referendum activity, interest groups have become more prominent in that process. In a few cases, established groups have been leaders in a campaign. For instance, the Maine Christian Civic League led the 1998 campaign to overturn the gay rights' law.

More recently, citizen's organizations have grown up around specific issues. A campaign in 2002 to permit casinos in Maine triggered the rise of a group calling itself Casinos No!, which was very effective in mobilizing voters against that proposal, raising millions of dollars to do so. Earlier, the establishment of terms limits in 1993 was managed by a group calling itself the Committee for Governmental Reform, which was led by prominent citizens in both political parties and financed by a usually non-political philanthropist.

In a few instances an initiative been so popular that the legislature has simply endorsed it, making it law without a referendum. Such an event occurred in 2007, when the legislature overwhelmingly approved a proposal to provide tax credits to reimburse educational loan payments for any Maine resident who earns a degree from a Maine college or university and remains to live and work in Maine. The tax credits have a value of $2,100 for each year the individual spent in college. The idea, sponsored by a recent graduate of the University of Southern Maine, gained thousands more signatures than the initiative process required.

Some observers believe that the use of referendums may be waning.[22] In the 1990s, Mainers voted mostly in favor of initiated measures. In contrast, between 2000 and 2004, voters supported only two of the eight proposals presented to them. A key problem was that the language in some of them was very broad. In the anti-bear hunting referendum described earlier, proponents sought to ban three hunting methods, not just the one—trapping— that had provoked the most controversy. The casino idea that lost in 2002 envisioned a very large, $650 million facility, whereas a smaller project might have gained more support. Lawmaking through the initiative and referendum procedure does not allow for negotiation, the hallmark of the legislative process. Maine voters may continue to resort to the referendum process to press the legislature to deal with certain taxing and spending issues, but they are likely to confine its use to making occasional—and relatively modest—changes in other policy arenas.

CONCLUSION

Politics in Maine exemplifies a loosely organized two-party system in which the key factor in a political campaign is the personality of the candidate. With voters divided among Republicans, Democrats, and independents, neither party has a permanent hold on the legislature, the governorship, or the congressional delegation. Each party has enjoyed its greatest successes when it has nominated the more attractive candidate for an office. Democrats have been able to nail down more state legislative districts than have Republicans, and the party has enjoyed majority control for most of the past three decades. The congressional delegation has been about evenly divided between the parties, with the Republicans having the more senior members. The state's congressional Republicans have been more liberal—and better attuned to Maine's political environment—than have many of the Republicans seeking seats in the state legislature.

In organizational terms, Maine parties have almost switched places with each other since the one-party system disappeared. At that time, the dominant Republicans were strong in the towns and counties, while the small organization that the Democrats maintained was focused on the state government, centering on such charismatic figures as Edmund Muskie. At the present time, Democrats are better organized in local areas, especially in the larger towns. Republicans must count heavily on nominating attractive statewide candidates to win, and their organizational efforts have largely centered on state, not local, politics.

For much of its history, Maine had a few very powerful interest groups that exploited its natural resources of wood and water, and took advantage of its amateurish state government to win favorable policies. With the great expansion of interests in Augusta in recent decades, the power of extractive interests has diminished. Nonetheless, interest groups and lobbyists remain key players in state government, as their information and experience are critical in policymaking, especially in an era of legislative term limits.

CHAPTER FIVE

The Constitutional Tradition

Like all state constitutions, Maine's charter provides the fundamental structures and guidelines from which all state policymaking must proceed. The various branches of the state government are supposed to act in accordance with the provisions of the Maine Constitution and the U.S. Constitution. If the legislature fails to follow these provisions, the laws that it makes can he thrown out by the courts as unconstitutional. The state charter also furnishes a window to the political and social growth of the state. To begin an examination of the Maine Constitution, a look at the differences between state constitutions and the U.S. Constitution is useful.

State charters resemble the federal Constitution in some respects, but they perform a very different function. Their primary purpose is to limit the exercise of power. This trait arises from the fact that the states inherited all the power of the British government after the American Revolution. Because of fears of unrestrained power, citizens quickly circumscribed state power with constitutional provisions. The U.S. Constitution, on the other hand, grants power to the national government, which otherwise would have no legitimate basis of existence.

State constitutions are also characterized by their accessibility to the people. Compared to the federal Constitution, state charters are much easier to amend. The Maine Constitution is amended whenever the legislature, by a two-thirds vote of both houses, proposes a constitutional amendment that the voters then ratify in an election. This ratification process contrasts with the more onerous procedure whereby the approval of thirty-eight states (three quarters of the states) is required to approve a federal constitutional amendment.

HISTORY OF THE CONSTITUTION OF MAINE

As part of the process of securing statehood, citizens of the District of Maine convened a constitutional convention in Portland in October 1819.[1] The convention was composed of nearly three hundred delegates, who were drawn from every incorporated town in the district. The delegates represented a wide range of occupations; some were shipbuilders and traders, others were farmers and fishermen, and still others were lawyers and politicians. The primary question the convention had to resolve was whether to write a new constitution for Maine, or to build the state's charter from the Massachusetts Constitution, under which the district was then governed.

Some delegates, such as William King, the state's first governor, wanted to strike out independently. But the majority seemed to share the view of William Pitt Preble, delegate from Saco, that the Massachusetts document should be relied on because the convention lacked "sufficient time . . . [for] such an ambitious undertaking" as drafting a very different charter.[2] The Massachusetts Constitution of 1780 would become, by the twentieth century, the oldest charter in the United States. Written by John Adams, it is considered a pioneering statement of political thought. Unlike other early state constitutions that established weak governments, the Massachusetts document "subordinate[d] the individual to society." Its political theory "taught . . . that a republican political system . . . must enjoy a wide latitude of action in the pursuit of the public good."[3]

The Maine Constitution was ratified in December 1819. As of 2007 it had acquired 171 amendments. It is a measure of the rapid expansion of state government that half that number (85) has been added since 1962— less than a quarter of the time Maine has been a state. In Maine, amendments are periodically codified into the text of the charter with the intention of keeping it comprehensible to the people. Thus, the charter reads as a single text, with no list of amendments at the end of the document, as is the case with the U.S. Constitution. The process of codification has been conducted by the Chief Justice of the Maine Supreme Judicial Court every ten years since 1875.

CONTENTS OF THE CONSTITUTION OF MAINE

In this section, we sketch first the contents of the contemporary constitution. Later we focus on the specific changes produced by amendments adopted since the 1820s.

The first article of Maine's Constitution, most recently codified in 2003, contains twenty-four sections known as the "Declaration of Rights." Of the ten articles, this has received the least alteration since 1819. Citizens are guaranteed, among other things, free speech and freedom from "unreasonable searches and seizures." They are promised that in all criminal prosecutions, they have the right to a "speedy, public and impartial trial," and they cannot be compelled to provide evidence against themselves. The rights set forth in Maine's charter and in other early state constitutions formed the basis for the Bill of Rights of the U.S. Constitution, which was adopted in 1791.

Maine's Declaration of Rights also incorporates language from the Declaration of Independence. Power is inherent in the people, in whose authority "all free governments are founded." The people have the right to institute, alter, or reform their government "when their safety and happiness require it." The Maine Constitution was, in some respects, more democratic than that of Massachusetts. It protected freedom of worship as well as speech, and it made no distinction between Protestants and members of other religious groups. The 1780 Massachusetts Constitution made it a duty to worship the "Supreme Being," required church attendance, and prescribed a certain amount of tax discrimination against Catholics and Jews.

Article II addresses the qualifications for electors. Universal suffrage is provided for all citizens age eighteen or older, except persons under guardianship for mental illness and persons in the military service stationed in the state. In addition, students residing at any "seminary of learning" are not entitled to vote in local elections in the place where the school is situated.

Articles III, IV, V, and VI outline the structure of the state government. Article III establishes the principal of separation of powers, while Article IV concerns the structure of the Maine Legislature. Apportionment is to be conducted by a joint commission. In the event that an apportionment plan is not produced within thirty days after the legislature has convened, the Supreme Judicial Court is required to make the apportionment. This court is also empowered to hear any challenge of inequitable apportionment.

Article IV also outlines the regular legislative sessions, stating that the legislature can convene "at such other times" on the call of the president of the senate and the speaker of the house. The legislature is given "full power" to establish all laws for the defense and benefit of the state's citizens. While Article IV grants sole power of impeachment to the house of representatives, the senate is given sole power to try all impeachments. The number of representatives is fixed at 151; the number of senators varies from 31 to 35.

Article V focuses on the executive branch. The governor is the only official elected statewide, and his or her term is set at four years (in 1819, it was a one-year term). The governor is required to have been a citizen of the United States for at least fifteen years, and a resident of Maine for at least five years. In addition, any person filling the governorship cannot hold any other office under the jurisdiction of the United States, Maine, "or any other power."

Article V states that the governor is the chief law enforcer of the state. The governor may, on "extraordinary occasions," convene the legislature. Except for judges of probate and justices of the peace, the governor is empowered to nominate all judicial officers. The last parts of Article V outline some of the duties of the secretary of state and the treasurer. The secretary is required to keep all records of official proceedings of the governor, as well as those of the legislature. The treasurer is empowered to appropriate the funds for the payment of the state's debts if the legislature fails to do so.

Article VI delegates judicial authority to a Supreme Judicial Court and to "such other courts as the Legislature shall . . . establish." Except for the positions of justice of the peace and member of the Judicial Council, no justice is allowed to hold office under the jurisdiction of the United States or any other state. The rest of Article VI outlines the tenure of judicial officers and the election by the people of judges and registers of probate.

Article VII deals with the organization of the state militia. The governor is given the power to appoint all commissioned officers as well as the adjutant general, while the legislature is required to establish the necessary qualifications to hold a commission in the militia.

Article VIII is divided into two parts. The first part, which has received little alteration since 1819, establishes the role of the state in the education of its citizens. The second part grants home rule to the state's municipalities, allowing them to alter and amend their charters on all local matters "not prohibited by this Constitution or general law."

Articles IX and X outline a number of provisions that touch on all three branches of the state government, and also establish the financial restrictions and powers within which the government must work.

The basic structure of the Maine Constitution stresses broad popular participation and a state government equipped with fairly extensive powers. This was apparent in the state's original constitution, where suffrage and civil rights were broader than they were in Massachusetts, and where the governorship was considerably more powerful than it was in most states at the time (Maine's governor had veto power as well as appointive power). The state legislature began as the primary branch of government, and it has since maintained its independence. Among the fifty state assemblies, the Maine

Legislature's constitutional independence has been a particularly salient feature. The continuity in Maine's Constitution is part of the moderation that characterizes the state's politics. This moderation, in turn, is reflected in the careful balance of power between the people and their government.

Over the years, the Maine Constitution has had to be amended to make it relevant to changing circumstances. Although the number of amendments is much larger than the number of federal constitutional amendments, it is not so by state standards. Maine's fundamental charter ranks among the third of the states with the shortest constitutions, a grouping that also includes all the other New England states. State constitutions tend to differ regionally. As a New England state, Maine has what Daniel J. Elazar has termed a "commonwealth constitution."[4] This type of charter is usually brief and concerned mostly with setting forth the essentials of government. States in other parts of the country have tended to develop longer documents. In those jurisdictions, the constitution becomes a bargain or contract among contending political forces. As the forces change, the entire constitution is sometimes discarded and replaced by a new charter. Louisiana, for instance, has operated under eleven constitutions since it entered the Union in 1812. In contrast, Maine has tended to show long-run agreement on political questions, at least about matters it wants to settle on a constitutional basis. That habit seems to be a characteristic of its moralistic, broadly participatory political culture.

For the most part, amendments have not generated significant political controversy. They have tended mostly to be statements about government and public policy that are widely shared by Maine citizens at the time of amendment adoption. As noted by Marshall Tinkle, the leading scholar of Maine's fundamental charter, constitutional change has been a "triumph of gradualism."[5] Amendments must be proposed by a two-thirds vote of each house of the legislature, and must be approved by a majority vote in a popular referendum. Nearly 90 percent of the proposed amendments have been adopted. The amendments have enabled the Maine Constitution to remain relevant to a governmental process vastly different, in many respects, from the one it was originally designed to direct. The constitutional areas especially affected have been state institutions, state-local relations, the suffrage, and public policy.

State Institutions and the Maine Constitution

Created as the most powerful branch of government by the original constitution, the legislature has retained its strength through certain amendments. Paradoxically, even the amendments that restrict the legislature conserve the institution's original power. This has happened because the adoption of restrictive measures often offsets powers accumulated by the legislature.

The bulk of the amendments extending legislative power have been budgetary in nature. They have been concerned especially with the issuance of bonds and the level of permissible state debt. Most of them constitute an exception to the sixth amendment of 1848, one of the most restrictive of all measures placed on the legislature. This amendment forbade the loaning of state credit and limited the state debt to $300,000. The original document had not set a debt limit

The sixth amendment was adopted with the sole intention of circumscribing the powers of the legislature. This amendment was the result of serious financial difficulties in which the state found itself during the 1840s. During this time, Maine had overextended its credit in order to meet the costs of government and the sudden onset of the Northeastern Boundary Dispute.[6] The sixth amendment was written more as a guideline and a pledge than as a realistic expectation. As such, exceptions to it (in the form of bond issues) have been rather numerous over the years. This is not to belittle the restriction set out in the sixth amendment, which is both literal and symbolic.

Beginning in the 1950s, a series of amendments placed some procedural restrictions on the financial powers of the legislature. Among these, there has been the seventy-fifth amendment (1951), which requires that a statement of the state's outstanding debts must accompany all proposals to the voters for the issuance of new state bonds. The 151st amendment (1984) has placed a time limit on the life of authorized bonds. In one sense, these amendments help to bring the tenor of the constitution closer to what it had been in 1848, when the sixth amendment had just been ratified, and to distance it from the tone of the document in the 1940s before the restrictions were imposed.

Other amendments have also affected the legislature. Among those that extend its power are the seventeenth amendment (1876), which promises that the legislature shall never "surrender" its power of taxation, and the nineteenth amendment (1876), which allows the legislature to convene a constitutional convention in order to amend the constitution (though this has never been exercised). More recently, the 115th amendment (1970) enables the legislature to call itself into special sessions, a power formerly lodged with the governor alone.

Among the amendments particularly restrictive to the legislature are the sixth, already mentioned, and the fourteenth (1876), which promises that acts of incorporation will be established under general laws and not under special legislation. The 127th amendment (1975) limits legislative amendment and repeal of laws initiated or approved by the people.

Maine's executive branch has not been immune to alteration. During the nineteenth century, there was a protracted battle over executive power. Initially, as mentioned, the governor had extensive appointive powers, which included the naming of judicial, civilian, and military personnel. In 1856 several of these offices were made subject to popular election (ninth amendment). These included judges and registers of probate, municipal judges, and county sheriffs.

Beginning in the 1870s, state politicians began to rethink some of their earlier actions against executive power. This was partly because there were many officials responsible to a governor who had no direct influence over their selection. In Maine, this new thinking resulted in the repeal of portions of the ninth amendment. Under the sixteenth amendment (1876), the appointment of judges of municipal and police courts reverted to the governor, and the governor's power to appoint the adjutant and quartermaster generals was restored under the twenty-eighth amendment (1893).

The governor has gained some significant powers during the twentieth century. The thirty-eighth amendment (1917) allows the governor to remove county sheriffs in certain instances, and the seventy-eighth amendment (1955) expands the governor's pardon powers. In 1957 under the eighty-fourth amendment, the governor's term was extended from two years to four. In 1975 the Executive Council was abolished by the 129th amendment.

The Executive Council, consisting of seven members elected by the legislature, had been created by the 1819 constitution. Although the council was meant to "advise the Governor in the executive part of government," it provided one of the most significant restrictions to early gubernatorial power in Maine. The Executive Council was a vestige of Revolutionary suspicion of centralized power, and Maine "inherited" its council from the Massachusetts Constitution.

If the council did not already hamstring a governor, it could become an obstacle when the governor's party was not in control of the legislature. Frequent efforts were made to remove the council—by constitutional commissions in 1875 and 1962, by Gov. Edmund Muskie, and by the Democratic Party for decades. When those attempts succeeded in abolishing the council under the 129th amendment (1975), Maine's governorship was finally concentrated into the hands of the chief executive. The 165th amendment (1995) provided the governor with a line-item veto. Maine had been among a handful of states that had withheld that authority from its chief executive.

While many states have incorporated into their constitutions specifications concerning the structure of their executive branch, Maine's document says relatively little on the matter. Most of the broad changes in the state executive, particularly its growth from a handful of employees in the 1820s to the approximately twelve thousand employees in its current workforce, have been accomplished through statutory revision.

The state courts have received the least amount of constitutional revision. With the growth of judicial business, the legislature has been able to establish new courts and new levels of courts without resorting to amendments. The only court officially sanctioned by the constitution is the Supreme Judicial Court. The major changes that have occurred in that court through constitutional amendment have concerned judicial tenure. Originally, justices were allowed to serve until age seventy. This was altered by the third amendment (1840), which established seven-year terms and removed the age limit. The 132nd amendment (1976) allows justices to serve for six months after the expiration of their term, or until their successor is named, whichever occurs first.

STATE-LOCAL RELATIONS AND THE MAINE CONSTITUTION Like local governments in all states, Maine's towns and cities are, in constitutional theory, "creatures of the state." The state may direct their actions as it desires, and its powers include the authority to create, modify, and abolish local governmental jurisdictions. The original constitution was silent on the topic, but several amendments have significantly developed this relationship.

One of these was the twenty-second amendment which, in 1878, barred municipalities from creating debts exceeding 5 percent of their property valuations. The legislature had earlier allowed localities to sell a limited amount of bonds for the purpose of constructing railroads. Pressures on the legislature for further relaxation of the credit limitations on individual communities were so intense that the amendment was adopted to regulate the situation across the state. The municipal debt limit was later raised to 10 percent, where it remains today.

In general, amendments to the constitution concerning the state's localities have provided them with additional powers. The most important came in 1969 with the 111th amendment, which granted home rule to the state's municipalities. Under the provisions of home rule, local residents were given the power to alter or amend their charters on all local matters not prohibited by constitutional or general law. Previously, all changes in municipal charters had to be approved by the legislature. Thus, the structure and functions of local government could more readily reflect the overall philosophy of government in any particular community. In 1992 voters approved the 162nd amendment that required the state to fund mandates imposed upon a municipality by statute or executive order.

SUFFRAGE AND THE MAINE CONSTITUTION   Another important dimension of the Maine Constitution is suffrage. At the time of the 1819 constitution, the states had sole power to determine who could vote. Gradually, the federal government began to circumscribe state power in this area, through amendments to the federal Constitution, such as those granting suffrage to blacks, women, and persons age eighteen or older.

The seventh amendment (1848) marked the beginning of a long struggle to alter the manner of electing state officials. The original constitution required winning candidates for the house, the senate, and the governorship to obtain a clear majority of all votes cast in the particular election. In the absence of a majority, reballoting was necessary in the case of the house. The senate decided elections where no candidate for the senate had received a majority. In the case of the governorship, the entire legislature was called on to settle the contest.

When splinter parties evolved in the 1830s and 1840s, the majority system of elections broke down. In the 1846 house elections, some 40 percent of the districts had no majority winners and required additional contests. The solution to the problem was plurality elections, in which the candidate with the highest number of votes (whether or not a majority of all votes cast) was declared the winner. The seventh amendment (1848) established this procedure for the house of representatives, but voters rejected the plan for other offices.

In 1868 and 1872 elections for certain senate seats had to be decided by the senate itself because of the absence of a majority winner. In 1875 the thirteenth amendment was enacted to establish the plurality rule for senate elections. The governor, though, was still being chosen by the required majority vote. In three successive gubernatorial elections, beginning in 1878, no candidate obtained a majority of the votes. In one of these elections, the legislature chose a candidate who had not even obtained a plurality. In 1880 voters finally approved the twenty-fourth amendment, establishing plurality elections for governor.

Continuing the tradition in Maine where a fairly considerable amount of power was invested in the hands of the people, amendments defining the right to vote have generally expanded the suffrage. In the constitution of 1819, electors were restricted to male citizens age twenty-one or older (excepting paupers and American Native Americans) who were residents of Maine for at least three months preceding an election. All of these provisions have been modified. The passage of the seventy-seventh (1954) and one-hundredth (1965) amendments ended the official discrimination against Native Americans and paupers, though in practice the limiting provisions had often been overlooked. The voting age was lowered to twenty by the 113th amendment (1969), and then to eighteen by the 116th (1971). Residency requirements were removed under the 123rd amendment in 1974. In addition, a number of amendments have facilitated voting in various ways, such as authorizing the use of voting machines (fifty-ninth amendment, 1935).

One of the most important suffrage amendments was the thirty-first. When this was passed, in 1909, Maine became the first eastern state to adopt the direct initiative and referendum.[7] The initiative allows the people to enact statutes without legislative consent. The referendum allows them to veto measures already enacted by the legislature, as well as to approve initiatives.

Since 1909 the initiative and referendum have been used fairly frequently, especially in more recent years. Partly because of this, there is a trend toward restricting the use of these measures. Among the amendments that restrict the thirty-first amendment is the seventy-second amendment (1951), stipulating that any measure adopted through referendum which fails to produce adequate revenues for its services will become inoperative. The 144th amendment (1981) specifies that no signature on a petition older than one year is valid. Under the 167th amendment, adopted in 1999, a petition for a people's veto must be voted on at the next statewide or general election, not a special election. The purpose behind these restrictions, as well as several others, seems to be to prevent interest groups and small numbers of voters from manipulating the referendum and initiative processes for their own advantage.

In considering other amendments that have restricted suffrage, it should be noted that Maine failed to adopt a woman's suffrage bill prior to the Susan B. Anthony amendment, which became a part of the U.S. Constitution in 1919. The twenty-ninth amendment, enacted in 1893, required that voters be able to read the Maine Constitution in English, as well as write their names. Already enrolled voters were exempted. Enacted during the period of heavy in-migration of French Canadians, as well as other nationalities, the amendment was regarded as nativist and was strongly resented in French communities.[8]

PUBLIC POLICY AND THE MAINE CONSTITUTION   To a considerable extent, the amendments authorizing new bond issues outline Maine's expanding public policy responsibilities. Among these amendments, which are numerous, are mandates for soldiers' bonuses (forty-fifth, 1920), for fostering industrial development (eighty-second, 1957) and recreational development (102nd, 1965), for student loans (105th, 1967), for fisheries and agricultural enterprises (108th, 1967), and for Native American housing (119th, 1972). Other amendments have addressed school financing and road building.

Maine's use of constitutional amendments to establish social policy invites attention to the twenty-sixth amendment, which in 1885 "forever prohibited" the use of alcoholic beverages. Although this amendment had already been established as a statute—the "Maine Law"—in the 1850s, it rested on an uncertain basis because of Democratic opposition. The intention behind the twenty-sixth amendment was to provide a more secure basis for the law. Indeed, the twenty-sixth amendment was effective until it was repealed in 1934 under the fifty-fourth amendment.

Ensuring the thoroughness and protection of civil rights has been an important aspect of Maine's amendment process. As already mentioned, suffrage restrictions on Native Americans were removed in the 1950s. Another anti-discriminatory measure is the seventy-ninth amendment (1955), which removes the requirement that the governor be a natural-born citizen of the United States. Under the 158th amendment, adopted in 1988, all sexist language must be removed from the constitution.

Another example of Maine's constitutional social policy is the fourteenth amendment. Passed in 1875 this act promises that charters of incorporation will not be created under special legislation, but under general laws. The intention behind this amendment was to wipe out privilege, favoritism, and monopoly, which began to be associated with charters of incorporation given out by special legislation. In this sense, the fourteenth amendment was an important symbol, and a guarantee, of egalitarianism. In proposing the fourteenth amendment, Maine's legislature significantly restricted the scope of its actions, but perhaps not as dramatically as one might at first suppose. The case of *Taylor v. Portsmouth, Kittery, & York Railroad* (91 Maine 193, 1893) established the rule of law that if the legislature should grant a special charter, which might have been formed under general laws, only the state itself (not private citizens) can inquire into such an act's validity.[9]

THE NATIONAL CONTEXT OF MAINE'S CONSTITUTION

Political scientists have sometimes analyzed the evolution of state constitutions according to certain time periods. One widely accepted analysis specifies three periods of state constitutional and institutional development.[10] The first period, lasting from approximately 1776 to 1870, was one of legislative supremacy and the extensive use of popular elections to fill public offices. Those practices reflected the great stress given to the value of representation in the states at that time. The second period, from 1870 to 1920, primarily witnessed an effort to limit the power of the legislature, which in many states had become irresponsible and corrupted by political machines. Political power in state government proceeded to be splintered among many independent boards and commissions. The third and most recent period (since 1920) has stressed coordination in state affairs, and hence has focused attention on the need for a strong governorship.

Maine's development has somewhat resembled that pattern. Starting with a strong legislature, the state experimented for a time with the popular election of certain officials during the 1850s, but abandoned that practice by the 1870s. The fourteenth amendment's requirement of general incorporation laws in 1875 circumscribed the legislature, with the intention of reestablishing a process that had been tainted. Maine has rarely used its constitution to arrange the details of its executive branch. Although a large number of boards and commissions were created in the late 1800s and early 1900s, they generally did not achieve constitutional status. When major executive reorganization took place in the 1970s, little constitutional change was required. However, the long-term impact of the state's constitutional growth in the twentieth century has clearly been one of enhancing the power of the governor and the legislature.

In the past decade the constitution has been drawn into the political process to a greater degree than in the past. The increased use of the initiative and referendum to make law has led to the introduction of bills in the legislature extending those procedures to amending the state constitution. Thus far the legislature has not acted on the issue. The legislature has also resisted suggestions that it convene a state constitutional convention, which could consider a wide range of changes. Another issue concerned a provision in the Maine Constitution that disqualified from voting persons under guardianship because of mental illness. Voters defeated an amendment to remove the clause in 1997 and again in 2000. Shortly after the second rejection, the Disability Rights Center of Maine, the state's designated protection and advocacy agency, filed a lawsuit in federal district court on behalf of three individuals affected by the provision. The court found the language in violation of the Fourteenth Amendment to the U.S. Constitution and the Americans with Disabilities Act.[11]

CONCLUSION

The most salient feature of Maine's constitutional politics has been the generally successful reconciliation of two potentially clashing elements—the need for competent government and for a politically effective citizenry.

Maine's borrowing from Massachusetts seemed to set the state on an effective course, since the Massachusetts Constitution of 1780 recognized the importance of both elements in a political society. The idea of balance can also be found in the long amending process. Many amendments pull and tug at each other. For example, while the legislature has acquired powers to issue bonds (thereby eroding the sixth amendment), its powers have been restricted more recently. As another illustration, the very considerable powers given the people through the initiative and referendum have been recently clarified and more sharply regulated as the use of the devices has become more frequent. The result of such balancing has been that the constitutional structure set out in 1819 has largely been retained and made relevant to changing circumstances. Most particularly, the amendments to the Maine Constitution have both reflected, and helped to maintain, a spirit of moderation in the state's politics.

CHAPTER SIX

The State Legislature

The year 1991 was a disastrous one for the Maine Legislature.[1] Governor John McKernan would refer to it as "the session from hell." Tensions between the legislature and the governor grew steadily almost from the start of the legislative session in January. In part the conflict was an aftermath of the bitter 1990 gubernatorial election. Incumbent Republican John McKernan, who had been behind in the polls, narrowly defeated former governor Joseph Brennan (1979–1987), who sought to recapture the Blaine House after having served two terms in U.S. House of Representatives. Some Democrats claimed that McKernan had deliberately misled voters about the condition of Maine's finances. Brennan, who had built a reputation for fiscal prudence as governor, had insisted during his campaign that the state was headed into a major fiscal crisis. He repeatedly attacked McKernan for failure to address the situation. McKernan said some budget problems existed, but maintained they were far less severe than his opponent claimed. A few days following the election—after the state budget office published new data—the governor acknowledged the state was facing a rapidly mounting deficit, and that spending reductions would be necessary in the next (115th) legislative session.

Conflict between Democrats and Republicans in the Democratic-controlled legislature reached crisis proportions in June. According to legislative rules, in each chamber a two-thirds majority was required for a measure to become law immediately following legislative enactment by the legislature and endorsement by the governor (so-called "emergency" legislation). A bill with only a majority vote would not take effect until three months following enactment. With the fiscal year ending June 30 the state budget fell under the "emergency" provisions. That meant that Democrats, who had about 60 percent of the seats in each chamber, needed Republican votes. Governor McKernan insisted Democrats in the house and senate agree to reductions in the state's workers' compensation program in return for Republican legislators' votes to pass the budget. The Democratic leadership, led by House Speaker John Martin, refused. The stalemate lasted for three weeks, forcing the state government to shut down all but essential services after July 1. State workers picketed the capitol, pleading for a resolution of the budget crisis. The confrontation was publicized nationally. Newspapers in Maine denounced the legislature in language rarely seen in editorial pages in the Pine Tree State.

A compromise was eventually reached and the budget was enacted. However, the effects on the legislature were profound and negative. Almost immediately, a citizen's organization was formed to promote the idea of placing limits on the terms of state legislators. Not long after, an initiative gained the necessary signatures to be presented on a ballot for a statewide referendum. In November 1993, voters overwhelmingly approved a measure that restricted state legislators to no more than four consecutive terms in the same legislative chamber. The provision took effect in the 1996 elections. With that provision, Maine became the only northeastern state to limit its legislators' terms.

Why did Maine voters react so strongly to the 1991 budget crisis? What compelled them to scrap a representational system—one permitting unlimited terms of office for legislators—that had prevailed since 1820? A general answer is that the legislature was caught in a duel over two political values that has conflicted state government in recent decades. The conflict may be described as a tension between participation and professionalism, between the ideas of citizen involvement in government and the necessities of infusing governmental policymaking with expertise and technical knowledge. Maine's governmental institutions were at one time heavily staffed by citizens themselves. More recently, a greater degree of technical skill has been required in the courts and in the executive branches as well as the legislature. The balancing of that professional element with attention to input from citizens took place fairly gradually, and without great conflict, in the judicial and executive departments. On the other hand, it caused a major upheaval in the legislative process. The Maine Legislature in the past two decades has not been able to agree on what model to follow. As a Portland legislator commented in a debate over a proposed legislative pay raise, "The big issue is: do we want to be like New York, or do we want to stay more like New Hampshire?"[2]

THE CONSTITUTION AND THE LEGISLATURE

In contrast to the current debate, the framers of the Maine Constitution were in agreement about the legislature's job. In 1820 it was regarded as the foremost institution of state government. Alone among the states, the legislature had the power to name the secretary of state, the treasurer, and the state auditor. In the 1850s, it gained the right to name the state attorney general. In 1970 a national study group asserted that the legislature's strongest feature was its formal independence from the executive branch.[3] Unlike the case in many states, such as New Hampshire, where the state constitution has historically restricted legislative salaries (they are limited to $200 per year in New Hampshire), the Maine Constitution places few limits on legislative power. The main restrictions have focused on financial procedures, such as the requirement of voter approval of bond issues, but these limitations have not proved to be onerous.

The principal legislative issue that plagued the framers of the Maine Constitution was apportionment.[4] That was understandable given Maine's scattered and rapidly growing population in the early 1800s, and its commitment to citizen participation in affairs of government. House seats were allocated to towns according to their populations, but with some limitations. No town was permitted more than seven representatives, and towns with fewer than 1,500 inhabitants were grouped to form separate districts, with the provision that the representative would rotate from year to year among the towns of the district. The framers could not agree on a fixed size for the house of representatives. Anticipating population growth, they specified only that the house would be between one hundred and two hundred members. The first house had 143 members. In 1841 after the house membership reached 200, a constitutional amendment reduced its size to 151 members, where it remains. With an average of 8,800 citizens per house district, Maine has fewer constituents per legislator than all but a handful of states. The small size of these legislative districts tends to reinforce the citizen quality of Maine government, even in a time of professionalism and technology.

The framers allocated senate seats according to counties. In 1820 the three largest counties—York, Cumberland, and Lincoln—had four senators each, while the smallest counties, then the northernmost counties of Penobscot and Washington, each had one. The first senate had twenty-one members.

Historically, the legislative apportionment systems used in the Maine house and senate overrepresented rural areas, but only moderately. In fact, in studies in the 1950s, Maine ranked among the top third of states in fairness of representation, and was one of only two New England states to fall in that category.[5] In contrast, until the early 1960s, Vermont allocated one seat in its House of Representatives to every town regardless of size, which meant that as few as 12 percent of its voters could elect a majority of house members. After the U.S. Supreme Court declared that state legislative apportionments must be based on the principle of "one person, one vote," Maine joined all other states in revising its house and senate districts.[6]

An interesting change since the mid-1960s relates to single-member districts. In 1966 the senate abandoned multimember districts, long defined by county boundaries, and established individual senatorial districts. The house switched in 1975 from a mixed arrangement of single-member and multimember districts to a plan composed entirely of single-member districts. Previously, nearly one-third of its members, mostly from urban centers, had been elected in multimember districts.

The two parties had to strike a bargain in the legislature to bring about single-member districts. Democrats liked the multimember districts because they believed that these districts provided the party with an advantage in legislative races in the larger cities. Because Democrats held a majority of the voters in most cities, they could win all of the legislative seats in those cities in an election. Republicans opposed multimember districts for the same reason, and sought to redistrict cities into separate single-member districts, some of which they could expect to win. For their part, Republicans were able to name all of the members of the Executive Council (the advisory body to the governor) in the early 1970s because they had a majority of the seats in the legislature. The Executive Council, empowered to confirm gubernatorial appointments, regularly hampered the administration of Democratic Gov. Kenneth Curtis (1967–75) and the development of Democratic programs generally. Because abolition of the Executive Council required a constitutional amendment, both parties had to agree to the move. In return for Republican acceptance of removal of the Executive Council, Democrats agreed to single-member districts for all 151 house members.

THE LEGISLATORS

The changes in apportionment were accompanied by a greater diversity of people who won seats in the house and senate. Historically, despite Maine's participatory culture, the political and social bases of the legislature were fairly narrow. In the 1941 session, for instance, the two chambers had a combined total of 159 Republicans and only 23 Democrats. Approximately half the members listed their occupations as farmers or owners of small businesses, and only four members were women.[7] In terms of public policy, the one-party Republican legislature of that era was conservative and usually very attentive to the concerns of the business community, especially the pulp and paper and textile industries. As one scholar has put it: business occupied "a virtually invulnerable position" in state affairs, with great emphasis on "a low-power, low budget government with a minimum of taxes and a minimum of restrictions on business freedom."[8] It is useful to examine the ways in which the legislative membership has changed.

In the past three decades, the legislature has had competitive political parties, with the Democrats in the majority in both chambers since 1983 except the 117th session (1992–94) when the Republicans narrowly controlled the senate. Democratic margins have been substantial, but not overwhelming. In fact, only three times in the past thirty-five years have either the Republicans or the Democrats held as many as two-thirds of the seats in the senate, and no party has enjoyed that proportion of seats in the house during that period. The figure of two-thirds is important because the rules require that certain legislative measures be passed only with that size of majority. The fact that neither party has enjoyed an overpowering margin has generally fostered a bipartisan approach to legislative issues, where bargaining and compromise are crucial.

Though most of the state's history, turnover in each chamber approached 50 percent. Beginning in the 1970s, as the legislature added staff and legislative sessions lengthened, legislative turnover declined, reaching a level of about 20 percent in the late 1980s. Some members started to regard service as a representative or a senator as a career. That all changed after the 1993 term limits referendum; legislators who had completed four consecutive terms of service were prohibited from running for reelection to the same chamber. The law took effect in 1996. Soon after, the average length of service in both the house and senate sharply declined, from seven years in 1991 to slightly more than four years in 1997.[9] On the other hand, "termed out" legislators began to move more frequently from one chamber to the other. In 2006 four former senators went to the house and six former representatives arrived in the senate.[10]

Since the advent of term limits, the senate has revealed an unusual depth of legislative experience because the shifting between chambers usually runs from house to senate. The 2007 senate was revealing in this regard. The chamber was composed of 27 incumbents and eight new members. Of the eight new senators four came directly from the house and two others had earlier served in that chamber. Altogether, nearly two-thirds of the senators in that year were former house members. The more experienced senate has particularly seemed to enjoy an edge over the house in bicameral negotiations over appropriations.

What are the principal occupations of Maine legislators? Mostly, they are jobs that permit legislators to build the wide circle of friends and acquaintances so necessary in politics. Legislative occupations must also permit a legislator to maintain a flexible working schedule.

In 2005, approximately 20 percent of the house members were retired; approximately 25 percent were in business or self-employed. In the senate, about half of the members were involved as business-owners, self-employed, or workers, and only four members—about 12 percent—were retired. Educators are a significant presence in the legislature, especially in the house. Including retirees, their numbers composed about 20 percent of the 2005 legislature. Through statute, the legislature has encouraged Maine public school teachers to run for legislative office. A measure enacted in 1983 requires an employer to arrange a leave of absence for a teacher for as long as the teacher remains in the legislature.

In contrast to educators, fewer attorneys appear to seek legislative office. In 2005 the senate had four lawyers while the ten attorneys held seats in the house. Those numbers are somewhat higher than comparable figures for the 1989 session when only six attorneys were present in the entire legislature. In some sessions it has been difficult to find adequate legal representation on such committees as Judiciary and Veterans and Legal Affairs. The modest legislative salary and the ability of lawyers to advertise their services (which reduces the importance of the visibility of legislative service as a form of advertising) have contributed to a decline of lawyer-legislators.

Maine's legislators usually arrive in Augusta with considerable political experience. In the light of the state's strong town-meeting tradition, and the distribution of its population among a large number of small towns and cities, it is not surprising that a high portion of legislators have local office-holding experience. Typically, about half of the senators and representatives have held positions in local government such as city councilor, school board member, or member of a town board. Another common type of political experience is that associated with nonprofit agencies, social service groups, and other organizations that are quasi-public, such as the Substance Abuse Council, the Maine Lung Association, an area Agency on Aging, and the Coalition for Maine's Children. Those organizations have grown rapidly in the past three decades, and most of them are involved in state policy-making.

An important change has been an increase in the number of women legislators. Their rise has made the legislature far more descriptively representative of the state's total population than in the past. Since 1991 about one-quarter to one-third of the legislators have been women. Maine has ranked, in some sessions in the past two decades, among the top five states in the percentage of women legislators. After the enactment of term limits, the proportion of women dropped in the house but rose in the senate. This seemed due to efforts by women senators in their fourth (and final) terms to recruit as their replacements women representatives in their senatorial districts nearing the end of their own terms. Women legislators have in recent years occupied the senior leadership positions in both chambers. Rep. Elizabeth Mitchell (D.–Vassalboro) was Speaker of the house in 1996–98. Senator Beverly Daggett (D.–Kennebec County) was senate president in 2002–04. She was followed by Senator Beth Edmonds (D.–Cumberland County), who served as senate president in 2004–06 and in 2006–08. The first woman legislative leader was Democrat Lucia Cormier of Rumford, who was the house minority leader in 1959. (In 1960 Cormier unsuccessfully challenged U.S. Senator Margaret Chase Smith. That senate race was the first in U.S. history in which both major parties nominated a woman.)

THE LEGISLATIVE PROCESS

The Maine Legislature must accomplish a great deal of work in a short span of time. In the 2005 session, the house and senate considered 1,692 bills and passed 612 of them. Many of these measures were controversial and complex. The legislators must try to ensure that as much public participation as possible take place as the legislature prepares measures, even as it adheres to the time deadlines it has established. The first regular session, which takes place in odd-numbered years, must adjourn by the third Wednesday in June. The second regular session, which occurs in even-numbered years, must adjourn no later than the third Wednesday in April, and is limited by the Maine Constitution to certain types of legislation, such as "budgetary" matters and "emergency" bills.

To understand the workings of the legislature, it is useful to focus on three arenas of decision-making—the presiding officers, the party caucuses, and the standing committees. The powers and activities of each have shifted during the past few years because of legislative efforts to cope with an increased workload while still remaining, for the most part, a citizens' assembly. The steps in the legislative process once a bill reaches the floor of the legislature are also examined.

The Presiding Officers

In part-time state legislatures, the role of the presiding officers is normally crucial. These officials usually have much more information concerning legislative issues and legislative politics than individual members. Their commitment of time to the process is also usually far greater than that of other members. Maine's legislature has traditionally had powerful presiding officers.

One of them, Thomas Brackett Reed, Speaker of the house in the late 19th century, later became Speaker of the U.S. House of Representatives. The authority of the Speaker and the president of the senate includes the power of naming all members of the standing committees, presiding over the debates in their respective chambers, participating in overseeing the legislative staffs, sending members to national and regional conferences, and representing the legislature to the public. In addition, legislative leaders have played increasingly strong roles in the nomination and election of the individual members.

The power of the leadership grew significantly in the 1980s, especially under the Speakership of John Martin. First elected to the house in 1964, Martin represented Eagle Lake, a French community in the impoverished northern portion of Aroostook County, which borders the Canadian provinces of Quebec and New Brunswick. Like the Liberal Party in neighboring Canada, Martin has long supported an activist state government. A particular example was the establishment of the Land Use Regulation Commission (LURC), which provides the state with zoning authority over the extensive lands owned by the paper companies. Martin's power rested heavily on an unrivaled knowledge of the legislative process. A Republican floor leader once referred to him as the "most technically perfect parliamentarian I have even seen."[11] Under Martin the house and senate budgets grew, their staffs greatly increased in size, and the legislature began to assume the status as co-equal partner with the governor in state government.

Even before the crisis of 1991, however, Martin's handling of the Speakership was seen as heavy-handed. In one celebrated instance, the Speaker removed the chair of the powerful Taxation Committee in mid-session, when the legislator's handling of an important tax measure provoked his ire. Among conservative house Republicans, dislike of the Speaker grew particularly intense. Beginning in the early 1980s, they regularly introduced bills to impose term limits on legislators. The measures at first had little support, but a scandal in the Speaker's office would crystallize the opposition. In 1991 a top aide to Martin was found to have attempted to alter ballots from a special election housed in a room in the statehouse awaiting tabulation. Martin was not involved in the incident, but his judgment was called into question. When he stepped down in early 1993 after a revolt in his party, the power once centered in the Speaker's office declined sharply. The diminished authority of the Speaker was made permanent with the adoption of term limits in November 1993.

While term limits has altered the entire legislative process, its greatest effects have been on leadership, which includes the presiding officers and the floor leaders of each party in each house. Those officials once progressed through several positions, especially committee chair positions, en route to a leadership post. Since 1996 the leadership has been much more transitory, and it has followed a different path to leadership positions. The house has had a new Speaker in every two-year legislative session since 1996. Each Speaker has been in his or her fourth (and last) term in the house on the occasion of taking over the gavel. They have been respected for their abilities and commitment, but they have not been able to wield the authority of John Martin or even that of Speakers in the distance past. A large part of the problem is their lame-duck status at the point of taking over the position. Another difficulty is their having worked their way to the leadership position through their party's caucus. Several Speakers have risen, for example, from the post of majority leader, which they held in their third term. Before term limits, leaders typically came from chairmanships of powerful standing committees, and had a depth of expertise in both policy and committee operations that current leaders had trouble matching. The consequence is that the legislative process in the house is less predictable and more freewheeling than in the past.

The office of president of the senate has had somewhat less turnover in the past decade. Senator Mark Lawrence (D.–York County) served two consecutive terms in the post (1996–1998 and 1998–2000), and Senator Beth Edmonds (D.–Cumberland County) likewise served consecutive terms (2004–06 and 2006–2008). Because of the chamber's small size, most senators in the majority party serve as committee chairs, beginning in their first term. The presiding officer and floor leaders thus arrive at their posts with substantial committee experience. Still, the advent of term limits has lessened the influence of the president. Before 1993 senate presidents occasionally served multiple terms, the importance of the position magnified by its being next in line to the governorship. In the heyday of one-party Republican rule, indeed, the post was more often than not held by a politician planning to run for governor.

Even though they are currently in office for relatively short periods of time, legislative leaders have certain key sources of power to enable them to manage the legislature's business. One is the legislative staff. The legislature employs about two hundred staff members. Approximately half are technical and professional personnel who work on a nonpartisan basis (for example, researchers who staff the standing committees). The remaining staff members mainly consist of partisan employees assigned to the majority and minority leaders in each chamber, and to such offices as the clerk of the house and the secretary of the senate, which are under the control of the majority party. Through their staffs, members of the legislative leadership are able to stay abreast of and quickly influence developments throughout the legislative process. The present pattern contrasts sharply with the scarcely half-dozen aides that served the entire legislature until the early 1970s.

The influence of staff has grown since the advent of term limits. Staff aides in the Office of Policy and Legal Assistance, which provides support for the standing committee, have become involved with the management of legislation, sometimes advising committee chairpersons on the handling of bills as well as providing research assistance. Because staff members often serve longer than legislators, they form a critical "institutional memory" for the chambers concerning the disposition of issues in previous sessions. In recent sessions, officials such as the clerk of the house, the secretary of the senate, and the revisor of statutes have played key roles in acquainting new members with the legislative process. Their responsibilities have grown in maintaining the deadlines, schedules, and procedures necessary to keep the legislature's business moving. The legislative staff budget in the mid-2000s was approximately $25 million, placing Maine fairly high among the states in legislative funding considering its population and per capita income.

A second source of power for the legislative leadership is the Legislative Council. Composed of the ten members of the leadership (five from each house), the council has several functions. One involves the selection of bills to be considered at the second regular session of the legislature. Under a 1975 amendment to the state constitution, the business of the second session is limited to certain categories of issues, such as "budgetary matters" and "legislation of an emergency nature." The council decides at the beginning of the session which of the many measures that legislators wish to introduce will be accepted. The council has less authority over the filing of bills in the first regular session, but it can determine whether a measure that a legislator desires to introduce after cloture (a calendar date after which no new legislation is to be introduced) can be granted an exception.

In the hectic closing days of a legislative session, the council supervises the scheduling of measures and plays a critical role in deciding which bills receive funding. Because of their leadership positions, council members become more decisive on budget matters than the members of the Appropriations Committee during this period.

A final part of the council's authority is related to activities between legislative sessions. The council establishes the research agenda for the standing committees between sessions, specifying which projects will be funded. It also manages the non-partisan legislative staff, including committee staff members, and oversees the legislature's budget. The council's most important employee is the legislative director, who is in charge of the day-to-day operation of the legislative staff. Although very powerful, the Legislative

Council is still subject to Maine's law governing public meetings, which means that the council's proceedings are normally open to the public, except when personnel matters are considered. In many other states, the work of the Legislative Council would be conducted by rules committees in the house and senate. Meetings of those units are generally secret.

The Party Caucuses

A second part of the legislative process is the party caucus. Each house has a Democratic and a Republican caucus, which is composed of all the party's members in that chamber. In the house, the caucuses meet occasionally in the early months of a session, and more frequently in the closing weeks. In the senate, the parties usually caucus weekly. Caucuses have historically played a major role in the Maine legislative process. Their traditional function was to provide a forum in which party members and their leaders could discuss legislation and legislative strategy during the session. The caucus was a kind of dress rehearsal for the floor debates and formal action on the floor. For the part-time legislator, the caucus provided an efficient means of gaining and sharing information, and of learning about and helping formulate party strategy.

In the 1980s, the caucuses were less central in the legislative process. The responsibilities for developing legislation tended to devolve to the standing committees, which by that time had acquired staff. The increasing complexity of legislation also was a factor, as the caucuses were too large and unwieldy to fashion lengthy, detailed measures. Presiding officers worked directly with the committees, leaving the caucuses mostly to inform members about bills and to provide an airing for grievances. Occasionally, they were a pivotal place for the development of a party position on an issue, especially when the governor's interests were involved. After term limits arrived in 1993 the standing committees became less effective in the legislative process and the caucuses began to resume the role they had historically occupied. More legislation was reported to the floor, leaving to them the task of sorting out bills for floor debate. One responsibility the caucuses have always had is nominating candidates for leadership positions at the beginning of the session.

The Standing Committees

Maine is one of a handful of states that uses the efficient, timesaving device of joint standing committees to consider legislative bills. The units are always composed of three senators and ten representatives. Committee seats are distributed between the parties in a manner roughly proportional to the seats that each party holds in the legislative chamber. In recent Democratic-controlled sessions, committees have generally had two Democratic senators and one Republican senator, and six Democratic house members and four Republican members. Until the mid-1970s, a senator was normally named the committee chair. Due in large part to the influence of Speaker John Martin, a system of house and senate co-chairpersons evolved. The two legislators usually take turns in presiding over committee sessions, and share in directing the committee's work. Each committee has a clerk. Recently, the legislature has maintained about twenty standing committees covering the major areas of legislative policymaking. Appropriations, taxation, state and local government, education, human resources, and transportation are among the most important units.

The presiding officers determine the membership and the chairs of the committees. In the senate every member of the majority party, including first-year members, usually chairs a committee. As a senator gains seniority, he or she moves from chairing a less-busy committee to heading a more powerful unit. In the house, members normally serve two or three terms before chairing a committee. The floor leaders try to select as chairs people who will manage the units competently, are politically congenial with the leadership, and have shown themselves to be effective in floor debates.

The committees' importance in formulating legislation seemed to start in the 106th session (1973), when the legislature first employed professional researchers as committee aides. Until then, the committees worked without staff and depended heavily on lobbyists and other outsiders for technical information. Currently, the Office of Policy and Legal Analysis (OPLA) is composed of approximately twenty persons, most of whom have graduate degrees, and provides assistance, including bill-drafting assistance, for the committees. One or two members of the office are assigned to a major committee. A single staff member may serve two less-active committees. Between sessions, OPLA staff members assist legislative study groups, appointed by the leadership, which are composed of committee members, other legislators, and representatives of the public to investigate policy questions that have arisen during the legislative session. Recent task forces have reported on such topics as "The Parity and Portability of Retirement Benefits for State Law Enforcement Officers;" "Municipal and County Law Enforcement Officers and Firefighters;" "Compliance with Maine's Freedom of Access Laws;" "New Payment Models for the Logging Industry;" and "The Implementation of the Privatization of the State's Wholesale Liquor Business."

As legislative policymaking grew more complicated in the 1970s and 1980s, the committees gained power. With the assistance of staff, committees were able to research bills, evaluate the testimony provided in public hearings, and determine how comparable issues were handled in other states. Committees tried to put bills in nearly final form before reporting them to their respective caucuses. The critical stage is a committee's "work session," which follows the public hearing on a bill and is still open to the public. During the work session, the bill is discussed thoroughly, amendments are drafted, and votes of committee members are cast. If the leadership has strong views on the legislation, they will be made known at this point. At times, work sessions can consume several days and even weeks.

Since the mid-1990s, the standing committees have been weakened because of legislative term limits. The increased turnover has diminished the level of experience committee members bring to their tasks, particularly among the most powerful committees, on which were once found the legislature's most senior members. In the 118th (1996–8) and 119th (1998–2000) legislatures, for instance, the Appropriations Committee lost about half its membership. Furthermore, turnover has caused most committee chairs to be relatively new at their jobs. The average length of experience in their chamber among house committee chairs dropped from 8.8 years in the 116th legislature (1992–4) to 4.7 years in the 120th legislature (2000–02). A party leader observed in 2001 that "some of the committees dealing with complicated issues are struggling. Taxation, Appropriations, Health and Human Services all have issues taking considerable time to learn. Term limits do not allow that time."[12] Because of the committees' diminished expertise, legislators no longer extend the degree of deference to committee reports they did in the 1980s.

In reporting legislation, standing committees can recommend that the legislation "ought to pass," "ought to pass as amended," or "ought not to pass." There are no written reports beyond this indication of the committee's preference. On a controversial measure, a committee may submit both a majority and a minority report. Bills reported with a unanimous "ought not to pass" need a two-thirds affirmative vote of the chambers before they can be considered (which almost never happens). All other bills are placed on a legislative calendar and, under the rules of procedure of the house and senate, must be considered promptly by the chambers. To facilitate the handling of a bill on the floor, committees perform a certain amount of advance lobbying. When handling a complex measure, the house and senate chairpersons may assign each committee member a certain number of legislators (not on the committee) to contact before the committee releases its report.

Floor Action

After a measure is reported from committee, it moves through several more stages. Initially, a committee report has to be accepted. Once it is accepted, the bill is given a first reading. In the house, a bill that has been favorably reported from committee by a unanimous vote is placed on the Consent Calendar. After two legislative days, it is considered as passed to be engrossed, or put into its final form. Any member by an objection can remove a bill from the Consent Calendar, in which case it will have to follow the normal procedure of separate readings. The senate has no procedure comparable to the Consent Calendar.

Other committee reports may not be accepted as easily. Complex bills sometimes generate split reports, wherein committee members submit different versions of a bill. Rejection of a favorable report or acceptance of an unfavorable report can kill a bill at this stage. For most bills, particularly controversial ones, the second reading is the most important stage. Debate and the consideration of amendments take place at this point. Amendments are generally offered to most complex bills. Since the advent of term limits, floor debates have become more protracted. The chambers now must deal with various issues once mostly handled at the committee level. A major reason is that committees face more difficulty securing unanimous reports on the disposition of bills. For example, the number of committee reports where there was only one dissenting member grew from just thirteen in 1993 to forty-seven in 1999. On the floor, nonunanimous reports move more slowly since debate time is allocated. Even when committees do present unanimous reports, they have occasionally been reversed in floor debates. As one member said, "Why should I follow the recommendation of people who have no more experience in dealing with an issue than I do?"[13]

The legislature keeps a complete record of its debates. Following debate and amendment, a bill is passed to be engrossed. This task is carried out by the Office of the Revisor of Statutes. A bill that has passed to be engrossed in one house must move through similar stages in the other chamber. Very occasionally, a conference committee composed of three members of each house appointed by its presiding officer may be convened to reconcile differences in the house and senate versions of a measure.

Once a bill is engrossed, it is ready for enactment. By long-standing practice, this is accomplished first in the house, then in the senate. Although the rules of both chambers are similar, the legislative process usually takes less time in the senate than in the house, partly on account of the senate's smaller size. The senate also seems to display somewhat fewer philosophical and ideological conflicts than the house. That difference may exist because senators represent broader, more diverse constituencies than house members.

CONCLUSION

The legislature's place in state government has fluctuated in the past three decades. Historically an almost entirely "citizens' assembly," the legislature grew in power in the 1980s and early 1990s as members remained in office longer, as staff aides strengthened the work of committees, and as experienced, powerful presiding officers competed with the governor for attention in the state media. Following the arrival of term limits in 1993 the legislature's authority and prestige diminished. Power flowed away from legislators to the governor, the executive departments, and the legislative staff. An entirely new group of generally inexperienced leaders came to be in charge of each chamber in each subsequent session. More recently, things have improved as legislative leaders have learned to cope with the problems of turnover. One strategy has been a tightening of internal procedures, such as enforcing the deadlines governing the introduction of bills and the schedules standing committees must follow during sessions in reporting measures. The legislature's role in policymaking, while not as strong as it was two decades ago, seems to be more substantial than in the first years following the term limits law. After many years of debate, the legislature voted in 2007 to extend legislative term limits from eight to twelve years, subject to approval in a referendum. In November of that year, voters rejected the idea by a wide margin.

The feelings of Maine people about their legislature are illustrated in a letter that Representative John Diamond (D.–Bangor), house majority leader during much of the 1980s, received from a constituent. The writer was upset with Diamond's endorsement of a certain health measure that affected the Bangor area. After explaining his concerns about the legislation, the writer broadened his criticism of Diamond's politics. He summed up the legislator's eight-year career in the house by stating that his service in government had been a betrayal of the public trust and that he had done "nothing whatsoever for the people of Maine." Despite that hostility, the writer wrote a final message that suggests the close, neighbor-like relations most Maine politicians have with their constituents: "P.S. My parents send their regards."[14]

CHAPTER SEVEN

The Governor and the Administration

The Maine governorship reflects a different dimension of the state's political culture than does the legislature. Whereas the mostly "citizen legislature" stresses participation, the governorship emphasizes leadership and coordination, such as the development of consistent policies throughout the state. The need for consistency is implied in the state's moralistic culture, in which a commonwealth or communitarian conception of politics is uppermost, and no group or section of the state can be ignored in decision making in Augusta. Recent governors have made reconciling gaps in economic advantage in different parts of Maine a central goal of their administrations. The effort to establish such policies is complicated by the state's geography. With its population scattered throughout nearly five hundred communities, some of them remote and inaccessible, effective implementation of state programs is often difficult.

Maine's location in the extreme northeastern part of the country has led to other geographically related problems. For instance, United States and Canadian trade policies often differ, which sometimes leaves Maine industries, such as fishing, caught in economic warfare with their counterparts in eastern Canada. The governor must deal with federal agencies, with Canadian provincial premiers, and with other state chief executives in defending the state's borders and coastal interests.

As Chapter 5 pointed out, the Maine Constitution has not seriously burdened the governor. While it has kept three senior administrators (attorney general, secretary of state, treasurer) away from his control, it has not been used to fix the structure of the executive branch. In 1971 Maine was able to move from an executive branch primarily dominated by boards and commissions to a very different cabinet system of governance without the necessity of a constitutional amendment.[1] Those changes that have been made in the governor's constitutional power in recent decades have strengthened the chief executive's hand in virtually every case. New powers have included a four-year term (beginning with the gubernatorial election of 1962) and important budgetary and fiscal authority that was, until 1975, assigned to an executive council.

THE GOVERNOR IN HISTORY

A look at the individuals who have held the Maine governorship since 1820 shows something of the evolution of this aspect of Maine politics.[2] Especially relevant are the kinds of backgrounds that politicians elected to the governorship brought to the job and the careers that they followed after leaving office.

Maine's earliest governors all served one-year terms, and about half left after the conclusion of the one term.[3] The state thus had a fairly large number of governors in the early years of statehood; twenty-one men served as chief executive between 1820 and 1860. Most of them were born in Massachusetts, New Hampshire, or southern Maine. A majority had studied law, but the governors represented a variety of occupations. Enoch Lincoln, who was governor from 1827–1829 and who died in office, was a well-known poet. Nearly all of the governors had occupied some public office before becoming Maine's chief executive; especially popular were state legislative positions, which one-third held when elected to the governorship. Another one-fifth of the governors were elected directly from the post of U.S. congressman. After completing their term as governor, more than half the former chief executives returned to legislative service, winning seats in the Maine House of Representatives, the Maine Senate, the U.S. House of Representatives, or the U.S. Senate. Three governors left office to become judges.

Maine's early governors were mostly public persons with long records of service. Their careers suggest that they were adept in dealing with both state and federal issues. Maine had come into the Union as part of the Missouri Compromise of 1820, and federal issues continued to intrude into state politics in subsequent decades. An example was the 1842 Webster-Ashburton Treaty with England, which settled Maine's northern border and averted a war between the United States and Canada. The substantial political experience of the early governors suggests that political skills were highly valued as Maine tried to manage its rapidly growing, relatively egalitarian, frontier society.

In the years after 1860 Maine shifted from a state in which political parties had been competitive to a one-party Republican stronghold. Of the twenty-seven governors between 1860 and 1940, all but four were Republicans. Most were born in Maine, but they continued to come mainly from small towns. Fewer than half were lawyers. Other common occupations included newspaper editor, physician, and business executive. One governor, William Cobb, had been the president of the Bath Iron Works, the state's largest shipbuilding firm, before he entered politics. Another, Joshua Chamberlain, had been a college president and a military hero for the Northern army at the Battle of Gettysburg.

Like the earlier chief executives, however, most governors in this period continued to have state legislative experience; about one-quarter of them were serving in the legislature at the time of their election as governor. The presidency of the state senate evolved as a popular steppingstone to the governorship. However, in contrast to the pre–Civil War period, fewer than half of the chief executives remained in public life after leaving the governor's office. Of those who did, most held federal positions, especially in the U.S. Congress. Former governors figured in the cohort of Maine Republicans who served prominently in the federal government in the late 1800s and early 1900s. An example was Nelson Dingley (governor, 1874–76), who chaired the Ways and Means Committee in the U.S. House of Representatives in the 1890s. Dingley became associated with one of the nation's most important tariff measures, the Dingley Act of 1897.

Governors elected since 1940 have revealed some new background characteristics. While law continues to be the most predominant occupation, chief executives have tended to come from the larger communities, such as Portland, Lewiston, Bangor, Rumford, Waterville, and Augusta. That pattern reflects the rise of the Democratic Party, whose partisans traditionally have been concentrated in urban centers. Like earlier chief executives, however, a majority of governors in the most recent decades had legislative service as part of the career route to the state's top office. Four of them (all Republicans) were president of the senate at the time of their election. That steppingstone was no longer used when Democrats began winning gubernatorial elections in the 1950s. (Although Democrats have held a majority of seats in the state senate since the 1980s, their senate presidents have not shown an inclination to use the office to run for governor.) About half of the governors took a federal position after leaving office. Two—Frederick Payne and Edmund Muskie—moved to the U.S. Senate; another, Joseph Brennan, was elected to the U.S. House; and two others, Kenneth Curtis and John Reed, initially took appointive positions in Washington and eventually became U.S. ambassadors (to Canada and Sri Lanka, respectively). Most of the others went into the private sector. One governor (Horace Hildreth, 1945–49) served as president of Bucknell University in Pennsylvania for many years after leaving office.

Thus, two career traits of Maine governors through history seem to be their holding legislative office before becoming the state's chief executive and their serving in federal office (either elective or appointive) after leaving the governorship. Because Maine has no statewide elective office other than the governorship, the legislature is a crucial place for a prospective governor to line up political support. Among the New England states, more governors in Maine have served in their state legislature at some point in their careers than have the chief executives of any other state.[4] The possession of both legislative and executive experience has undoubtedly aided governors in building successful federal careers after leaving office.

THE ROLES OF THE GOVERNOR

In performing the job of governor, the chief executive plays several roles, which sometimes conflict, including the functions of chief of state, legislative leader, chief of administration, party leader, and ombudsman. While these tasks have always been associated with the gubernatorial office, they have grown more complex with each succeeding gubernatorial administration. The current governor, John Baldacci, elected in 2002 and reelected in 2006, is served by an executive-office staff of approximately twenty people. These staff members assume various functions that the chief executive once handled virtually alone. Like members of the legislature, the governor struggles to maintain personal contact with Maine citizens even as he oversees a government now spending about $3 billion per year.

Chief of State

In the role of chief of state, the governor speaks for all of state government, even though he officially heads only one branch.[5] The role may be particularly important in Maine because the direction of its politics depends heavily on the personality and style of its leader. Political parties have become highly candidate-centered, but even their nominees are not always successful. Twice in recent decades, independent candidates possessed with charisma and a strong message resonating well with voters won the governorship over the best efforts of the parties.

That governors greatly symbolize the state government's activities has contributed to wide fluctuations in the public's evaluation of them. When the state executive branch nearly closed down in 1991, in a tumultuous conflict between Gov. John McKernan and the state legislature, McKernan was one of the least-popular chief executives among the fifty states. A decade later, with the state economy growing and the executive and legislative branches operating in relative harmony, Gov. Angus King enjoyed a ranking as one of the most well-regarded governors in the country. In his first term (2003–2007), Gov. John Baldacci's poll numbers ranged from about two-thirds of voters' approving his performance in office in his first year to less than 40 percent doing so in his third year, after several controversial issues had been in the spotlight.

To maintain popular support, Maine governors typically rely on a few overarching themes. Those ideas are usually part of their inaugural addresses. The declarations deal as much with their approach to the process of government—an always important topic in this state—as with requests for new programs. Governor King stressed a need for bipartisan cooperation, especially in finding ways to encourage economic growth. Governor Baldacci proposed a variety of new programs, especially in health and education, and stated that his approach would be incremental. Both King and Baldacci proposed ways to mitigate economic disparities among Maine's regions, in order to ease the "two-Maines" problem. And both King and Baldacci tried to encourage Mainers to be optimistic about the possibilities of growth and progress in their state. Beyond establishing general directions, governors carry out the role of chief of state through an assortment of specific tasks. The governor greets visiting dignitaries, serves as honorary chair of various civic and charitable committees, attends all manner of social and sporting events, gives college and high school commencement addresses, cuts ribbons for new buildings and parks, and talks to many citizens' groups. All that involves much travel around the state. Maine is mostly a state of small towns—almost five hundred—and its expansive geography always shapes its politics. Governors typically try to visit as many communities as possible. Governor Baldacci's staff estimated that in the months of July, August, and September 2005—to take one period of time—he visited forty-six Maine towns, several of them more than once. Some visits were connected to a local celebration, such as Rangeley's 150th anniversary as a town; others helped further a gubernatorial program such as economic development (by recognizing the expansion of a potato processing plant in Mars Hill).

Governors arrange their travel differently. John Baldacci usually visited a town on his own or with at most one or two other state officials. In contrast, former Gov. John McKernan made traveling into a more formal event. Under a program dubbed "capital for a day," McKernan directed state affairs from the locality he visited during the time he was there. On such a visit, most of his cabinet officers would accompany him. Once in town, they would seek out their counterparts in the local government to discuss state–local relations. At some point, a town meeting would be held at which the citizens could ask questions of the state leadership. The visit would also include news releases of state governmental actions affecting the community.

As chief of state, the governor also represents Maine in meetings with the national government and with officials of other countries. In his first term, Governor Baldacci was successively vice chair and chair of the Northeastern Governors' Conference. Maine governors are also members of the National Governors' Association, the New England Governors' Conference, and the New England Governors' and Provincial Premiers Conference, an organization that brings together U.S. and Canadian officials to consider border problems. Governors Brennan and McKernan each chaired that organization during their years in office. Overseas travel in conjunction with trade and economic development projects is also an essential part of a governor's work. Recent chief executives have committed two to four weeks annually to that activity, primarily in visits to European nations.

Another important task is crisis management. Maine's rugged terrain and climate sometimes present governors with severe weather challenges. In early January 1998 the state experienced a severe ice storm, which lasted nearly a week and caused about three-quarters of the state's population to lose electricity. After declaring a state of emergency, Gov. Angus King spent most of his time with the president of Central Maine Power Company, appearing regularly on news broadcasts to discuss the status of repairs to the state's power grid, arranging assistance for persons in remote parts of the state and lining up federal financial assistance. Gov. John McKernan faced a similar emergency a decade earlier (in April 1987), when large areas of central Maine were flooded because of a sudden thaw after an above-average winter snowfall. As one governor's aide expressed it: "when a crisis like that hits, everything else stops."

Legislative and Policy Leader

A second gubernatorial role is that of legislative and policy leader. Although the Maine legislature tries to protect its independence, it has long depended on the governor to provide leadership in policy formulation. The chief executive's program is usually the focal point for legislative debates. The program is announced in various ways: through the governor's state-of-the-state message at the beginning of a legislative session in January, through occasional special messages, and, above all, through the executive budget that the governor recommends to support state operations. Fiscal issues have assumed particular importance in the past decade, and the governor's legislative powers have grown accordingly. Appraising Governor Baldacci's impact on first session of the 121st legislature in 2003, during which the central issue was a $1.2 billion gap in the state budget, a Republican legislative leader acknowledged, "He absolutely set the agenda. I'd be hard-pressed to name a major initiative that came out of this session that wasn't introduced by the governor."[6]

Under the state constitution, the governor has some specific legislative powers. One is the authority to call the legislature into special session. Chief executives typically call the legislature into special session to consider emergency measures and items remaining from the regular sessions. Special sessions generally last only one or two days and are focused on the subject matter in the governor's call, sometimes a particularly controversial topic. During the Baldacci administration, Democrats and Republicans fought over the amount of borrowing that the state should undertake for long-term projects involving the environment and the conservation of land. The governor called several special legislative sessions specifically to resolve those questions. The governor also has a major voice in determining, with the Legislative Council, what measures are to be considered during regular sessions of the legislature.

Another power is the executive veto. If a governor vetoes a bill, the legislature must pass the measure by a two-thirds majority in each chamber for it to become law. Maine chief executives have customarily used their veto power sparingly, but with great success. During his eight years in office (1979–87), Gov. Joseph Brennan vetoed thirty-three measures, of which the legislature later passed only four over his objections. Although the Republican Party was in the minority in both chambers during Republican Gov. John McKernan's tenure (1987–95), the legislature overrode only one of his 90 vetoes. Independent Gov. Angus King (1995–2003) compiled a similar record: he vetoed fifty-two measures and on only two occasions did the legislature muster a two-thirds vote to override. In his first three years (2003–2005), Governor Baldacci vetoed three bills, none of which were overridden.

Even though the veto is important to the governor as a means to prevent a measure from becoming law, the threat of a veto can be even more potent in securing legislation desired by the governor. Gov. John McKernan was particularly adept at that process, as suggested in a newspaper report summarizing the results of the 1989 legislative session:

McKernan told Democrats he would veto the entire state budget if it did not include 85 new positions at the Augusta Mental Health Institute. He said he would veto any property-tax relief package if it did not contain the GOP-backed homestead exemption. . . . And he warned that he would only accept "sin" taxes to finance an omnibus health care package. He got his way in each case.[7]

When the legislature is in session, the governor devotes more time to legislative business than to any other responsibility. Most of this work involves informal negotiation. Meetings with legislators range from personal conferences in the governor's capitol office, to working lunches at the Blaine House (the governor's official residence) across the street from the capitol, to organized meetings with the legislative leaders of both parties. Observers believe that the imposition of term limits on legislators, which took effect in 1996, has significantly strengthened the chief executive's influence with the legislature. That seems to have been especially the case with Angus King (1995–2003), who as a political independent had no formal political base of support in the legislature. In its eight years, the King administration was consistently able to shepherd major legislation through the house and senate, often overcoming opposition from legislative leaders. Particularly effective was the expert testimony King officials offered the standing committees when those units studied administration-related legislation. Because of term limits, the institutional "memory" the committees once enjoyed had faded, making them more dependent on information from the executive department. Of course, governors do not always prevail in legislative matters. Both Governors King and Baldacci found themselves unable to resolve certain major tax and budget problems during their respective tenures.

Among Maine governors in the past several decades, only independent James Longley (1975–79) was mostly unsuccessful in his legislative relations. Longley's combative approach toward many issues angered legislators, and he never developed a dependable core of supporters. More than half of the more than one hundred vetoes he cast during his term were overridden. For other governors, the fact that they have had to deal with legislative chambers occasionally controlled by the opposing party has not posed a major obstacle. As an example, Edmund Muskie (1955–59) faced legislatures where the Republican Party held about two-thirds of the seats. Muskie reportedly won passage of about 65 percent of the bills he supported, and about 90 percent of the most important bills, by working cooperatively with the Republican leadership.[8]

Today, the outcomes are similar, although the process is more involved because legislation is generally more complex. The staff of the past three governors' has included three senior policy aides, each of whom specializes in the activities of approximately one-third of the administrative departments. The clusters include natural resources, human services, and economic development. Departments forward their requests to the group, which in turn helps the governor fit the proposals into his overall legislative program. The policy aides also assist the governor in overseeing the implementation of policy in their respective cabinet departments.

Chief Administrator

A third role the governor plays is that of chief administrator. Unlike the tasks of chief of state and legislative leader—which have long occupied a prominent place on the governor's schedule—the responsibility of overseeing the executive branch has only recently claimed a major part of the governor's time. It was not until 1971 that Maine provided its chief executive with significant appointive powers. Before that time, the governor lacked administrative authority over many state operations. Beginning with Kenneth Curtis (1967–75), each succeeding governor appears to have devoted increasing attention to program implementation.

The governor supervises a cabinet composed of about twenty departmental commissioners, who are appointed by the chief executive (with the consent of the senate) and serve at his pleasure. The cabinet normally meets once a week. Those present include both cabinet officers and senior members of the governor's staff, such as the chief of staff, the policy aides, the communications director, and the legal counsel. Discussions generally focus on the governor's agenda, particularly his legislative priorities during the months when the legislature is in session, but they also cover many other issues. In a September 2004 cabinet meeting, for instance, the items considered included, among other matters, a status report on Maine troops overseas, a report on the two-year budget to be submitted in January to the legislature, the level of unemployment in the state, certain agricultural issues, an upcoming gubernatorial trade mission, and the state chamber of commerce's position on a forthcoming referendum seeking to cap local property taxes.

Part of the governor's success as administrative chief depends on his relations with the state workforce. Maine has approximately twelve thousand executive-branch employees, about two-thirds of whom work in the Augusta area. All governors try to improve employee morale and performance, and in so doing place their respective stamps on the state bureaucracy. Governor Brennan (1979–87) divided an existing Department of Finance and

Administration, such that a separate cabinet department (Department of Administration) could focus specifically on management problems. Within that department a new bureau of employee health was established. Under Governor McKernan (1987–95), the Department of Administration created a Maine Executive Institute in cooperation with the Department of Public Administration at the University of Maine to provide seminars for state agency managers. Gov. Angus King (1995–2003) promoted the use of computers to link state departments to the public. His efforts led to Maine's becoming a leading state in "e-government," with citizens able to obtain approximately 130 different licenses from its website (www.maine.gov). In his first term, Governor Baldacci brought about a merger of the Department of Human Services and the Department of Behavioral and Developmental Services to form a new Department of Health and Human Services. The aim was to enable the state to address client problems in a more coordinated fashion. Baldacci also worked closely with all departments in his first year in office in order to effect a workforce reduction necessary to close a large gap in the state budget.

Political Party Leader

In addition to the three roles discussed, the governor also serves as head of his or her political party and as such is called upon to help recruit candidates for office, to assist in fund-raising efforts, and to oversee the development of party policy in the legislature. During his tenure, Governor Baldacci held regular meetings with Democratic leaders during legislative sessions, separate from the bipartisan leadership meetings. In 2004 and 2008 he led the delegation to the Democratic national conventions, and helped direct the party's presidential campaigns in the state. Nonetheless, the governor's role in leading his or her political party is probably less important in Maine than in states with more robust party organizations. Governors have relatively few patronage jobs to dispense, and more important, tend not to use party loyalty as a major criterion in awarding positions. Only about 15 percent of John Baldacci's appointments in 2003 involved individuals who had financially supported his campaign the year before.[9] Most significantly, candidates generally win office in Maine on the basis of their own personal and political organizations. The party structures alone are too weak to be relied on.

Ombudsman

The role of ombudsman for the state's citizens is another part of the governor's responsibilities. Historically, a portion of the gubernatorial workweek was given over to visits with private citizens. Citizens would present individual problems and requests to the chief executive, who would then follow through with the matter or assign it to an assistant. The governor would often interview people personally before nominating them to state offices and commissions. Modern-day governors are too involved with their administrative and legislative responsibilities to engage heavily in this type of work. Recent governors have committed less than 10 percent of their working time to one-on-one meetings with private individuals.

Still, in Maine's participatory politics, some aspects of the ombudsman role remain. Governor Baldacci's staff estimated his communications from constituents included, on a daily basis, about 150 E-mails, 50 letters and 20 FAXes. The governor made some kind of reply to all of them. A staff assistant directed many requests to the appropriate administrative agency for resolution. The most common problem involved child support, and those messages were forwarded to the Department of Health and Human Services. Once the aide ascertained the department's decision, she informed the governor, who then wrote a response to the constituent.

A related responsibility affecting private citizens is the filling of positions on Maine's approximately three hundred independent, part-time boards and commissions. Governors annually name about a thousand individuals to boards ranging from the Maine-New Hampshire Bridge Authority and the Board of Examiners on Speech-language Pathology & Audiology to the Advisory Board for the Licensing of Guides and the Board of Commissioners for the Portland Harbor. While most vacancies are filled solely at the governor's discretion, a few positions also require senate confirmation. Organizations with ties to specific boards usually suggest candidates. Andrew Cashman, who handled appointments for Governor Baldacci in his first term, regarded his job as accommodating as many qualified persons as possible, and sought alternative positions for individuals not selected by the governor.

STATE ADMINISTRATION

Development of the Maine executive branch since 1820 has witnessed the gradual centralization and structural integration of many separate agencies under the authority of the governor. The primary reason for administrative change has been the growth in the complexity of executive activities. At the turn of the century, there existed "an administrative organization which totaled some 27 offices, commissions, and boards."[10] Soon afterward came such new state units as the Industrial Accident Commission, the Highway Commission, and the Department of Charities and Corrections. By 1932 there were twenty single offices and forty-five boards and commissions. Under Gov. William Tudor Gardiner (1930–32), some limited consolidations were accomplished, but the state continued to add functions. In 1955 when Edmund Muskie took office, there were more than one hundred separate agencies, many of which were headed by administrators whose terms exceeded that of the governor. Finally in 1971 Maine adopted the cabinet form of state administration. Under this form, nearly all administrative activities are organized into cabinet departments, each headed by a commissioner who is named by the governor and serves at his or her pleasure.

How do Maine's citizens view their state's bureaucracy? Generally, they seem to have a love-hate relationship with it. In a survey a few years ago, they agreed by an approximately two-to-one margin with the statement that "it's government's responsibility to assure such basics as housing and health care."[11] A substantial majority also indicated that they felt they could influence the government; only one-third agreed with the view that "people like me are unable to affect or change the policies of government." Mainers divided fairly evenly on the proposition that "the state bureaucracy is so strong that things will stay pretty much the same no matter whom we elect to office." The various administrative agencies have grown dramatically in influence in recent years, and will continue to be major players in the state's efforts to meet the challenges of an ever more complex society.

SOME MAJOR DEPARTMENTS

One of the largest departments in the executive branch (2,400 employees) is the Department of Transportation (DOT).[12] The department's evolution is fairly typical of the way state administration as a whole grew. It emerged from the State Highway Commission, which was created in 1913 to build roads after the invention of the automobile. The commission was a three-member body, whose chair had a seven-year term. It was made a part of DOT in 1971 along with units regulating ferries, railroads, and airports. The department has seven field offices, which are responsible for maintaining 30,000 miles of state road. Its biennial budget of approximately $1 billion is heavily financed by the state gas tax of twenty-six cents per gallon, which can be used only for road and bridge construction and maintenance. Additionally, about one-third of DOT's funds come from the federal government. Unlike some states, Maine's transportation policies are rarely affected by partisan changes in the governorship. The current commissioner of DOT, David Cole, was formerly the President of the Eastern Maine Development Corporation, a nonpartisan position. Two of his predecessors as DOT commissioner had earlier served as city managers of Presque Isle and Old Town, respectively.

The Department of Health and Human Services (DHHS) is responsible for the second largest budget in state government, spending over $1 billion annually. The department began in 1885 with a six-member State Board of Health. In 1913 the legislature created a five-member Board of Charities and Corrections. The boards were merged into a Department of Health and Welfare in 1931, and eventually into the present department in 2003 as part of a major reorganization of the Baldacci administration, which brought together formerly separate units dealing with welfare services, physical and mental health services and children's services. The current structure tries to make the department accessible to citizens in all areas of the state. DHHS has three regional offices and eight district offices. The new department structure is designed to provide a holistic approach to families and individuals in need, who often require several different types of services. To that end, field offices of the formerly separate units have been merged where possible. Many of the activities of the department are carried out in conjunction with citizen advisory groups, such as the Maine Council on Alcohol and Drug Abuse Prevention and Treatment, the Advisory Committee for the Division of Deafness, and the Maine Human Services Council. Consistent with Maine's nonpartisan style of managing state functions, DHHS and its organizational predecessors have shown little attention to ideology from one gubernatorial administration to another.

Some administrative departments have relatively small numbers of employees, but major responsibilities because of the way the legislature formulates their mission. A good example is the Department of Education (DE), which has only a few hundred employees even though the state commits the largest share of its budget to this department. Most funds are funneled to localities where the vast majority of education personnel are concentrated. The department began in 1846 with a Board of Education, composed of one member from each county. The board named the education commissioner until 1971, when that power shifted to the governor. DE provides technical assistance and regulations for Maine's local school districts. A major educational dilemma in the state is the gap between the rates of graduation in Maine high schools—which are among the highest in the country—and the relatively low levels of college attendance by high school graduates. Under the urging of Governor Baldacci, the state established a new system of community colleges in 2004, designed in part to address this problem.

The Department of Marine Resources began in 1867 with the establishment of two commissioners of fisheries, and assumed its present form in

1973. It is concerned with the conservation and management of marine resources, and with seafood safety and boating safety along Maine's 3,500
miles of seacoast. Among state agencies, the department has an unusually
high level of involvement with groups and organizations outside of Augusta. Specific advisory councils assist the department in setting rules for the
management of various types of sea life. Five lobster zone councils regulate, for instance, the number of licenses issued in five separate areas of
the coast. The department works closely with the New England Fisheries
Management Council and the Atlantic States Marine Fisheries Commission
to protect the state's coastline. Within state government, the department is
closely monitored by the legislature's standing committee on marine resources, whose members include many legislators with coastal constituencies. The committee oversees departmental rules and takes an active interest
in its management.

The Department of Conservation, created in 1973, brought together several independent natural resource units. Its mission is to promote responsible, balanced use of Maine's land, forest, water, and mineral resources.
With seventeen million acres of forestland, Maine is the most heavily forested state in the United States. A critical responsibility is the management
of about ten million acres of unorganized territory in the northern part of
the state, the largest contiguous undeveloped area in the Northeast. A major
unit in the department is the Land Use Regulation Commission, created in
1971, which serves as the planning and zoning authority for that area. With
few local governments, the state is required to handle those regulatory matters. The department is often a center of conflict over development issues, as
more land becomes available with the decline of the paper industry.

Another part of the administrative structure is the Executive Department
itself, which houses three units: the governor's office, the State Planning
Office, and the Office of Public Advocate. The governor's office consists
of approximately twenty employees, who assist the chief executive in the
several areas of his responsibilities. In 2005 the office included a chief of
staff, three policy advisors, each assigned to work with certain cabinet departments, a communications director, a legislative aide, a director of constituent services, a director of boards and commissions, a legal counsel,
and several other assistants. Displaying that partisanship is irrelevant in the
selection of some gubernatorial staff, Governor Baldacci retained three personal aides, including his office receptionist, who had served in the same
positions in the King administration.

The governor's office is at times the home for new functions the governor regards as particularly important and which carry his stamp. A good

example is the Dirigo Health Care Program, which was a key piece of legislation in Baldacci's first term. It involves arrangements to control health insurance costs for small businesses, which employ about 70 percent of the state workforce, thus enabling them to offer insurance coverage to their employees. The state works with insurance companies to develop policies that small business can afford, and helps low-income workers with their premiums. After the legislature approved the program in 2003, it was housed in the Office of Health Policy and Finance, which was part of the governor's office.

The State Planning Office occupies an important role in Maine state government. It has about fifty employees. Its research staff assists the chief executive, and to some degree the legislature, in setting long-term goals through economic analyses and forecasting, and it also has several operational responsibilities. It oversees programs that generally fall between the jurisdictions of the cabinet departments, particularly intergovernmental programs. The office administers federal funds related to such programs as reducing coastal hazards (under the Coastal Zone Management Act of 1972) and providing community service volunteers (under the AmeriCorps program). It also coordinates energy conservation policies. In regard to local governments, the Planning Office is involved in such activities as land use planning, the training of municipal code enforcement officers, and establishing community waste management and recycling programs.

The Office of Public Advocate represents the interests of citizens before independent regulatory bodies, such as the Public Utilities Commission. It is responsible for arguing public concerns that might not otherwise be voiced in regulatory proceedings. Since its creation in 1982 the office claims its efforts have saved Maine rate-payers over $200 million. The office is fairly small—about eight employees—and has on occasion become embroiled in legislative budget battles that threatened to reduce its size even further. Democrats generally support the agency more than Republicans.

What types of backgrounds do the officials who head the executive departments bring to their jobs? Looking at the group of commissioners who composed the Baldacci cabinet in 2005, those officials were mostly long-time Maine residents who brought to their jobs fairly extensive experience in state and local government. Six commissioners (Administration and Finance, Defense, Environmental Protections, Health and Human Services, Professional Licensure and Financial Regulation, and State Housing Authority) had attained their positions through promotion from within their own units, or from senior positions in other state departments. Another five commissioners (Education, Inland Fisheries and Wildlife, Public Safety,

Transportation, and Workers Compensation) assumed their posts after occu-
pying local administrative positions in the state. Such posts included county
administrator of Aroostook County, school superintendent of Windham,
and executive director of the Eastern Maine Development Corporation. Two
more commissioners (Conservation, Economic and Community Development) had each served several terms in the state legislature. Another cabinet
member, the Director of the State Planning Office, had served as the Director of the Legislature's Office of Policy and Legal Assistance. Two commissioners (Finance Authority of Maine and Labor) were recruited from the
private sector. Reflecting the state's nonpartisan tendencies, the remaining
three commissioners (Agriculture, Corrections, and Marine Resources) had
first joined the cabinet of Independent Gov. Angus King and continued under Democratic Gov. John Baldacci.

Recent governors have only rarely looked outside of the state to find their
cabinet nominees. In 2005 all but two of the department heads had been
born in and/or received their education in the state.

The profile of the Baldacci cabinet supports the idea that Maine state
government's transformation from a modest caretaker operation to one with
a major, ongoing impact on the lives of its citizens has helped produce a political class in the state. Nearly all of the top officials in the executive branch
in the mid-2000s were career public servants, some holding public positions
for twenty or thirty years. Their careers revealed much professional mobility. Cabinet officers had earlier moved among different state executive agencies, different branches of the state government, different levels of government, and, in some cases, between public interest groups and governmental
positions. Maine's political class is a product of the state's participatory
culture, but it particularly reveals the modern technological component of
that culture—the blending of civic involvement and activism with the professional skills needed to administer complex policies.

LEGISLATIVELY FILLED OFFICES

The Maine legislature selects four administrative officials: the attorney general, secretary of state, state treasurer, and state auditor. The most powerful
of these officials is the attorney general (AG), who is the state's chief law
enforcement officer and the legal representative of the state. Although the AG
speaks for the governor and the legislature in the state courts, he or she has
the final authority to determine what cases to pursue. Additionally, no state
agency can proceed to court without the AG's approval. The office is made
up of approximately one hundred lawyers, most of whom staff the several

administrative departments. About one-quarter of the attorneys, for instance, are assigned to the Health and Human Services to work on cases ranging from child abuse to challenges to the licensing procedures for foster homes.

In recent years, the office has taken on greater importance by virtue of joint activities with other states' attorneys general in consumer protection, health care, and antitrust issues. As part of a settlement with major tobacco companies over illnesses caused by cigarette smoking, Maine obtained approximately $60 million per year, which it commits to solving public health problems. Under Attorney General Steven Rowe (2001–09), Maine was been particularly active in pursuing cases involving consumer fraud by interstate businesses. Another growing responsibility is enforcement of drug laws. In 2004 the AG's office prosecuted some six hundred cases involving cocaine, heroin, marijuana, and other drugs. Six assistant attorneys general are employed as Drug Task Force Attorneys, and work with the various district attorneys around the state in those prosecutions.

The attorney general has the sole responsibility in Maine for prosecuting homicides, and works with local district attorneys on other criminal cases. In recent years, the office of attorney general has proved attractive to gubernatorial aspirants. Governor Brennan broadened his political support through his handling of the Indian Land Claims cases while attorney general (1975–79). His AG successor, James Tierney, the 1986 Democratic nominee for governor, had pursued numerous cases on behalf of consumers and environmental groups. Attorney General Rowe is regarded as a possible Democratic candidate for governor in 2010.

The secretary of state maintains the state archives. It is the office that preserves the articles of incorporation for businesses incorporated in Maine. In addition, some of the more controversial aspects of state government are located here. The secretary of state is responsible for the management of all state elections, including ballot printing, tabulations, and maintaining the financial records of candidates. It also is responsible for the registration of motor vehicles and the issuance of motor vehicle licenses.

The department has been at the forefront in using technology to make information and services available to Maine citizens. Approximately twenty online services are available, including vehicle registrations and drivers' licenses, access to motor vehicle driving records, access to absentee ballot applications, and information in the Maine archives. Further, the department operates several programs to encourage voting, such as holding mock elections in high schools and registering first-time voters. It annually gives an eighth-grade citizenship award that recognizes outstanding community service in every Maine middle school.

The state treasurer's main job is to manage the income accruing to the state from various taxes and federal grants, and to sell bonds. The office processes a total of about three million checks per year, exclusive of unemployment compensation payments. State Treasurer Dale McCormick (1997–2005) was active at the national level as well as in Maine. She helped found the National Coalition on Corporate Reform, which worked with the Federal Securities and Exchange Commission in setting new rules for corporate governance.

The state auditor is responsible for conducting an annual audit of the accounts of all state agencies and for reporting its findings to the legislature. Maine law requires that localities also have their finances audited once each year. The state auditor assists communities in meeting that responsibility. A member of the auditor's staff visits a locality and provides recommendations for improvement of internal controls. The report is sent to appropriate municipal officials and to the state representative and senator from the district. The assistance is designed primarily for towns that have fewer than five thousand residents.

CONCLUSION

The governor is the central player in the state government. Notwithstanding the importance of legislative deliberations, the governor's place in the processes of both policy formulation and policy implementation is critical. In modern-day state government, the governor is the most visible state official, the figure most often in the news, and the person who commands the largest sources of information through overseeing the state bureaucracy. Maine's special location seems to add to the prominence of the governor, who deals with international as well as national issues. The governor's power is, however, predominantly the power to persuade. The level of conflict in state government is greatly affected by how the governor uses that power. The chief executive must work with an unpredictable legislature, a technically sophisticated bureaucracy, and a court system whose decisions affect more and more areas of public policy.

CHAPTER EIGHT

The Court System

Like the other two branches of the state government, Maine courts reflect the distinctive features of the state's politics. Unlike the legislative and the executive branches, however, judges in Maine (with the exception of probate judges) are not subject to popular election. Instead, Maine is one of several New England states that choose judges through gubernatorial selection. However, because the constitution has never provided much detail about how the courts are to work, the elected branches of state government and, broadly speaking, the electorate itself have been able to shape the court system. Since gaining statehood in 1820, Maine's courts have probably changed more fundamentally, in both structure and operation, than have the other two branches.

This chapter examines how the court system's structure, working style, and decisions relate to the state's politics. Mainers seem to take a great deal of pride in their courts, which are one of the most efficiently organized state judiciaries in the country. Courts are frequently visited by high school and college classes. Its judges, particularly members of the Supreme Judicial Court, are highly regarded. The current challenge Maine's courts face is providing appropriate access to all people throughout the state—consistent with the participatory culture—even as courts grapple with complex legal, technical, and geographical issues, an increasing caseload, and a relatively low level of financial support. The courts struggle continually to modernize their practices. In the past decade, new attention has been given to ways they can work with other state agencies to help solve social problems that raise persistent legal issues.

THE CONSTITUTION AND THE COURTS

An understanding of the courts begins with the state constitution. The system that the constitution put in place in 1819 included "one Supreme Judicial Court and such other courts the Legislature may from time to time establish." The legislature has periodically revamped the court system and modified the jurisdictions of the various courts. The first supreme court consisted of a chief justice and two associate justices, and had both original and appellate jurisdiction.[1] It sat with either two or three justices at least once a year in each of the counties, which then numbered nine. The trial court, called the Court of Common Pleas, had duplicate jurisdiction with the supreme court in handling original cases. It was composed of a chief justice and two associate justices who held jury trials throughout the state. In 1839, it was replaced by a district court made up of four justices who performed the same function in different parts of the state. In 1852 the legislature abolished the district court and for a time assigned all jury trial responsibilities to the justices of the supreme court. Individual justices of the Maine Supreme Judicial Court would sit as trial justices in the various counties, and when needed would come together for appellate work. To enable the court to perform both trial and appellate work, the legislature expanded the number of justices to seven in 1852 and to eight in 1855.

That arrangement lasted for about three-quarters of a century. In a few large counties, rising caseloads slowly required separate trial judges. Thus, in 1920, such justices were in place in four counties (Cumberland, Kennebec, Penobscot, and Androscoggin), but the members of the Supreme Judicial Court handled trials in the remaining twelve counties. Finally, in 1929, the legislature created the present superior court, whereby one or more trial justices serve in every county. Because of lessened trial responsibilities, the number of supreme court justices was reduced to six. However, until the early 1970s, about half of the working time of supreme court justices still consisted of trial court work (usually called "single justice work"). Since that time, increased appellate caseloads led to the virtual disappearance of that activity. Single justice work, which lasted in Maine longer than in almost any other state, seemed to have had a beneficial impact. The Institute for Judicial Administration, in New York City, described the system in 1969 when it was still fully in operation:

> [I]t allows the justices to maintain closer contact with the public and with the members of the practicing bar. This helps the public image of the judicial system and makes for cohesiveness within the legal profession,

contributing to the maintenance of high professional standards. [It also] contributes to judicial realism.[2]

THE DISTRICT COURT

Like all states, Maine has courts to handle minor cases, such as traffic cases, hunting and fishing violations, and civil cases involving small amounts of money. These courts have limited jurisdiction. They are the courts with which most citizens come into contact; persons appearing before them generally do not have to be represented by an attorney. The courts hear a large number of cases, most of which are disposed of fairly quickly. Their judges work without juries. Until 1961 Maine's courts of limited jurisdiction consisted of a confusing group of tribunals. They took the form of approximately seventy-five municipal and trial justice courts, each of which was created by a separate statute. The courts were staffed by part-time judges. Most judges were lawyers, but some had their primary occupation in business or agriculture and performed the role of judge with little or no legal training. The local magistrates were familiar with local conditions. However, their verdicts, especially traffic fines, varied greatly from county to county. Reformers stressed the need for more uniformity in the administration of local justice.

The arrangement ended in 1961 with the creation of the Maine District Court. It was composed of twenty-five judges organized into thirteen districts, who held court in thirty-three locations. Every county was served by at least one district court judge. Maine for the first time had professional judges serving in all its courts. In the mid-2000s, there were thirty-three judges serving in thirty-one locations. The number of cases they handle seems huge. Case filings in 2004 amounted to slightly over 129,000. An even larger group of cases (138,673) was handled by the Maine Judicial Branch Violations Bureau, based in Lewiston, which is an adjunct of the district court. Added together, the two numbers are sufficient to have involved one of every four Maine residents as a plaintiff or defendant.[3] Violations Bureau cases involve uncontested traffic violations in which the offender pays a fine without having to go to court. The bureau exemplifies a district court effort in recent years to streamline its operation. Before the mid-1990s, the processing of traffic violations was lodged with each of the district court's sites.

Apart from traffic offenses, the largest category of district court cases embraces adult criminal matters, such as disorderly conduct and theft. While elsewhere often referred to as misdemeanors, in Maine they are styled Class

D and Class E crimes. They are offenses that carry penalties which do not exceed one year in jail or $1,000 in fines. Civil violations and general civil matters compose the next largest group of cases, followed by small claims. The district court on particular days of the month offers the services of a small claims court, where individuals can pursue cases where the money judgment is less than $4,500. The process is fairly informal (lawyers are generally not involved.) The volume of business in the various locations of the district court varies widely. The Madawaska District on the state's northern border with Canada processed some 693 cases in 2004, while the Portland District in the same year handled 19,303 cases and had two judges working full-time. No juries serve in the district court. Judges settle issues after hearing both sides of a question. Certain categories of decisions—such as institutional confinement, the revocation of probation and DNA testing— are appealable to the superior court, but most appeals go directly to the Maine Supreme Judicial Court.

In recent years, the district court has been at the center of judicial efforts to find new ways to address certain social problems, such as substance abuse, that compose a large part of the caseload of all Maine courts. In 1998 the state created the Maine Drug Court, which operates in five district court locations. The drug court offers a defendant in a substance abuse case a reduced sentence if the individual is willing to undergo treatment and supervision by a case management officer. The officer typically is employed by the Department of Health and Human Services or the Department of Corrections. The program takes about a year. In a similar vein, the district court maintains the family court, which employs eight case management officers who work with children involved in divorce proceedings and family disputes.

THE SUPERIOR COURT

The district court's senior partner is the superior court, Maine's trial court of general jurisdiction. Unlike district court judges, who are mostly assigned to one location, the sixteen superior court justices travel throughout the state holding terms of court in the state's various counties. The superior court shares jurisdiction with the district court over minor criminal and civil cases; the superior court will normally be used if the defendant in a criminal case or the plaintiff in a civil case wishes to have a jury trial. The superior court has exclusive jurisdiction over serious criminal offenses, such as murder, arson, rape, aggravated assault, and burglary; civil cases where the monetary amount of damages sought exceeds $30,000; and injunctions.

In 2004 the superior court had 15,381 cases, of which about one-quarter were civil and the remaining three-quarters criminal matters. As for civil cases, personal injury matters accounted for the greatest number of dispositions, followed by contract disputes and damage cases. Criminal cases came mainly from two sources. About half the caseload consisted of transfers of minor criminal cases from the district court because the defendant had requested a jury trial. Most of the remaining cases stemmed from indictments by grand juries. In these instances, a grand jury had concluded (based on information supplied by a district attorney) that sufficient evidence existed to indicate that a serious crime had been committed and to charge a defendant.

Although the superior court is the only court in Maine to use juries, the vast majority of cases that come before it are settled without a jury. In a recent year only 4 percent of the criminal cases and 3 percent civil cases were resolved with the assistance of a jury. Why are juries used so rarely? One reason is that people believe that judges are more objective and better able than juries to handle complex sets of facts, especially in civil trials. Another factor is the greater cost of jury trials. Further, many cases are concluded before a trial can get under way. About half of the civil cases in recent years have ended with the voluntary dismissal of charges by the plaintiff or a stipulation agreed to by all parties. In these instances, the judge brings the parties to the case together, but does not impose a verdict. As far as criminal cases are concerned, a guilty plea is typically entered in about half of them. In another one-quarter of the cases, the district attorney will dismiss the complaint at some point before the proceedings are concluded.

If only those cases in which the trials were completed are considered, then juries are employed somewhat more frequently than the overall figures of 4 percent and 3 percent would suggest. In recent years, several dramatic murder trials in the state have used juries and have called attention to their importance in the judicial process. In fact, Maine appears to be resisting a national trend toward the reduced use of juries to resolve civil disputes. In a 1985 ruling, the Maine Supreme Judicial Court held that under the state constitution, the right to a jury trial exists on any claim in which an award of money is sought.[4]

A longstanding issue in the operation of the district and superior courts was the problem of guaranteeing the constitutional right of jury trial in a criminal case without overburdening the superior court with large numbers of minor cases. At one time, defendants who lost their cases in the district court would request jury trials (*de nova* trials) in the superior court. The practice resulted in a fair amount of plea bargaining between the prosecution and defense in order to save judicial time, and was widely criticized. In

1982 the legislature enacted a measure regulating the handling of criminal cases that may be heard in either the district court or the superior court. The measure authorizes a defendant to waive the right to a jury trial and to be tried in district court. If the defendant wants a jury trial, he or she must make an affirmative request for it within twenty-one days of a plea entered in district court. Otherwise the right to a jury trial "shall be deemed waived."

In the past decade, Maine has tried to bring about greater coordination between the district and superior courts. The legislature authorized in 1999 a major study on court unification, headed by retired Supreme Judicial Court Chief Justice Vincent McKusick. The study led to important changes in the trial courts. District and superior judges were encouraged to preside over each other's courts where such work would expedite the completion of court calendars. The salaries of the two groups of judges were equalized. The staffs of the two courts were coordinated, particularly in rural counties, such that employees of one court could support the work of the other court as needed. New efficiencies were found in the handling of cases. In murder cases, for example, where both a district court judge and a superior court justice had typically become involved in separate aspects of a proceeding, one superior court justice is now assigned to handle the case from beginning to end.

Despite the heavy caseload of some Maine courts, per capita crime rates in the state are among the lowest in the country. In 2002, Maine ranked 45th in crimes of all types, 46th in violent crimes and 47th in the number of prisoners per capita.[5] The state's relatively low level of crime has helped its judiciary to operate with a fairly small number of judges.

A TRIAL JUDGE AT WORK

What is involved in the work of a trial court judge? In a 1987 article in the *Maine Bar Journal*, Kermit V. Lipez, who was appointed to the superior court bench the preceding year, described some of his experiences.[6] He observed that new trial justices are normally assigned to locations outside of their home county for the first year, so that they have an opportunity of "making mistakes" away from the view of former colleagues. As a newcomer, Lipez found it helpful to write out certain of the statements and presentations he was to make orally in order to avoid mistakes. He prepared a bench book on such topics as the Rule II proceeding, which takes place when a defendant pleads guilty to a Class A, B, or C offense, and for the task of charging a jury. He also provided the attorneys with copies of his jury charge since the judge's charge to the jury is often the basis for an appeal.

An important task for any justice is maintaining decorum in the courtroom, and the responsibility sometimes poses novel challenges. In one instance, Lipez discovered that the jury foreman had marked the special verdict form provided to the foreman before the jury had even deliberated, recording a unanimous verdict for the defendant. The foreman was excused, and an alternate juror was found to serve in his place. Lipez thinks the judge's charge to the jury should not necessarily be limited to matters raised in the trial. He believes juries make assumptions about factors not brought out in the trial (for instance, the amount of insurance held by a defendant in an automobile negligence case), and he thinks a judge should sometimes speak to such concerns. In one instance, jurors asked him to cover in his charge to them several matters not raised in the trial. Supervising the courtroom also means a judge becomes involved with members of the press. Lipez discovered that the court reporters in the different counties have different working relationships with judges. Some will try to remain in the judge's chambers when conferences are taking place with attorneys, in the event that a judge hands down a ruling. Others will depend on the judge to inform them of his or her rulings.

After his first year on the bench, Justice Lipez found that sentencing was the hardest part of the job. It involves "an unwieldy mix of statutory goals, personal beliefs, inadequate information, limited resources, [and] conflicting demands . . . ." He thinks there is a tendency to ignore the victim at the time of a sentencing hearing. Accordingly, the judge may need to speak to that matter. Another difficult problem for a judge is dealing with expert medical testimony. So many cases involve medical evidence that Lipez concluded that being a judge "is a bit like going to medical school." Finally, Lipez noticed that a depressingly large number of controversies in his court were caused by alcoholism and drug abuse.

THE SUPREME JUDICIAL COURT

As its title implies, the Supreme Judicial Court, the only tribunal mentioned in the state constitution, is the highest court in Maine. It accepts appeals from lower courts. Appeals from its decisions, if they involve a question of U.S. constitutional law, are directed to the U.S. Supreme Court. Before discussing Maine's high court, two points need to be made about semantics. The apparent redundancy in the title ("Judicial Court") exists because the term "court" was used in colonial Massachusetts, from which Maine borrowed its institutional arrangements, to refer to legislative bodies as well as to judicial agencies. (The Massachusetts legislature is officially still called the Great and General Court.) Second, in the state's legal community, the Maine Supreme Judicial Court is commonly called the "Law Court," a term that arose because, historically, so much of the work of supreme court justices was single-justice (trial) work. The reference of "Law Court" is to the collective work of supreme court justices as they perform their appellate function of reviewing lower court decisions.

The Supreme Judicial Court has seven members, presided over by a chief justice. Its main job is to hear appeals from civil and criminal decisions in the superior and district courts and to decide questions of law arising from those cases. In 2004 the law court disposed of 751 cases, including 157 with signed opinions. (The other cases were disposed of through shorter memorandum opinions.) Approximately two-thirds of its caseload involved civil matters, and about one-third embraced criminal proceedings. The law court typically alters the decisions of lower courts in only about ten percent of the cases. It has been most likely to find grounds for reversal in environmental and public utility issues. In contrast, it has only rarely altered a trial court's decision in disputes involving workman's compensation and divorce settlements.

The relatively small portion of cases heard by the supreme court that end in a reversal resembles the pattern found in other states which, like Maine, have but one appeals court. Supreme courts in these states must review all cases appealed from the various trial courts, whether or not the cases raise novel or important points of law. The top courts in the smaller states differ from the supreme courts in those states, mostly large urban states, which use intermediate appeals courts. In those jurisdictions, the lower appeals courts first screen the cases, leaving only the most difficult and controversial issues for the top court.

In addition to reviewing cases from lower courts, the Maine Supreme Judicial Court has certain specialized functions. One is the appellate review of sentences. Until 1965, the court could review only the legality of sentences imposed by trial judges, not their propriety. In that year, the court established an Appellate Division, composed of three judges, which had the authority to add to or reduce a convicted individual's sentence. In 1989, the division was replaced by a Sentence Review Panel, composed of three judges with the power solely to grant or deny leaves to appeal from sentences. If the panel grants an appeal, the full supreme court reviews the sentence and hands down its judgment. Although modifications of the work of trial judges are infrequent, the supreme court's concern with sentencing practices seems to have helped make those practices more uniform among Maine courts.

Another function of the court is to provide, on the formal request of the

governor or either house of the legislature, an advisory opinion on "important questions of law" being considered by the other branch of government.
The justices of the court write about one advisory opinion per year (they
sign the opinion individually). In 2004 the court advised the legislature that
an initiated bill altering the basis for property taxation would violate the
state constitution because it improperly created different classes of property
owners according to when the owners purchased the property. In 2002 the
court advised Governor King that he had no authority to accept or reject
ballots in disputed legislative elections. Instead, the court found that power
rested with the Secretary of State. Other opinions have dealt with such issues as forestry taxation, legislative procedures relative to the overriding of
the governor's veto, and state ownership of certain lands.

A third responsibility of the Supreme Judicial Court is to deal with occasional problems of judicial misconduct. In instances of alleged misconduct, the Committee on Judicial Responsibility and Disability, composed of
lawyers, judges, and laypersons, first undertakes a study of the allegations
of misconduct. It recommends a course of action to the court, which makes
the final decision. In 2002 the law court found that a probate judge in Aroostook County had violated the Judicial Code of Conduct when he ran for a
seat in the state senate while still holding his judgeship. In 2003 the court
held that a probate judge in York County had improperly reduced the salary
of a county employee. In a widely publicized dispute in 1985, it fined, and
suspended for one month, a district court judge in Skowhegan County who
had ordered the jailing of persons in three cases in which imprisonment was
not an allowable punishment under Maine law.[7]

A fourth task of the court is to establish policies for the judicial branch.
While the legislature must approve major changes in the operation of courts
(for instance, the creation of new judgeships), the Supreme Judicial Court
oversees the operation of the trial courts on a day-to-day basis. Regulations
governing the filing of cases, the hours of courthouse operations, the procedures followed in criminal and civil cases, and the personnel arrangements
for the nearly five hundred employees of the judicial branch are among its
tasks. The chief justice, who is the central figure in this work, serves as a
half-time administrator as well as a judge.

Maine's Law Court has no building of its own (the only state without such
a building), and convenes generally in the Cumberland County Courthouse
in Portland, which is also home to a superior court and district court. Occasionally, it meets at other locations around the state, providing citizens with
an opportunity to view its proceedings. In 2006, for instance, the court held
sessions in Caribou, Lewiston, and in the South Portland schools. While the

justices sit together to hear a case on appeal argued orally and discuss it in a conference, some perform the actual opinion-writing tasks in chambers in their home county court houses, circulating the opinions among themselves by mail or the internet.

Compared to other state supreme courts, the law court has traditionally revealed a high degree of consensus. Fewer than 10 percent of the cases decided on appeal have registered a dissenting opinion. When a dissenting opinion is presented, it usually seems to reflect the personal views of the justice or justices writing it. A survey several years ago among the justices found no one who recalled an instance where a dissenting opinion later became a majority opinion.[8] The absence of dissent from Maine Supreme Judicial Court opinions undoubtedly has cultural roots. The court, like other state political institutions, seems inclined to follow a moderate course on most issues. Its justices generally see their role as "law-interpreters" rather than as "lawmakers." Nonetheless, the growing number of policy questions presented to the justices in recent years has seemed to impel the justices to become more expressive. An interesting decision was *Alden v. Maine* in 1997.[9] The case questioned whether the Eleventh Amendment to the U.S. Constitution, which prohibits citizens of a state from bringing lawsuits against governments of other states, bars state employees from suing their own state government in a state court. Alden and his coworkers had sought overtime pay from the Maine Department of Corrections. The Law Court interpreted the Eleventh Amendment to say such suits were prohibited, but the justices split 5 to 2. Lengthy opinions were delivered on both sides. On appeal, the U.S. Supreme Court affirmed the Maine Law Court in a 5 to 4 decision.[10] The holding became a landmark statement on federal-state relations in the 1990s.

Judicial Backgrounds

What backgrounds do the justices of the law court bring to their work? If that question were asked a century ago, the answer would be "mostly private practice experience." Attorneys well-known in their counties and active in the dominant Republican Party typically won nomination for vacancies on both the county courts and the Supreme Judicial Court. That pattern was consistent with the practice of supreme court justices performing "single justice" work, that is, trial work, since their appellate duties did not constitute a full-time responsibility. In the years between 1900 and 1920, according to one study, less than one-quarter of Maine Supreme Court justices had as much as five years of judicial experience of any kind.[11] That pattern has gradually shifted to one where lower court experience is generally expected of a nominee to the top bench. In 1990 three of the seven members of the law court had no judicial experience prior to their appointment; in 2005, only two of the seven jurists were in that category.

Four of the members in 2005 had earlier served on the superior court, and three had had experience on the district court. Three justices had also held the post of chief justice (or judge) of the superior or district court before their elevation to the law court. Justice Leigh Saufley, who was named to the Supreme Judicial Court in 1997 and became chief justice in 2001, was the first member of the top court to have served on both trial courts. The greater careerism among judges is also reflected in the superior court. In 2000 ten of its sixteen justices had served on the district court bench.

For much of Maine's history, a background in state politics was necessary for an attorney to win appointment to the supreme court. Justices would count among their members former legislative leaders, candidates for Congress, state party chairmen, and other persons with experience in electoral politics. That type of resume is still found, though less frequently. Justice Robert Clifford, for instance, joined the law court in 1986 after having been mayor of Lewiston and a member of the Lewiston City Council. More recent justices have tended to come from major posts in specific legal organizations and advocacy groups, such as executive director of the Pine Tree Legal Assistance organization, chairman of the Maine Family Law Advisory Commission and member of the Board of the National Legal Services Corporation. Such careers reflect the judiciary's new concern with social problem-solving. They also suggest political parties play a diminished role in recruiting persons for top judicial posts.

Most Supreme Judicial Court justices have Maine roots. Four of the seven members in 2005 had an undergraduate degree from a Maine college (three from Bowdoin, one from the University of Maine). On the other hand, all but two obtained their law degree from an out-of-state law school.

The most important judicial appointment a governor makes is filling the chief justiceship. Reflecting the rise of a career judiciary, three of the last four chiefs have been elevated from the position of associate justice. Governors generally name individuals with whom they are politically compatible. In 1971 Gov. Kenneth Curtis promoted Armand Dufresne Jr. to the position of chief justice. Observers believe that in naming Dufresne, Curtis wanted to recognize the state's French community, which had strongly supported him in his election campaigns. In 1977, Independent Gov. James Longley nominated Vincent McKusick, a Portland attorney with close ties to business organizations. He seemed to fit Longley's preference to have a chief justice with a strong interest in judicial administration. McKusick's successor as chief justice, Daniel Wathen, named in 1992 by Republican Gov. John McKernan, was a highly regarded conservative jurist. Wathen left the bench after eight years to seek the Republican nomination for governor. The current chief justice, Leigh Saufly, was appointed by Gov. Angus King in 2001, after having served four years as an associate justice. She became the first woman chief justice in Maine history.

The past three decades have witnessed a new prominence of the office of chief justice. The official has become an important spokesperson for the entire court system, The chief provides an annual report to the legislature and meets with the governor regularly on court business and, especially in the past few years, on financial problems affecting the courts. Maine's judiciary ranks low among states in budgetary support (the courts receive slightly less than 2 percent of the state general fund). A recent concern pressed by Chief Justice Saufley has been finding funds to improve court security, especially for the screening for weapons among persons attending court hearings. In 2006, a total of twenty-nine weapon-related incidents were reported to have occurred in Maine courts.

Court Decisions

The law court has handed down several important rulings in recent years. In *Davies v. City of Bath* (1976), it permitted Maine citizens for the first time to sue the state and its political subdivisions under certain circumstances.[12] This ruling overturned the longstanding practice by Maine courts of shielding those government divisions against suits by citizens on the basis of the doctrine of governmental immunity. In 1989, the court handed down a critical ruling on a different problem. In *Bell v. Town of Wells*, the court effectively closed what had long been regarded as a public beach in that town.[13] It maintained that landowners' deeds gave them ownership of Moody Beach from a seawall to the low-tide mark, and that the public's right of access extended only to such activities as fishing and boating. This case was important because most of Maine's coastline is privately owned, and because only about thirty-five miles of the coast, like Moody Beach, is sandy and usable for swimming. After the decision, the Town of Wells began action to purchase some of the properties so that townspeople and tourists would have access to the beach.

Other significant cases have involved the liability of private companies for certain acts. In a 1986 case of a shipyard worker who died from exposure to asbestos, the court held that manufacturers can he held responsible for injuries caused by their products even though the exposure took place before the state's strict liability law went into effect. It further ruled that widows of victims could collect damages under Maine's Wrongful Death Act. On the other hand, in 1988 the court dismissed a $1 million award to victims of a traffic accident caused by an employee of a company who had consumed liquor at the company's Christmas party, in light of the fact that the company had a policy against the consumption of alcoholic beverages on its property, and the employee had purchased the liquor elsewhere. The court believed that to hold the company liable would be to "prescribe a paternalistic duty upon employers generally." In 2001 in *Budzko v. One City Center Associates Limited Partnership*, the court decided for the first time what responsibility a business owner has to its employees and customers concerning the accumulation of ice and snow during a storm.[14] It held that some remedial actions may be expected while a storm is taking place. In that respect, it set a stricter standard than states that follow a "storm in progress" doctrine whereby an owner is not obliged to remove snow and ice until a storm has abated. The Maine court also indicated that the appropriate level of care is related to the number of people affected by snow-and-ice conditions.

Judicial Review

As part of its work, the Maine Supreme Judicial Court performs the important task of judicial review, whereby it determines the consistency of Maine laws with the state and federal constitutions. If it finds that a law is contrary to either constitution, it will declare it void. To illustrate, the court has been aggressive in protecting the right of free speech, which is guaranteed in both the U.S. and Maine constitutions. In *State v. Events International, Inc.* (1987), the court declared void a provision in the Maine Charitable Solicitation law that required solicitors for charitable organizations to report, in certain instances, the percentage of each dollar contributed that was actually received by the charity.[15] Earlier, in a 1983 case, the court had invalidated an order of the Maine Labor Relations Board banning dissident faculty members at the University of Maine from distributing information concerning a collective bargaining agreement.[16] In 1999, the court vacated a rule of the Maine Public Utilities Commission requiring the Central Maine Power Company to file with the PUC educational materials concerning retail access to electricity generation services before they were distributed to the public.[17] The court found the rule to be a prior restraint on free speech.

In other policy areas, the law court has "readily sustained legislation against a wide variety of attacks."[18] This posture is exemplified in the court's handling of cases concerned with legislative delegations of power to executive agencies and regulatory boards, especially ones dealing with environmental concerns. Here the court appears to have shifted its views. The Maine Supreme Judicial Court gave a fairly restrictive interpretation of the Wetlands Act of 1970 shortly after its enactment. However, in more recent times, it has upheld regulatory legislation according to standards that are highly deferential to the executive and legislative branches. For instance, the court has held that a plaintiff seeking to overturn a law on substantive due process grounds must undertake the difficult burden of establishing a "complete absence of any state of facts that would support the need for the legislation."[19] It seems unlikely that in the near future the court will exercise the power of judicial review much beyond the area of civil rights.

SPECIAL COURTS

Maine uses special courts for certain types of cases. One example is the probate courts, which have had constitutional status since 1819. The probate court in each county handles estates and trusts, adoptions, name changes, and guardianship cases. Initially, the governor named the probate judges, but since 1855 these judges have been elected on a partisan ballot. The judges, who serve four year terms, are part-time and work without a jury. As part-time officials, probate judges are permitted to practice law and appear before the courts, including other probate courts. The system has come under criticism because of its involvement in county partisan politics. In 2001 the legislature considered, but did not enact, a measure to consolidate probate courts into the state judiciary.

An administrative court was created in 1973 to consider cases concerned with the suspension and revocation of licenses issued by administrative agencies, as well as agency refusal to grant licenses. The court's two judges were appointed by the governor and worked without a jury. Because its caseload always remained small, the legislature abolished it in the 1990s, transferring its responsibilities to the superior court where they had earlier resided.

A third specialized court is the small claims court—really a special session of the district court—which is convened in every district location on certain days of the month. Procedures are more informal than during regular sessions of the district court, and individuals involved in small claims disputes generally do not need attorneys. Small claims proceedings must be limited to cases where the contested amount is less than $4,500.

In 2007, the legislature created a business and consumer court, modeled somewhat after the small claims court. The new court handles regulatory matters, contract disputes, and issues involving trade secrets, and operates as a session of the district court. Aware that trial court judges have in recent years given a priority to settling criminal cases involving families and children, various businesses and attorneys pressed the legislature to create a court to deal specifically with commercial disputes. The business and consumer court accepts cases through an electronic filing system and uses video conferencing to facilitate meetings of counsels. For a case to go before the court, one party must be a business.

Periodically, discussion takes place over the need for an intermediate appeals court to assist the Law Court. Maine is one of about a dozen states that does not have such an intermediate body. Interest in the idea grew in 2000 when the court's signed opinions swelled to more than three hundred. Subsequently, the court's workload has lessened because of the changes in the appeal process for workmen's compensation cases and the greater use of memorandum opinions by the justices. While an intermediate appeals court is not likely to appear soon, the issue will continue to provoke debate.

COURT ADMINISTRATION

The Maine courts have become big business in recent years. With case filings now nearing three hundred thousand per year, judicial administration has grown in importance. Historically, the principal tool available to the Supreme Judicial Court was power to review lower court decisions. The high court had little control over trial courts because, historically, these courts were locally financed and staffed by the counties and towns in which they were located. Beginning in 1961 with the creation of the district court, the state began to take over the funding of trial courts. In their present status as fully financed state agencies, both the district court and the superior court have gradually become subject to centralized management. In 1975, Maine established the Administrative Office of the Courts, directed by a state court administrator who is appointed by and reports to the chief justice of the Supreme Judicial Court. The office prescribes and maintains fiscal records, prepares the judicial budget, examines dockets to determine where delays may exist that require additional personnel, oversees clerical functions, and looks after court facilities and matters of court security. The office has locations in Portland and Augusta.

The management of the court system is handled through four senior administrators with specialized statewide responsibilities. The officials oversee four areas: court facilities, court services and programs, court clerks and their staffs, and court reporters and judicial secretaries. They report to the state court administrator. Additionally, they work closely with the chief justice of the superior court and the chief judge and assistant chief judge of the district court. A particular responsibility is to maintain effective relationships with local and county officials and local developers to ensure that adequate court facilities exist in each county. Under current scheduling arrangements, within each of eight regions a superior court justice and a district court judge coordinate the handling of all cases in the trial courts in their region. Schedules are announced several months in advance. The new practices appear to have expedited the handling of many types of cases. The chief justice reported that in 2006 the courts cleared all family cases filed in that year, whereas fewer than half of those filed in 2001 had achieved a comparable level of completion.

One task involved in judicial administration is developing ways whereby certain categories of disputes can be settled without resort to the courts. The Maine Court Mediation Service provides for the mediation of domestic relations cases, small claims, landlord-tenant disputes, major civil and commercial cases, and environmental and land-use conflicts. Since 1984 Maine law has required mediation in all domestic relations cases in which minor children are involved and in those cases in which a trial is requested. Approximately one-hundred mediators, distributed among seven regions in the state, work with the various district court and superior court judges on a part-time basis. The Mediation Service handles approximately ten thousand cases annually, resolving about half of them without a trial.

The Judicial Department also operates a Court Appointed Special Advocate Program (CASA) under which trained volunteers look after the needs of abused and neglected children in child protection cases. The volunteers replaced state-paid attorneys who had earlier performed the work. The CASA volunteer, who receives considerable training, is a party to all administrative and judicial matters affecting the child. About five hundred children are involved in the program.

CONCLUSION

That Maine has been able to operate successfully with a relatively small judiciary (approximately fifty judges) may be attributed in part to its participatory culture. The state manifests a substantial degree of consensus on political values. While the courts establish important rules of public policy, they only rarely encounter and attempt to settle strongly partisan or ideological conflicts. When such issues do arise, the tendency of the Supreme Judicial Court as the state's only appeals court is to write opinions that adhere closely to the facts of the case. Decisions of the courts are widely accepted.

Unlike some other state courts, the Maine judiciary is not a battleground among competing political or legal viewpoints. As a dean of the University of Maine Law School has commented, the reason seems to be simply that "there isn't much ideology in Maine politics."[20]

The consensus on values has also permitted the courts to evolve into one of the nation's most-centralized and well-coordinated state judiciaries. In the past, the courts, like the legislature, operated intimately, in an almost neighborhood-like fashion, with citizens. That process is no longer possible. The centralization that has taken place in the courts has produced some tensions. However, because public officials and citizens alike tend to share the same values, the centralization has not created a gulf between the courts and the citizens. The quality of justice remains high, and judicial administration is almost certainly more efficient than in the past. The most pressing issues facing the judiciary are determining how the trial courts can operate most efficiently, and addressing social problems within the confines of a restrictive budget.

CHAPTER NINE

Maine's Budget as Policy

The ability and willingness of citizens to pay government taxes and fees impacts the type and quality of services government provides. There is no question that state fiscal matters have driven policymaking in the new century. The state budget both fuels economic policy and responds to economic events. This budget does not take place in a vacuum; the actions of federal, state and local policymakers are linked more tightly than any one would prefer. Anyone from Maine will tell you it is a high-tax state. They will not know its exact rank among all states, but they will know that they pay high property, income, and sales taxes. They won't differentiate between local and state taxes because it is a nuance that doesn't change the end result. Their bottom line is, where does the money go, how much is spent, and is it spent wisely?

This chapter looks at the process of managing the fiscal affairs of the State of Maine as determined by its budget, and all the other aspects captured within it including the budgetary process, results of the process as measured in revenues and expenditures, and servicing debt. The property tax with its special relationship to state and local finances in paying for education, and local revenue sharing will be highlighted.

The first edition of this book stated that in the study of state policymaking, the budget is not always appreciated for its central role. In the nearly two decades that have passed since it was written, there is no longer any question about the budget's pivotal role in public policymaking. Every issue is framed as a budget issue. Since the first edition, the state has gone through three economic downturns that severely decreased revenue sources, making either increasing taxes or reducing services necessary. Governors have been forced to deal with structural deficits (projected revenues not able to support projected expenditures) before they became real deficits.

THE BUDGET PROCESS

The budget process determines how decisions are made, what rules are followed, and the role each participant plays. The process is dynamic, as policymakers adapt to changing environments and internal power changes. What has held constant since Maine achieved statehood is the constitutional requirement of balancing the budget. Unlike the federal government, the governor in Maine must present and the legislature must approve a balanced budget.

Political parties, interest groups, the governor, executive agencies, the legislature, the courts, the media, and, of course, the public are all players in the process. Among the constraints are the revenue available, total debt, projections of federal assistance, unfunded mandates, statutory and constitutional limitations, and very importantly, the previous budget. Each approved budget reflects the values, services, and social and economic polices of its government.

In the budgetary process, preparing the budget is the first step. This takes place in all state agencies and departments, which prepare budget requests, sometimes called "biennial budget requests," because they outline the state government's needs for the next two fiscal years. Maine is one of twenty states that use a biennial budget cycle.[1] The legislature once met every other year but changed in 1975 to better monitor the budget. The budget is approved during the Maine legislature's first session (in an odd-numbered year), and the budget is revised during the second session (the following even-numbered year). The fiscal year begins on July 1.

Under Maine law, on or before the first of September in even-numbered years, all state departments and agencies requesting state funds must submit their requests to the Bureau of the Budget. The governor receives the budget requests through the bureau. Reviewing each agency's requests, the governor, working with the bureau, makes adjustments as deemed necessary. When this review is finished, all the budget requests, as well as the recommendations of the governor, are assembled into a budget document. This usually occurs in late December and January. The budget bills must be transmitted to the legislature in January unless there is a governor-elect, who has one additional month to submit the budget by early February. There are three budget bills provided by the governor to the legislature: a supplemental budget, sometimes referred to as an emergency budget bill; the Part 1 unified budget; and the Part 2 supplemental budget bill. We will discuss them more later.

Until about two decades ago, the budget requests did not reflect all of the revenue expected to be available. Instead, the legislature budgeted only for the expected general and highway revenues, as well as liquor and lottery revenues. The legislature decided in the early 1980s that it needed more information for its budgetary decisions, and all funds including federal funds were included in the budget requests.

The budget document is divided into two principal parts. Part I consists of funding requests for existing programs, including personnel needs, or what state officials call requests "to keep the store open." Part 2 is devoted to requests for new and expanded programs and staff. It also contains funds for capital improvements and construction. Like the biennial schedule, this format has long been popular with the legislature, and it has resisted change.

The governor's budget estimates shift as new information becomes available, complicating the legislature's work. In June 1989 Gov. John McKernan, confronting a slowdown in the state economy, lowered his tax collection estimates for the existing fiscal year and for the upcoming biennium (1990–91) by more than $100 million. He also scaled down his original spending requests by more than $60 million. The revision came just two weeks before the legislature was scheduled to adjourn, when lawmakers were struggling to make final decisions on spending requests. The event highlighted a need for changes in the forecasting of revenues for the state budget.

During the 1990s, several adjustments to the budget process were instituted. They included professionalizing the forecasting of economic and revenue assumptions that the state government used for budget decisions, equipping the governor with line-item veto power, mandating certain performance indicators for state government departments and agencies, and greatly limiting unfunded mandates the state could impose on local governments. Each one is described below.

In 1992, a Consensus Economic Forecasting Commission and a Revenue Forecasting Committee were formed by executive order to provide an independent process for state economic and revenue forecasting. The assumptions and analysis used by the commission in forecasting state economic conditions provide the conceptual base for the revenue committee's estimates of future state revenues. Both groups have been codified into law, maintaining both the structure and intent of the original executive order. The intent of these groups was to provide objective professional criteria to support budget assumptions. The legislators now have to agree only on where to spend money, not how much money is available.

In 1997 the law changed the role of the Revenue Forecasting Committee from an advisory body to one making the actual revenue projections the executive branch uses in setting budget estimates and recommendation. The committee was also expanded to six members. It is required to report its findings no later than December 1 and March 1 to the governor, legislative council, and the Appropriations and Financial Affairs Committee. The revenue forecasts are developed using econometric models for the sales and use tax, individual income tax, corporate income tax, fuel tax, and cigarette tax. Forecasts for the remaining lines are developed using trend data, national economic assumptions, and other analysis.

The Consensus Economic Forecasting Commission, composed of five members, is required to develop two-year and four-year economic forecasts for the State of Maine. No later than November 1 and February 1 annually, the commission must develop its findings for the same audience as the Revenue Forecast Committee. The Revenue Forecast Committee must use the economic assumptions and forecasts of the commission in developing its four-year revenue projections. Both groups are critical to the budget preparation process.

Another change in the budget process in the 1990s was the move to performance-based budgeting. Each state government program has a strategy with performance measures connected to it. Department or agency goals and objectives are linked to the strategy. The state received some unwelcome publicity when *Governing* magazine gave the state an overall above-average grade of B- for performance, but called attention to the lack of a legislative computer system to test the performance measures that the administration had provided.[2] The practice of providing performance measures is now part of the budget preparation process. Lawmakers and the public can compare the actual performance to the planned performance.

On November 7, 1995, a constitutional amendment was adopted giving the governor a line-item veto over the expenditures of state funds. The measure allows a majority of the elected members of the house and senate to override a veto. The legislature voted in 1997 not to pass on any new unfunded mandates to local governments. It was largely seen by the public as a symbolic measure that appeared not to give taxpayers relief from current unfunded costs. It probably did, however, set a tone for lawmakers to be vigilant about adding new costs to local governments.

Legislative approval is the second step of the budget process. The legislature receives the budget proposals from the governor in the form of several bills. The legislature refers the budget document to the Joint Standing Committee on Appropriations and Financial Affairs. The Appropriations Committee then holds public hearings on the requested funding for each department or agency. When the hearings are completed, adjustments to the bills are made by the Appropriations Committee, which then votes on the new drafts. The legislature receives the committee's reports on the bills for final approval by June of odd numbered years, because the fiscal year begins the next month.

The procedure described above applies to Part I of the budget ("existing programs"). For Part II of the budget ("new and expanded programs"), bills are first referred to the relevant standing committee whose jurisdiction embraces the subject matter of the proposed measure. For instance, a bill to restructure land use laws would most likely be handled by the Energy and National Resources Committee. The committee reports its recommendation to the Appropriations Committee. Once bills that affect the general fund have passed they are assigned to the appropriations table. At the end of the session, after the budget bills are accounted for, the Appropriations Committee and the legislative leadership determine which bills will be funded. Motions are then made in the senate to remove bills from the appropriations table and to enact, amend, or indefinitely postpone them. If enacted in the senate the bill then goes to the governor for approval.

Budget bills with two-thirds of the support of the legislature become law with the governor's signature. Budgets passed by a simple majority don't take effect until ninety days after the legislature adjourns. Since the budget year starts on July 1, the legislature needs to adjourn by the end of March for a majority budget. If both political parties do not agree on a budget, or if the governing political party has less than a two-thirds majority, the legislature risks failing to enact a budget at a later point, in time to meet the July 1 deadline.

The third step of the budget process involves its execution. Each agency or department submits an annual work program that outlines the year's expenses to the Bureau of the Budget. The program is classified to show distribution of funds by categories—personal services, capital expenditures, and all other department expenses. Generally, the Bureau of the Budget approves allocations on a quarterly basis. Only then can the agency expend its funds. Revisions to the budget within departments require the approval of the state budget officer and the governor. These adjustments, however, cannot change the total amount of funding, nor can they transfer appropriations between departments. Only the legislature can approve those changes. The state controller authorizes all expenditures based on the work program.

After the execution of the budget, the final step is the audit. The Maine State Auditor is elected by the legislature by a joint ballot of the senators and representatives in convention.

The term of office is four years, or until a successor is elected and qualified. The state auditor is responsible for auditing all accounts and other financial records of state government or any department or agency of state government, including the judiciary and the executive department of the governor, except the governor's expense account. The auditor must report annually on the audit, and at such other times as the legislature may require. The financial report is designed to provide a general overview of the finances of the state and to demonstrate the state's accountability for the money it receives.

Reading about the stages of the budget process does not by itself capture the richness of the experience. Taking a closer look at the FY06–07 general fund budget provides an illustration of the process. Governor Baldacci developed his budget with a looming structural deficit of $733.4 million, the difference between the projected revenues and projected expenses identified by the Revenue Forecasting Committee. This was after the state budget had experienced three previous years of structural deficits. This gap was later lowered to $687 million as revenues were projected to increase more than originally identified. In the previous budget, the structural deficit had been filled, in part, with one-time revenue generators such as selling the state liquor stores and reductions in services.

The governor's proposed budget for FY06–07 required $250 million of new spending for aid to local school districts due to a citizen initiated referendum passed the previous year. He had made a public commitment not to raise broad base taxes and was also concerned about the impact of excessive cuts in government services, especially in the state Medicaid program. He decided to propose what became a highly controversial strategy, namely, to raise funds by selling off ten years' of the state's lottery revenue for about $250 million in order to balance the Part I budget. The plan was reviewed and adjusted by the Appropriations and Financial Affairs committee. The majority of legislators rejected it, deciding to issue revenue bonds instead. It appeared that a consensus budget, likely to get two-thirds support, was not in the making.

Since the state government shutdown in 1991 because of the legislature's failure to pass a budget, governors have sought to avoid repeating the problem. One strategy is to pass a budget by a simple majority in March, so it will be effective on July 1. This early adjournment was first implemented by the 118th legislature in 1997, which provided the precedent for resolving the budget in 2005.[3] Voting along party lines, the Democrats passed the FY06–07 Part I "Current Services" Budget in March. The house and senate then voted to end the regular session. Shortly thereafter the governor called the legislature into special session to finish its work.

Legislators barely had started working on the Part II when some members of the Republican Party started collecting signatures to implement a "people's veto" of the borrowing. The people's veto requires that if sufficient citizen signatures are collected, the citizens can repeal a legislatively enacted measure. The timing would have put the matter on the ballot in November 2005.

A series of external events occurred that made the governor rethink the borrowing plan for the Part I budget. First, the federal Base Realignment and Closure Commission announced that the Defense Department had recommended that three of Maine's military bases be closed. If the commission were to approve that move, approximately seven thousand workers would be unemployed, negatively impacting the Maine economy. Later, Moody's Investor's Services lowered the state's bond rating from AA2 to AA3, thus leading to higher costs to the state in issuing debt. In lowering the bond rating the agency cited years of slow progress restoring depleted reserves, tight liquidity leading to four years of cash flow borrowing, the use of one-time revenue solutions to balance the states operating budget and the uncertainty that the people's veto brought to the budget.[4]

The Part II budget is referred to as "New and Expanded Programs" although it certainly seemed misnamed for the FY06–07 budget. One of the primary reasons Part II was needed was to address a shortfall in the Medicaid system. It also restored funding to a hospital settlement funds for treating Medicaid patients that the state had been seriously underpaying for more than a decade, and that the Part I budget had removed.[5] Those needs were addressed without borrowing more funds. The budget won the unanimous vote of the Appropriations Committee and was enacted as emergency legislation in early June.

In an unusual move a so called "Part III" of the budget was proposed by the governor. The purpose of "Part III" was to replace the borrowing section of Part I. Although all parties were in agreement on the need to reduce the borrowing, they did not agree on how to proceed to find the $250 million needed to do so. The Republican leadership wanted no new revenues or fees, locating the funds entirely through cuts in services. The Democratic leadership favored deriving half of the money from a $1-per-pack increase in the cigarette tax, and the remainder from across-the-board cuts in spending. The Democratic plan won. However, the Part III budget, which passed on June 18, did not get the two-thirds vote needed for immediate implementation. Thus, the cigarette tax did not go into effect until September.

The Maine budget has been driven for the last several years by projected budget deficits. The causes of budget deficits can be temporary, such

Table 2: Maine expenditures compared with all state by funding sources, fiscal year 2003

	Maine	All States
Federal grants	32.9	28.7%
General funds	41.8	43.9%
Bonds	1.7	3.1%
Other state funds	23.6	24.3%

Source: National Association of State Budget Officers. *2003 State Expenditure Report* (Washington DC: National Association of State Budget Officers, 2004).

downturns in the economy, or structural, such as expenditures outpacing revenue growth. The efforts used to manage deficits—short-term or stopgap measures, cutting the budget, or raising revenues—have driven the legislative agenda. While the $5.7 billion FY06–07 budget approved was balanced, a $400–$450 million structural gap appeared for FY08–09 general fund budget.[6] Fortunately, the gap was lower than the ones in some previous budgets. Since all states at times experience shortfalls, rainy day funds are important because they can fill in the gap. However, if the reserve is too small or there are too many years of budgeted deficits, those funds will not be effective.

REVENUES

It is useful now to analyze revenues and expenditures in some detail. By separating the revenue into its major sources, we can examine how these sources have affected policy decisions. Through tracing the major expenditures, we can see how these policies and the responsibilities they support have changed historically.

State revenues grew from $24,000 in 1820, the first year of statehood, to more than $5.4 billion in 2004–2005 biennium budget. It would be a mistake, however, to think that the gap between these figures is due only to the distance in years. During the 1820–2005 period, the sources of the state's income changed significantly.

As table 2 illustrates, Maine is similar to other states in revenue policies, except in federal grants, which have constituted a larger portion of the Maine budget than they do of the budgets of most other states. One reason is that Maine has usually been in the bottom-third of the states in per capita income. Like most other states in that category, Maine has customarily received above-average levels of federal funds because many federal

Table 3: Federal spending in each state per dollar of federal taxes, fiscal year 2004

State	Expenditures per dollar of taxes	Rank	State	Expenditures per dollar of taxes	Rank
U.S.	$1.00	—	Mont.	$1.58	9
Ala.	$1.71	6	Nebr.	$1.07	28
Alaska	$1.87	2	Nev.	$0.73	45
Ariz.	$1.30	19	N.H.	$0.67	48
Ark.	$1.47	12	N.J.	$0.55	50
Calif.	$0.79	43	N.M.	$2.00	1
Colo.	$0.79	41	N.Y.	$0.79	42
Conn.	$0.66	49	N.C.	$1.10	27
Del.	$0.79	40	N.D.	$1.73	5
Fla.	$1.06	30	Ohio	$1.01	32
Ga.	$0.96	35	Okla.	$1.48	11
Hawaii	$1.60	8	Ore.	$0.97	34
Idaho	$1.28	21	Pa.	$1.06	29
Ill.	$0.73	46	R.I.	$1.02	31
Ind.	$0.97	33	S.C.	$1.38	17
Iowa	$1.11	25	S.D.	$1.49	10
Kans.	$1.12	23	Tenn.	$1.30	18
Ky.	$1.45	14	Tex.	$0.94	36
La.	$1.45	13	Utah	$1.14	22
Maine	$1.40	16	Vt.	$1.12	24
Md.	$1.44	15	Va.	$1.66	7
Mass.	$0.77	44	Wash.	$0.88	37
Mich.	$0.85	38	W.Va.	$1.83	3
Minn.	$0.69	47	Wis.	$0.82	39
Miss.	$1.77	4	Wyo.	$1.11	26
Mo.	$1.29	20	D.C.	$6.64	—

Source: Office of Management and Budget, Tax Foundation.

grant-in-aid programs are based partly on need. The Tax Foundation, a non-partisan tax research organization based in Washington DC, has reported that for every dollar Mainers paid federal taxes in FY 2004, $1.40 was returned, making Maine the largest receiver of per capita federal funds in New England. As table 3 shows, Maine ranked sixteenth in the nation in terms of per capita federal aid, while Vermont followed at twenty-fourth. New Hampshire, which still does not have an income or a sales tax, ranked

Table 4: Maine state-local tax burden compared to U.S. average (1970–2005)

Year	State		U.S. Average
	State-local tax burden	State rank (1 is highest)	Average state-local tax burden
1970	10.8%	9	9.8%
1971	11.3%	6	10.1%
1972	11.8%	6	10.4%
1973	11.8%	5	10.2%
1974	11.5%	5	10.2%
1975	11.4%	7	10.2%
1976	10.6%	12	10.3%
1977	10.5%	14	10.2%
1978	10.5%	11	9.8%
1979	10.2%	12	9.4%
1980	10.4%	6	9.4%
1981	10.6%	7	9.4%
1982	10.9%	7	9.7%
1983	10.9%	6	9.7%
1984	10.9%	8	9.8%
1985	11.0%	7	9.9%
1986	11.3%	5	10.0%
1987	11.8%	5	10.2%
1988	11.8%	3	10.2%
1989	11.6%	4	10.2%
1990	11.5%	6	10.3%
1991	12.0%	5	10.5%
1992	12.3%	3	10.6%
1993	12.1%	5	10.5%
1994	12.2%	3	10.5%
1995	12.5%	2	10.5%
1996	12.7%	2	10.4%
1997	13.2%	1	10.3%
1998	13.5%	1	10.4%
1999	13.1%	1	10.4%
2000	13.2%	1	10.4%
2001	13.3%	1	10.5%
2002	12.7%	1	10.2%
2003	12.9%	1	10.1%

	State		U.S. Average
Year	State-local tax burden	State rank (1 is highest)	Average state-local tax burden
2004	13.0%	1	10.2%
2005	13.0%	1	10.1%
2006	13.5%	1	10.6%

Source: Bureau of Economic Analysis, Department of Commerce, and Tax Foundation calculations.

forty-eighth among the fifty states in per capita general expenditures and per capita federal grants.[7]

Of the total federal funds paid to Maine in FY 2004, the largest category, Medicaid, comprised 59 percent of the payments.[8] The other categories that received funds were transportation (9 percent), education (7.3 percent), public assistance (1.8 percent), and all other (23 percent). Maine has been proactive in utilizing federal funds, especially for healthcare of citizens with low income and disabilities. See Chapter 10 for more on the state's health policies.

In FY05 Maine generated state revenues from two major taxes: the individual income tax and the sales and use tax. The tax on individuals was the largest single source of revenue, making up 42.16 percent of total revenues. The sales and use tax yielded 32.62 percent. The third-largest source of revenue was the corporate income tax (4 percent), followed by the cigarette tax (3.6 percent). All other revenue sources provided about 17.6 percent They included such items as court fees, estate tax, and public utilities tax, among others.

The Tax Foundation has ranked Maine's local/state tax burden as a percentage of income as the nation's highest each year since 1997. In 2006 the local/state tax burden was 13.5 percent of personal income, compared to a national average of 10.6 percent.[9] As table 4 shows, the tax burden has been increasing since the 1980s. This ranking has been challenged by the Maine Center for Economic Policy, an independent nonpartisan research organization. The center reported Maine ranked the second highest when somewhat different data (from the U.S. Census) were used. The center also argued that the state would rank only fifteenth among the states on tax burden if adjustments were made for the high proportion of Maine property taxes paid by nonresidents (17 percent).[10]

History of State of Maine Revenues

Changing times require new tax policies. Funding sources used at the turn of the twentieth century differ from the ones providing resources necessary in the twenty-first century. A brief review of the history of state revenues shows that until the 1840s, Maine was against the principle of direct taxation, considering it, in the words of the state treasurer in 1836, the "most odious and the most expensive way of sustaining the government."[11] Revenues were instead based on the sales of public lands, which activity boomed in the 1830s. Shortly thereafter, changes in the national and state economy, and a border dispute with Canada, caused the state to borrow so heavily that its credit was nearly ruined. By 1840 Maine had no choice but to levy a property tax, which would become one of the most important sources of state revenue.[12] Maine's reliance on the property tax, like that of most other states, began to diminish around 1900. The property tax remains the primary source of revenue for local government today, as it is in the other New England states. It will be discussed later in this chapter.

Sales and Use Taxes

In 1951, the state established a general sales tax of 2 percent on all retail sales, with various items such as food exempted. Once established, the sales tax rose quickly (it reached 5 percent in 1969) to become the state government's primary source of tax revenue, and it remained as such until 1989. The sales and use tax revenues are based on two factors—the rate of the tax and the base on which the tax is levied. When the tax was originally adopted—and for many years thereafter—it captured most of the economic activity of the State. In fact, in 1960 it generated 75 percent of Maine's own source revenue. As economic activity moved from the production of goods to the delivery of services the tax has not easily captured those changes. Further, since 2000, sales of autos and home building supplies have accounted for 30–40 percent of sales tax revenues in Maine. That makes the sales tax so sensitive to shifts in the economy that its annual revenue varies significantly and sometimes unpredictably.[13]

In most states the rate of the sales taxes has risen. Of the forty-five states that had adopted the sales tax by 1970, twenty-four had rates below 4 percent, and only one state was as high as 6 percent. In 2003 only two states had rates below 4 percent and seventeen states charged 6 percent or more. Fourteen states allowed combined state and local rates to rise above 8 percent.[14] Maine exempts both food and medicine from the tax. Of the twelve states with sales tax that do not offer the food exemption, only five have tax rates higher than Maine's. Also, five of the twelve states that do not offer food exemptions—Hawaii, Idaho, Kansas, South Dakota, and Wyoming— allow an income tax credit to compensate low-income households.

In 1991, the legislature raised the sales tax from 5 percent to 6 percent due to severe budget shortfalls. Lawmakers promised to lower it once the economy improved. In 1993 lawmakers actually put a trigger to automatically reduce the sales tax if revenues grew by more than 8 percent. The first trigger was implemented in October 1998 yielding one-half-of-one-percent drop to 5.5 percent. The legislature, facing surpluses during the 1999 session, voted to reduce the sales tax to 5 percent effective July 1, 2000. If the Legislature had not changed the statute, the trigger would have been pulled again in October 1999, providing a one-half-of-one-percent reduction nine months earlier. As of 2006 the sales tax rate was 5 percent, which was the national median. There was, however, a 7 percent tax on lodging and prepared meals and a 10 percent tax on rental cars.

The sales tax has not generated the forecasted revenues in the 2000s, leading some policymakers to call for a broadening of the base to include more services, such as administrative services and various personal services. The challenge state government faces today is that tax policy not only competes with other states, such as New Hampshire, which levies no sales or use tax, but also with foreign countries due to the global economy. Government reliance on the sales and other consumption taxes has fallen worldwide since 1965.[15] It seems likely that if the sales tax is to generate more revenues, the increased funds will have to come from a broader base, not a higher rate.

Income Taxes

The legislature established personal and corporate income taxes in 1969. Under challenge, it was approved by the state's voters in a 1970 referendum to the surprise of many state officials. Since its passage, the income tax's portion of state tax revenue has grown impressively, largely because of the tremendous increase in wages over the last three decades. Nationally, the combination of state sales and income taxes has grown from 36 percent of state tax revenue in 1970 to 70 percent in 2001.[16] Those tax increases, without legislative action, grow as the economy increases. Economists refer to them as "elastic." The risk to states is that the same taxes also decrease when economic activity slackens so they do not provide the stable source of income the property tax does. This can be problematic since the personal income tax is the single most important source of state tax revenue.

Between 1969 and 1987, Maine's income tax rates were revised only once, in 1978. In 1987 substantial changes took place when the legislature passed a measure to incorporate the changes made by the federal Tax Reform Act of 1986 into Maine's income tax law. The move was necessary because Maine's provisions are coupled to federal income tax requirements. As an example, most deductions that are permitted under federal rules are permissible under state law. When the federal government enacted the 1986 revisions, it reduced its tax rates and eliminated many deductions. Until the state reduced its own rates, Maine taxpayers paid an excess of dollars to the state government because they could not claim the deductions permitted in previous years. The governor and legislature grappled with the problem in 1987 and 1988, when most Maine tax-payers received rebates.

In 1989 legislators reshaped the state income tax code. The revisions were based on recommendations of a nonpartisan consulting firm from Washington DC, which had been commissioned to review the state's tax system. The reforms resulted in tax decreases for about 90 percent of Maine's taxpayers.[17]

Maine's provisions for the most part conform to the federal income tax law. A notable exception is the decoupling of the standard deduction for married taxpayers who file jointly, which was passed by the 122nd Legislature in 2005. The federal government had increased the standard deduction, which resulted in a decrease of taxes owned by couples. Maine could not afford to implement that change. On the other hand, the state has phased in other federal changes, such as one for equipment depreciation.

Maine has recently lowered its top personal income tax rate. In 1992 the state had the highest marginal income tax rate of any state (at 9.9 percent). By 2005 Maine's rate of 8.5 percent was exceeded by five other states—California, Iowa, Montana, Oregon, and Vermont. Maine's personal income taxes are comprised of four brackets. The highest marginal rate starts at a relatively low level of income, $17,350 (in 2004). This low base raises a question of how progressive the income tax really is in Maine. It appears more similar to a flat tax since the marginal tax rates are 2 percent for incomes under $4,350, 7 percent for under $8,650 and 8.5 percent for over $17,350. Governor Baldacci would like to lower the top marginal rate to 8.45 percent. In addition, his tax reform plan would remove approximately forty thousand low-income taxpayers from the tax rolls by increasing the threshold of taxable income from $2,000 to $4,750, therefore improving the tax code's progressivity.

Across the globe more countries are decreasing marginal rates than hiking them, a trend that has gone on for five years.[18] In some Baltic and central

European countries, flat taxes have been adopted recently, modeled after Hong Kong's decades-old system. The advantages reported are increasing revenues through better compliance and economic expansion. Although there is discussion in the legislature about the need to reform Maine's personal income tax system, it is not clear what form it will take.

Property Taxes: A State and Local Challenge

A continuing feature of Maine's tax policy is change, created out of the need to develop new revenue sources and to modify old sources to meet new circumstances. This is illustrated by glancing at the state's original form of revenue—the property tax—over which controversy has raged in recent years. Because property taxes are assessed according to real estate values, but must be paid out of current income, they have been particularly onerous in those parts of the state where property values have skyrocketed within the past two decades. This strain has caused closer examination of all aspects of the property tax.

Local governments in Maine depend heavily on the property tax. Levied at the local level, it pays for the cost of local government services. The tax represents about half of the overall revenues of local governments in Maine.[19] There is simply no viable local alternative for raising needed revenue within the current legal constraints. The legislature has considered local options taxes, such as a sales tax, that would permit the local communities to decrease property tax dependency, but after consideration has gone on to reject them.

There is a direct relationship between local property taxes and the state budget. Across the country, state governments have taken on more responsibility in funding local governments through revenue sharing, property tax relief programs, education, and other services once solely provided by local government. This has reduced the burden of raising funds through the property tax. However, it has not reduced the burden as much as citizens in Maine expected during the last two decades. In fact, the property tax burden in Maine, according to the governor, was in 2005 second highest of all states, rising from fifteenth position in 1982.[20]

The major expenditure category of local governments is K-12 public education, which makes property taxes play a central role in the financing of local education. Substituting state funds for local funds is a way to both reduce reliance on local property taxes and deliver equal educational resources to students. States greatly increased their share of funding for elementary and secondary education during the twentieth century.

Table 5: New England property taxes per capita, growth rate, and percent of income, 2002

	Per capita property tax $	Per capita income $	U.S. capita income rank	Property tax percentage increase 1988–2002 (in adjusted dollars)	Percentage income for property taxes
New Hampshire	1,703	34,055	7	120.8	5.00
Connecticut	1,733	42,545	2	125.1	4.07
Rhode Island	1,369	31,475	16	129.2	4.35
Massachusetts	1,358	38,975	4	129.2	3.48
Vermont	1,337	29,245	24	117.2	4.57
Maine	1,477	27,713	34	169.0	5.33

Source: U.S. Census Bureau, Tax Foundation.

After years of debate in Maine about the role of the state in financing of public primary and secondary education, the School Finance Act of 1985 was passed. One of the key components of the act was that the state was to assume 55 percent of educational costs, while the local communities paid the remainder. After general purpose school aid increased 32 percent from 1985 to 1989, the expectation was that the state share of costs would increase and reliance on the property tax would decrease. But this did not occur. By 1990 after average annual state subsidy increases of 8 percent (during 1980–1986) and of 17 percent (between 1986 and 1990), the state share had only slightly increased its state share to 43.4 percent from the 1980s average of 42.8 percent.[21] After the recession of the early 1990s, during which the legislature essentially flat funded the state's share of the education subsidy to local communities, no further progress was made. In fact, by 2005 the state share was essentially the same as before the act passed—43 percent—a mere two-tenths of one percent increase in the state share of education costs since the reform measure was enacted.

By a number of measures, Maine's property tax burden has been increasing since the late 1980s. This was a result of the greater sensitivity of other sources of revenues, such as sales and income taxes, to economic downturns. Because the property tax generated more stable revenues, more school expenses shifted to the local property taxpayers. In 1988 the property tax accounted for 32 percent of all state and local taxes, and was the lowest property tax per capita in New England. In contrast, it currently produces 40 percent of tax revenues. As Table 5 shows, by 2002 Maine had had the largest increase in property taxes of any New England state—169 percent, moving it to the third-highest in New England and fourth in the United States during the period 1988–2002.

In New England, Mainers also paid the highest percentage of personal income for property taxes, 5.33 percent. The two New England states with higher property taxes per capita, Connecticut and New Hampshire, were ranked second and seventh, respectively, in per capita income, while Maine ranked thirty-fourth. Increases in the property tax and, especially, the crossing of the threshold of 5 percent, have been identified as key factors leading to property taxpayer revolts. Maine has experienced both conditions and it is no surprise that rising property taxes have recently provoked sharp reactions.

Several legislative study groups, business groups, and academics called attention to the lack of substantive progress in school funding and property tax relief. Maine's State Law and Legislative Reference Library counts eighteen studies conducted during the 1986–2003 period that addressed school-funding issues. After decades of inaction, a series of events culminated in the 2005 passage of a citizens-initiated property tax relief measure in a referendum, directing the state to pay a greater share of K-12 funding. A review of these actions highlights the slow and arduous road to property tax relief.

In 1995 and 1996 property tax reformers gathered signatures to place a citizen referendum on the ballot. The measure proposed was similar to the granddaddy of property tax relief programs, California's "Proposition 13" tax cap. The proponents were unable to gather enough signatures to put it on the ballot. Again in 2002, a group called the Maine Taxpayers Action Network collected signatures for a property tax cap. That effort failed when the Secretary of State determined that approximately three thousand of the 42,101 signatures necessary to place the measure on the November 2002 election ballot had been gathered incorrectly.

That same year, the Maine Municipal Association (MMA), for the first time in its sixty-six-year history, endorsed the idea of accomplishing tax reform through a citizen initiative. The MMA had earlier supported several legislative attempts at reform which failed.[22] The MMA's proposal required the state to pay at least 55 percent of the costs of elementary and secondary education including 100 percent of special education costs. It was calculated that such a move would shift $264 million of costs from the local to state government. MMA teamed up with the powerful Maine Educational Association (MEA) to advocate for the referendum. Meanwhile, the legislature passed a slightly different competing measure to phase in a 55 percent state contribution to education and expand property tax relief. There also was a third alternative (C), rejecting both the A and B choices. On November 4, 2003, voters faced choices IA, IB or IC. When the results were tallied the citizen initiative received 38 percent of the vote, the competing legislative measure followed with 35 percent, while IC (keeping the status quo) received 27 percent. In such a situation, the Maine Constitution requires that the measure obtaining the most votes (and gaining at least one third of all votes) be placed on a ballot for approval or rejection by itself. On June 8, 2004, the citizen initiative easily passed with 55 percent of the vote.

The second citizen referendum that year was known as the Palesky tax cap, named for Carol Palesky, a long-time Maine political activist. It sought to roll back property tax assessments to their 1996 level, hold increases in town valuations to not more than 2 percent a year, cap town mill rates at ten and prohibit the legislature from amending the system. On Nov. 2, 2004 it was rejected by 63 percent of voters. The tax cap was perceived as too harsh, often referred to a "meat ax approach to tax reform," which would damage needed services.

While signatures were being gathered for yet another citizen initiative for property tax relief, Governor Baldacci delivered a dramatic proposal on the first day of the 122nd Legislative Session, in January 2005. It was titled LD 1 "An Act to Increase the State Share of Education Costs, Reduce Property Taxes and Reduce Government Spending at All Levels." Because of the wording of the tax cap referendum, if lawmakers did not pass the governor's proposal by January 20, 2005, any tax bill passed after that date would wind up on a statewide ballot. After a bipartisan legislative committee approved the governor's plan, it was passed by legislature on the last day before it would have required a citizen's vote. The plan approved increased education funding to local communities by $250 million, increased property taxpayer relief with a higher exemption for the homestead exemption, and increased eligibility and funds for the circuit breaker program.

For the first time, the state imposed spending caps on all levels of state, county, and local budgets. Under the provisions L.D. #1, the permissible rise in annual state spending was limited to the rate of growth of Maine's average personal income plus the state's average population growth in the preceding year. In 2005 for instance, state income growth was 2.58 percent compared to population growth of 0.53 percent, permitting a maximum increase of 3.11 percent. For municipalities, the cap is determined by the state's average personal income growth plus a municipality's property growth factor—a measure of new development in the community. The local legislative body can increase the cap by majority vote. Since 2005 the

state government, county governments, and about 60 percent of municipalities have held spending within the intended limits. On the other hand,
expenditures of most school districts have exceeded the caps. The goal of
the bill was to reduce the overall state tax burden to the national average in
ten years. In the meantime the governor's office estimated that the average
property taxpayer in Maine would see a $207 annual reduction.[23]

At this point it is not clear that the goal of lowering property taxes will be
realized, especially to the extent voiced by the governor. A weakness of the
legislation was the lack of linkage between increased state funding for local
education and actual reductions in the property taxes of Maine citizens. As
noted, a municipality's governing body can override the spending cap with
majority vote in approving the budget. The state increased the homestead
exemption, but it required local communities to raise half the costs. The
state also increased the property tax circuit breaker program substantially—
to a cap of $2,000. This had the effect of shifting property taxes from resi-
dent homeowners to owners of second homes and businesses. For property
taxpayers to receive the relief LDI has promised, the overall cost of local
government must be reduced, or at the very least, held steady.

Before the impact of LDI could be measured, property tax reformers
were collecting signatures for still another proposal, one to be placed on the
November 2006 ballot. After a ruling by the Maine Supreme Judicial Court
upheld the right of Secretary of State Matthew Dunlap to accept signatures
after the statutory deadline, the so called Taxpayers Bill of Rights, commonly known as TABOR, appeared on the ballot.[24] It was modeled after the
Colorado initiative that reduced the state budget to the rate of growth of the
state population coupled with an inflation factor. The timing was somewhat
surprising, in the light of the fact that Colorado—the only state with such a
measure—had suspended the provision in 2005 when faced with declining
revenues and the prospect of about $400 million in cuts to state programs.[25]
Maine voters narrowly defeated TABOR in the November election.

EXPENDITURES

The expenditures made by Maine's government since 1820 chart the changes
in various policies and the growth of government responsibility. In 1820, the
state's expenditures of $38,000 were essentially devoted to setting up and
sustaining the new institutions of government. The greatest outlays were
spent on the legislature and on government administration, while education
followed in third place.[26] By the eve of the Civil War, state spending priorities had changed. Except for the redemption of the funded debt, brought on

by the excessive borrowing of the 1830s, education experienced the greatest outlay of state funds, followed by government administration and then by the legislature.

That pattern of spending was fairly consistent until 1915, when outlays for highway construction and maintenance mushroomed, triggered by the automotive revolution. Continued heavy spending on highway construction (1917–32) coupled with the onset of the Great Depression, left the state in debt, and most allotments to highways were sharply curtailed for the next few years.[27] By the end of the 1930s, however, allocations to highways increased to the extent that transportation was the primary recipient of state funds—typical of rural states of that period. By the 1960s, the picture changed again. Education's share of state funds began to surpass those earmarked for transportation. Although this change reflected a more liberal climate in Augusta, education had become a high priority of both political parties.

The majority of state government expenditures are payments to local governments. The largest expenditure category of the Maine State Budget is for elementary and secondary education. The other categories included in grants to local governments are revenue sharing, welfare payments, and community development.

Another counterintuitive fact is that some categories in the budget on the expenditures side have really been tax relief measures. The costs associated with these programs increase the overall reported expenditures for state government but are essentially giving back sources of funding. In order to accurately represent Maine's real tax burden in FY05 the 121st Legislature adopted moving the "Circuit Breaker" program for Maine property tax relief from a general fund appropriation to an offset of revenue. In the FY06 budget, the Business Equipment Tax Reimbursement (BETR) program followed. This change impacted the state revenue sharing program with localities because the amount shared is based on 5.1 percent of the revenue generated by all sales, corporate, and individual tax revenue. So reducing the revenue by BETR against income tax revenue has led to a decrease in funds in that program.

As table 6 indicates, Maine spends more on Medicaid than most other states. The Medicaid program is funded under a cost-sharing arrangement between the federal and state government to meet the healthcare needs of low-income people. The state reimbursement rate is based on the income of a state's citizens. Although Maine has had one of the higher Medicaid match rates (at 64.89 percent), the rate was lowered to 62.90 percent in FY06, which added an estimated $78 million to the state's cost of the program.

Table 6: Maine spending compared with all state average expenditures as a percentage of total state expenditures, fiscal year 2003

	Maine	All States
Elementary and secondary education	17.7	21.7
Higher education	3.7	10.8
Public assistance	2.6	2.2
Medicaid	28.2	21.4
Corrections	2.0	3.5
Transportation	8.2	8.2
All other	37.5	32.2

Source: National Association of State Budget Officers. *2003 State Expenditure Report* (Washington DC: Association of State Budget Officers, 2004).

Overall, Medicaid has since 1990 surpassed higher education as the second-largest state program.[28] Maine has supported a series of expansions of its Medicaid members through federal government waivers. In 2004 approximately 240,500 Mainers, or 18 percent of the population, were enrolled in MaineCare, the state Medicaid program.[29] The program continues to exert pressure on the state budget; it has had a series of expensive problems that have required the State to come up with more funds than planned for.

States across the country are concerned with health care costs, which are projected to increase between 8 and 9 percent a year, a level exceeding projected revenue growth rates.[30] Upon taking office, Governor Baldacci developed Dirigo Health to address the high cost of health care in Maine and be able to offer health insurance to the over 130,000 uninsured Mainers, 77 percent of whom work. Maine has the fifth-highest health-care costs in the country on a per capita basis. The goals of the program are to contain costs, ensure access, and improve the quality of health care. It was enacted with the support of two-thirds of the legislators in 2003. The state seeded the start up of the program mostly with funds derived from selling the nonprofit Blue Cross/Blue Shield to a private insurer, Anthem, and has covered other costs through state appropriations.

Another area that has shifted over time is welfare assistance. In 1989 welfare expenditures accounted roughly for a one-fifth larger portion of the Maine state budget compared to the average of all state budgets.[31] That was about the same portion as is shown for FY03 in Table 6. There has been a change since the TANF (Temporary Assistance to Needy Families) program, created by the Welfare Reform Law of 1996, replaced AFDC (Aid to Families with Dependent Children). TANF has provided Maine with the lowest level of cash assistance of any New England state—lower, in fact, than the national average in 2004. The maximum benefit a family of three can receive is only 36 percent of the federal poverty level. That is much lower than the levels of 58 percent and 52 percent Maine families received in 1979 and 1990, respectively.[32]

Interestingly, Maine spends a bit more on its state government, as measured by the percentage of funds in the total state budget, than other states. The amount expended on government administration placed it sixteenth among all states, in line with its overall ranking of thirteenth on state expenditures per capita.[33] The extensive network of administrative field offices needed to cover its scattered, rural population contributes toward larger than average administration expenditures. Another reason is that the state is still modernizing its bureaucracy, a process propelled by the extensive economic development of recent years. Further, the state's fairly liberal orientation to social and environmental polices contributes to a substantial state workforce.

Budget Stabilization Fund

One interesting area of the budget is the Budget Stabilization Fund, previously known as the Rainy Day Fund, which the legislature established in its present form in 2003. It is intended to provide the necessary resources to deal with times of budget shortfalls. The balances in this account, unlike other general fund accounts, carry forward each year. Prior to 1991, it was capped at $25 million. In 1991, it had a cap of 4 percent of the general fund revenues, which increased to 5 percent in 1999.

Because of the recession in the early 1990s, the fund did not actually start to grow until the later part of 1995. Between then and 1999 the fund increased to $137 million. The Maine budget had surpluses up to the year 2000. However, an unexpected shortfall in the 2001–2002 budget year required the state to use the Rainy Day Fund to balance the budget. By 2003 the reserves were depleted. Bonding agencies informed state officials that the reserves were too low, and could decrease the rating of the state-issued debt. It was under this constraint that the new Budget Stabilization Fund was formed, with a cap of 10 percent of the total general fund in the immediately preceding fiscal year, double the rate of the previous cap. The cap was later increased to 12 percent of general fund revenues. Under the governor's tax reform package submitted in 2007, it may not fall below 1 percent of revenues.

The 2003 legislation established a mechanism for both funding the Budget Stabilization Fund and addressing the unfunded liability of the state retirement system. It required that 32 percent of any future budget surpluses go to those two areas. It also required that another 16 percent go into the operating capital reserve within the general fund, and 20 percent to programs that were initially cut by the lawmakers but deemed as deserving. At the close of the FY 05, when the budget ended with a $75.2 million surplus, the funds were already dedicated based on the formula. In FY 2005 Maine was one of seven states whose end of year balances, as a percentage of expenditures, was less than 1 percent.[34] That lack of reserves was a factor in the reduction of Maine's bond rating in the spring of 2005.

Bonds

The yearly interest payments of State of Maine bonds are an appropriated expenditure in the general fund budget. If too many bonds are issued, interest payments may take up too large a share of the current revenues. Yet for projects that have benefits lasting more than one year, it is important to spread the costs over a number of years. Bonds make it possible for current taxpayers to escape part of the financial burden of projects that benefit future taxpayers. This is a key concept in tax fairness. State bonds are used in stimulating economic activity, meeting infrastructure needs, and in the case of Maine, preserving land for the public.

The Maine Constitution requires state bonds to have voter approval before the state treasurer can authorize their sale. The legislature decides which projects it believes should go before the voters, and the governor can sign or veto the measures. The voters then approve or reject each proposed project by a simple majority.

Tax supported debt is comprised of general obligation bonds, Maine Governmental Facilities Authority bonds, and lease purchase agreements. Maine pays off each bond issue after ten years, earlier than any other New England state. The state limits debt according to the "5 percent Rule," meaning it caps its tax supported debt payments to no more than 5 percent of the general fund and highway fund revenues. On June 30, 2005, the state was well within its limit, at 3.72 percent.[35] This has led to the question: should Maine bond more? Bonding can provide the opportunity to leverage funds to improve economic activity. However, the historically conservative nature of Mainers causes them to resist incurring debt.

Governor Baldacci proposed a $197 million bond package to legislators early in 2005. Republican lawmakers, who had opposed a bond package the previous year, fought to reduce the amount. In July, an agreement was reached for an $83 million package. It included $34 million for transportation, $20 million for research and development, $10 million for land purchases, $10 million for environmental projects, and $9 million for education. The funds were distributed in a way that those activities with more ability to leverage investments into the state coffers received the biggest amounts. For instance, federal highway grants have large matching formulas, and they were the largest single category in the proposed bond. The $20 million for research and development was large due to past investments, which returned $7 for every $1 invested. The *Bangor Daily News*, which often takes conservative positions on state issues, supported the bond package due to the opportunity to leverage funds. In November 2005, voters supported every bond except one dealing with higher education. Observers believed that the difficulty with that bond was voter concern about the mission and spending priorities of the University of Maine system.[36]

CONCLUSION

The tragic events of September 11, 2001, supplied the backdrop of one of the worst fiscal situations the states have had to deal with in the last sixty years.[37] Maine was no exception. Debate over taxes, especially property taxes, produced continued fireworks as the state budget and bond packages moved through the legislature. Maine's budget policy reflects both the choices of federal, state, and local policymakers and changing economic conditions. Whether or not Maine makes substantial progress in lowering its citizens' tax burden, it is clear that improvements in financial management, such as the creation of the budget stabilization fund and the processes for economic and revenue forecasting, have set the state on an improved path to managing its finances. The obligation of the state to provide services to a relatively small population of 1.3 million—which has a lower per capita income than the rest of New England even as it covers a land mass of nearly equal size—will continue to provide financial challenges.

CHAPTER TEN

Contemporary Policy Concerns

This chapter examines some key issues in Maine's public policy environment. These tensions reflect distinctive features of the state's politics as
Maine is called upon to make trade-offs among conflicting demands on its
resources. The focus is on the directions being taken by state government,
and the trends likely to be present in the next several years.

JOBS VERSUS THE ENVIRONMENT

A traditionally low-income state blessed by an unusually handsome physical setting, Maine has long been concerned with balancing environmental
protection with job creation. State government involvement in environmental problems began when the legislature created a Sanitary Water Board in
1941. The state has long depended on its rivers as a source of power for its
industries, especially the textile industry. A significant part of the state's
population settled along the several rivers running between the northern
wild lands and the seacoast. The abuse of the rivers by effluent discharges
from factories called attention to the problem. Edmund Muskie in *Journeys*
writes about his early impression of the problem:

> It was our river, the Androscoggin, that stirred public concern and indig-
> nation even before World War II. The Androscoggin begins its run to the
> ocean in the high, clear mountain streams and lakes in the northwestern
> corner of Maine. It flows into New Hampshire, then back into Maine, pick-
> ing up pulp and paper wastes in Berlin, New Hampshire, Rumford and
> Livermore Falls, Maine. In those days . . . , the wastes were visible long
> before the river reached Lewiston. There was a tremendous stench, and the
> paint on houses began to peel.[1]

The pollution problem caused by the pulp and paper industry was acute. By one measure (the biochemical oxygen demand of the wastes), three paper mills could produce more effluents than all domestic and municipal sewer systems in the state.[2] Although Maine made a few efforts to enact pollution legislation in the 1940s, the efforts were largely unsuccessful. This was a period in Maine politics which Duane Lockard has characterized as one dominated by "pine, power and paper."[3] Lobbies for the paper companies were sufficiently powerful that antipollution legislation was often emasculated. One measure enacted in the late 1940s set fairly rigorous limits on the amount of permissible discharges into rivers, and then proceeded to exempt from its provisions most rivers in the state.

The rise of environmental regulations began in the 1960s. Several political developments contributed to a changed climate for legislation.[4] One was the rise of the Democratic Party to a position competitive with the Republican Party. In 1966 Kenneth Curtis, a liberal Democrat with pro-environmental policy interests, was elected governor. Curtis was able to enlist the support of key Republicans in the Republican-controlled legislature for his measures. Another factor was the proposed federally funded Dickey Lincoln Dam. The project would have flooded thousands of acres of northern Maine for the construction of a hydroelectric power plant, whose power output would have lowered electric power rates. The huge scope of the enterprise helped to coalesce environmental interests against the dam. The project eventually failed for lack of funding.

By the end of the decade, the *Maine Times*, a widely read environmentally oriented weekly newspaper, had begun publication, and the Natural Resources Council of Maine, the largest environmental lobby in the state, had established an office in Augusta.

The pattern of future environmental legislation was thus established. A wide array of groups could be counted on to support environmental projects. In addition to the Natural Resources Council of Maine, they included the Maine Audubon Society, the Maine Chapter of the Nature Conservancy, the Maine Coast Heritage Trust, the Sierra Club, the Conservation Law Foundation, and many others. Even more important, environment interests would enjoy the support of both political parties. Despite a history of neglect of its natural resources, when the state finally joined the environmental movement, it did so in a very broad-based fashion—a reflection of its participatory political culture.

Beginning in 1970 major present-day environmental statutes were put in place.[5] One involved site location of new facilities and projects. The provisions required prior approval of the Maine Board of Environmental

Protection (BEP) before the construction or operation of such developments as subdivisions in excess of twenty acres, parking lots or paved areas exceeding three acres, buildings with a ground area in excess of sixty thousand square feet, and large-scale milling and excavation activities. One requirement is, for example, that a development will fit "harmoniously into the existing natural environment," and that the developer have the financial and technical ability to meet state air and water pollution control standards. The BEP, which is part of the Department of Environmental Protection (DEP), has authority to place terms and conditions on its grants and permits.

Two other major environmental statutes are the Solid Waste Management Act of 1973 and the Alteration of Coastal Wetlands Act of 1975. The Solid Waste Act authorizes BEP to adopt rules governing the location and construction of solid-waste facilities. Part of the law provides communities with a state subsidy equivalent to 50 percent of the cost of maintaining a facility, as long as it is in "substantial compliance" with state regulations. The measure is especially important in Maine because a large portion of the state's groundwater is close to the land surface and susceptible to pollution from waste sources. In the mid-1970s, the state began regulating more than 450 dumps throughout the state; because of opposition, DEP had to prioritize dumps according to those most seriously damaging to the environment.

In 1989 the legislature created the Waste Management Agency to oversee efforts to deal with the waste problem. Major attention was given to recycling, with the aim to reduce by 50 percent the amount of trash created by Maine residents. The state's existing bottle law, which had required deposits on beer and soft-drink containers only, was expanded to cover virtually all nondairy beverages. Plastic cans and certain other types of containers are banned. Buyers of refrigerators, tires, and other goods difficult to dispose of are subject to special fees to finance trash-disposal programs.

The evolution of Maine's environmental policy from primarily technical regulations to programs involving a range of issues and choices is illustrated by the Rivers Protection Act of 1983. Earlier pollution-control efforts were focused almost entirely on protecting people from the effects of certain types of private activity on private property that threatened the public's health, welfare, and safety. Factories were limited, for instance, in the amount of effluents that they could discharge into the waters of nearby streams. Under the 1983 Rivers Protection Act, the emphasis was shifted to provide the greatest benefit for the public in weighing proposed uses of rivers. As an example, the measure specifies that, for the thirty-one thousand miles of Maine rivers on which hydroelectric projects may be built, the public gain from a project must outweigh anticipated environmental losses. The BEP is asked to consider such factors as the impact of a project on soil, water quality, wildlife, fisheries, historic resources, public access, and flooding, in addition to energy benefits. The thrust of recent solid-waste and river-quality legislation has been to stress the interdependence of environmental factors. This, in turn, has put more power in the hands of state agencies to balance environmental and economic needs.

For many years, a battle was fought in Maine under the rubric of "payrolls vs. pickerel." Advances in environmental regulation were considered a threat to jobs in the pulp and paper companies and in other industries. In 1986 political fireworks erupted in the legislature over the "Big A" Dam. The Big A was a proposed hydroelectric project of the Great Northern Paper Company on a branch of the Penobscot River in central Maine, at the point of the Big Amberjackmockamus Falls. The politics of the project illustrate the tensions between the goals of job creation and preservation of the state's environment.

The desire of Great Northern to build the Big A Dam stemmed from the company's financial problems. The company argued that it needed the additional power source to cover the cost of upgrading its mills and to save approximately one thousand jobs. With the additional cheap power, Great Northern claimed it could even add several hundred jobs to its plant. Opponents maintained that the proposed dam would endanger popular salmon fishing and destroy a major area for commercial whitewater rafting. Because the dam was in a part of Maine with no organized local government, Great Northern's application was initially reviewed by the Land Use Regulation Commission (LURC), an agency created in 1969 to handle zoning and development in the state's unorganized areas. LURC applied the standards of the Rivers Protection Act and concluded that the economic benefits outweighed the environmental losses. The vote was 4 to 3. The company's struggle did not, however, end with LURC. Because federal water-quality standards were involved, the application also had to be approved by BEP. In the early 1970s, BEP had been assigned the responsibility of examining the compatibility of hydroelectric projects with federal standards. Great Northern lost this second round of the process. In early 1986 BEP found by a six-to-two margin that water quality would be adversely affected by construction of the Big A Dam.

The battle next moved to the legislature. Supporters of Big A attempted to enact a measure overriding the BEP decision by directing the commissioner of the Department of Environmental Protection, BEP's parent organization, to stipulate that water-quality standards had been satisfied. House Speaker John Martin, a strong advocate of Great Northern's position, was so incensed by BEP'S rejection of Big A that he suggested BEP members who voted against the project should resign for—in his opinion—violating state law as reflected in certain provisions of the Rivers Protection Act. He suggested that impeachment proceedings be started if they were unwilling to step down. After lengthy debate, the house approved the bill overturning the BEP decision by a vote of 85 to 45. The senate, however, stalled the measure. At that point, Great Northern abruptly withdrew its application, even though it had expended about $6 million in its preparation for the project, which was estimated to be valued at about $100 million. Although environmentalists had succeeded in overcoming legislative efforts to repeal the BEP decision, many business leaders believed that the uproar damaged the climate for economic development.

The outcome of the battle over the Big A was one that has rather typically occurred in Maine in environmental politics; in a struggle to regulate the activities of a particular plant or industry, environmental forces have usually prevailed. Another part of the story has been the state's tendency to concentrate on large specific polluters, and mostly to ignore small-scale activities that in aggregate produce equivalent hazards.[6] Maine enacted a Water Pollution Control Act in 1967 and has strengthened it in various ways since that time. The Act has led to a significant improvement of the state's waterways by reducing the amounts of effluents major point sources, such as the pulp and paper companies, are permitted to discharge into streams and rivers. However, approximately half the water pollution in the state comes from thousands of individual camps, farms, and small businesses, which are subject to relatively little control. In some cases, they are "grandfathered" into legislation setting forth the new regulations.

A related example can be found in the policies to improve air quality. Maine has been a leader in seeking national legislation to control airborne wastes from midwestern public utilities that, among other hazards, produce acid rain that falls on its forests. The state has also pursued various legal avenues to accomplish the same goal. Yet daily emissions from the thousands of cars on Maine roads constitute an even greater source of air pollution. The state has not been able to develop a long-term solution to that problem. It tentatively began an auto emissions testing program in 1993, but dropped it in 1995 when the legislature was threatened with a referendum to repeal it.

The environmental hazards of non-point source pollution of air and water have grown in tandem with population changes in the state. In the past two decades, the fastest growing towns—ones that account for nearly all of the state's population growth—are communities located ten to thirty miles from the major towns and cities where most people work and shop. To illustrate, in 1960 some 58 percent of the state's population lived in Maine's 69 principal "service centers," but in 2000 only 44 percent did. This dispersion, or sprawl, has increased environmental hazards such as auto emissions and lake degradation. Ironically, the movement away from urban centers has been encouraged by large-lot zoning practices, action once favored by environmentalists as a means of preserving open space and protecting a rural life style. As a later section describes, state involvement in local planning is a major part of Maine's environmental strategy.

Another element in the strategy is energy conservation. In the late 1970s, the state set forth energy conservation standards for buildings and began to regulate energy audits. In 1999 the State Planning Office was required to submit to the governor and the legislature a resource plan every two years, which included conservation plans. In 2001 the legislature required energy providers to adopt conservation plans. Maine's economy has seemed to become more energy efficient. One study reported that between 1985 and 2000, the state domestic product grew 50 percent while energy consumption rose only 26 percent, although some of that gain was due to the decline of traditional manufacturing industries.[7] The need to balance energy efficiency with environmental risks remains an ongoing challenge. Between 1972 and 1997 the state experimented with nuclear power in the form of a nuclear power plant, Maine Yankee, located in the mid-coast town of Wiscasset. Concern over the very difficult problem of waste disposal led to its eventual closing. More recently, liquefied natural gas (LNG) from the Middle East is seen as a possible significant energy source, but the location of LNG terminals on the coastline has raised still new environmental and security issues.

Despite some setbacks, Maine's environmental ethic remains strong. One of the most interesting initiatives in recent years is the Land for Maine's Future Program (LMF), which began in 1987. The program seeks to preserve lands that have exceptional natural or recreational value. Voters have thus far approved slightly more than $100 million in bonds, through which LMF has purchased 180 million acres and gained easements on another sixty million acres (insuring public access while the land remains in private hands), including more than three hundred of shorefront. A board composed of five state department commissioners and six citizens oversees the program. Local land trusts and other groups nominate parcels of land for inclusion in the program. Once a parcel is approved, the board purchases the land on a matching basis, with land trusts and various philanthropic organizations providing the matching funds. Since 2000 the program has secured more than two dollars for every dollar it has expended. The approximately one hundred land trusts in the state perform much of the day-to-day administration of the LMF program.

PROMOTING ECONOMIC GROWTH: FOR HOW MANY?

Maine governors in recent decades have made economic development a centerpiece of their administrations. That posture is hardly unique; most state chief executives make improving economic conditions for their constituents a goal—often the principal goal—of their tenures. Yet the Maine idea of economic development has some special features. A major characteristic is the transformation of an economy long dependent on natural resources to one based on services and, most recently, on knowledge and creativity. That massive change has, in turn, impelled economic growth strategies to be closely connected to many other public policies.

An example of the link is education. Until the 1970s, Maine high school graduates—finding high-paying jobs in industries such as pulp and paper manufacturing—saw no particular advantage in pursuing a college education. The state had a relatively low level of college attendance among persons between the ages of 18 and 22, and a low rate of public support for higher education. As businesses offering services began to supplant Maine's traditional industries, the need for a workforce with college training grew. Every governor in recent decades has made education reform, at all levels, a critical ingredient of his economic development strategy. Governor Baldacci is no exception. His focus in 2003–04 was to translate the state's vocational/technical institutes into a broader system of community colleges, facilitating the eventual enrollment of greater numbers of high school graduates in the state's four-year colleges.[8]

Another interesting dimension of Maine's economic development has been its concern with targeting. Maine's expansive geography and political culture have generally made it difficult for state officials to provide development benefits to some citizens and not to others. Except in welfare programs, where the provision of assistance to needy persons (based on income categories) is accepted, state assistance tends to be distributed very widely. When the U.S. Department of Homeland Security began providing grants to states in 2003, the Maine Emergency Management Agency (MEMA) directly dispersed the funds (approximately $20 million) to more than a hundred communities. Other localities also accessed funds through separate financial pools MEMA established in each of the sixteen counties. A tendency exists for all counties and towns to share in state-sponsored aid.

On the other hand, the rise of the "two Maines" idea in the mid-1980s alerted the state government to the possibility that regional differences might continue to grow. The situation was of particular concern to the Mc-Kernan administration (1987–1993). As the first Republican administration in twenty years, it did not wish to be identified primarily with the more-affluent southern region. Although many of its key staff members lived in the Portland suburbs, it faced a Democratic house and senate whose leadership came predominantly from the northern half of the state. The administration sought to diffuse the potentially politically explosive notion of "two Maines" in part by targeting development funds to economically distressed areas.

One McKernan program was the identification of "job opportunity zones" in four areas of central and northern Maine, which zones were defined by having unemployment rates approximately double the state average. Businesses that added "full-time quality" jobs were eligible for state grants of about $1,000. The zones were considered priority areas for the repair and upgrading of highways, especially where the roads were immediately involved in commercial development. Like its predecessor, the King administration (1995–2003) paid special attention to areas afflicted by high employment, and initiated several programs designed to assist small businesses in them. On a statewide basis, Governor King strongly emphasized the application of technology to improve economic conditions. "When people think of Maine," he told a reporter, "they think of lobsters and vacations. What I (want) to do is broaden that to have people see Maine as a technological leader."[9] Perhaps King's proudest achievement in that regard was persuading the legislature to enact a program providing every seventh- and eighth-grade student in Maine's public schools with a laptop computer at state expense. The program, implemented in 2002, gained national attention and placed Maine at the forefront in instructional technology in K-12 schools.

Soon after taking the office in 2003, Gov. John Baldacci announced his economic plans. While featuring several new proposals, especially the expanded use of technology, the governor's program also extended several policies of previous administrations. For instance, the targeting of funds to economically distressed areas was continued, although the way eligible recipients were determined was modified. The Baldacci plan identified some eight "Pine Tree Development Zones" (PTDZS) throughout the state. Each zone could comprise as many as five thousand acres in twenty noncontiguous parcels. Qualified businesses in the zones in manufacturing, technology, and financial services that engaged in certain new activities or expanded existing operations were eligible for several financial benefits, including a state income tax credit for five years, and reimbursement of state payroll taxes and a sales tax exemption for construction costs, each for ten years. As of mid-2005 the Department of Community and Economic Development had awarded sixty PTDZ designations to companies and businesses which, it estimated, had created three thousand jobs in the preceding two years.[10]

It is difficult to determine the success of Maine's economic targeting strategies. Regional differences continue to persist. Despite efforts to develop new businesses in Washington County, on Maine's eastern border with Canada, unemployment hovers near 18 percent. That is in stark contrast to towns in the southern counties bordering New Hampshire that in the past decade have formed the outer suburbs of Boston. Some observes believe Maine should use its economic development funds differently, for example, to forego local tax cuts in favor of programs that may be more effective in securing good employment, such as college scholarships. However that debate is resolved, Maine's economy—with its expanding service sector—now resembles the structure of the national economy more than ever in its history. That convergence has been accompanied by a significant rise in the state's per capita income, which moved from 80 percent of the national average in 1980 to 88 percent in 2000.

In recent decades, income inequality in Maine has risen, though not as fast as in other states. For instance, between the late 1970s and the late 1990s, the incomes of Maine's wealthiest one-fifth of families grew by 55 percent while the income of its poorest fifth increased by 22 percent.[11] Nationally, the contrast was greater. During the same period, the wealthiest one-fifth of families in the United States saw their incomes rise by 42 percent while the income of the lowest fifth actually declined, by a margin of 1 percent. Several state policies combined to cushion the effects of federal changes in the 1980s and 1990s that cut welfare support to low-income Maine families. One was the state's steeply progressive income tax. Another was a state-funded program that provides a property tax or rent refund to low-income individuals (usually called the property tax "circuit breaker"). A third was a generous set of programs, developed principally during the Angus King administration, which included financial assistance for women on welfare to attend college, expanded Medicaid coverage for low-income children and child care and transportation support for working parents. Maine's relatively low rate of unemployment during that period (under 5 percent) also helped prevent a greater rise in income inequality.

Since the mid-1990s, the state government has paid increased attention to three areas largely neglected in earlier economic development programs. One is research and development. Maine's investment in research and development grew from about $2 million in 1991, when it ranked last among the states, to about $60 million in 2004. The state's new interest in research is reflected in the creation, under the Baldacci administration, of an Office of Innovation in the Department of Community and Economic Development. A second area of attention is the "creative economy," a sector composed of high-tech specialists, cultural workers, artists and scientists such as biomedical researchers. Such jobs account for about 10 percent of all wage and salary employment in Maine. Governor Baldacci has made the creative economy a key element of his economic development plan, noting that "our natural heritage makes the state an obvious destination" for its workers.[12] He initiated as series of regional meetings in 2003 and 2004 attended by about one thousand people, and established a Creative Economy Steering Committee comprising state agency representatives.

A third area of concern is the long-neglected tourism industry. Maine's automobile license plates have carried the moniker "Vacationland" for more than sixty years, but the state did surprisingly little to entice visitors as a matter of public policy.[13] As recently as the early 1990s, Maine ranked last among states in governmental spending on tourism. State officials were reluctant to encourage travel to the state because of complaints about congestion, especially along the coast. Occasionally, there were political problems. In the 1980s, for instance, the tourism industry, many of whose employees are seasonal and part-time, fought the Brennan administration's efforts to raise the state minimum wage. More recently, however, tourism has been viewed as a major economic resource. Visitors to the state jumped from under 5 million in 1974 to 26 million in 2003. At that time, the number of employees in the tourism industry approached eighty thousand, making it Maine's largest employer, accounting for about 7 percent of the state's gross product, more than twice the national average. In 1996 Gov. Angus King commissioned a major study to explore the state government's responsibilities for tourism. The report issued in 2002 recommended that Maine encourage more first-time visitors, foster greater year-round tourism and increase the budget for the Office of Tourism. The Baldacci administration has moved to attain those goals.

The new emphasis on tourism underscores the important connection between economic issues and environmental questions. Although the two types of issues overlap in every state, their relationship is of particular importance in Maine. When Maine people say that their state is special, they almost invariably make reference to its physical environment. Protection of the environment is a major concern. A recent poll found that 81 percent of a sample of residents agreed with this statement: "The natural beauty of Maine should be preserved even if it means spending more public money or interfering with private investment decisions."[14] Responding to a somewhat different phrasing of the issue, only 22 percent of the sample agreed that "our first priority should be to get quality jobs, not to preserve natural conditions." State politicians of both parties adhere to the premise that growth must take place on Maine terms, which means that it must be consistent with environmental protection.

DEMOGRAPHIC CHANGE, SUSTAINABLE GROWTH AND SPRAWL

Demography is the statistical study of human population, and is especially significant to the foundation and growth of the local units of government within any state's boundaries. It is a fundamental variable in the quest for sustainable development. In Maine, historically this would prove to be an influential factor, especially with reference to population size, density, and distribution. This dynamic driving force of population (especially with regard to Maine's low density and capacity for expansion or decline) would have much to say about where local governments could first be established and how they would be influenced by future demographic change.

The 2000 Census confirmed many of the previous trends that had been identified by demographers—the exodus of Mainers from northern Maine to the coast and south, and in some cases well beyond the Kittery Bridge to other states. Population movement usually occurred because people either sought better jobs or a starter job. Since 1990 Maine's four northern counties (Aroostook, Penobscot, Piscataquis, and Washington) collectively lost six percent of their total population. In fact the City of Bangor experienced a 5 percent decline in its population, while the fifteen community Bangor metropolitan area lost only 765 persons in a region where some suburban growth had been occurring over the past three decades. At the same time, York and Cumberland, the two most southern counties, grew by 11 percent (forty-five thousand people).

In its *Special Report Census 2000: Two Maines Chasm Growing* the *Bangor Daily News* published a thorough analysis of the following five demographic trends that inevitably impact local government:

Maine has the fifth slowest growth rate of any state

Maine has the fourth oldest population

Maine young adults have the lowest birth rate

The state is predominately white, with its very small percentage (<3%) of racial minorities

Maine's young workers left the state (approximately one-third of the population between ages 20–34 departed) with few people to replace them

Since 1990 Millinocket has lost 25 percent of its population, East Millinocket lost 16 percent, and Medway lost 23 percent. These communities in northern Penobscot County were built by Great Northern Paper Company, which has scaled back the plant's operations and sold off much of its land. Local government and school districts began discussing ways of achieving more economies of scale through sub-state regional cooperation with interlocal agreements and possible consolidations.

The closing of Loring Air Force Base in 1994 decimated the town of Limestone, which declined in population from 7,500 to 2,361 in 2000, and nine other nearby communities. Aroostook County's population stood at 86,936 in 1990 and declined to 73,938 by 2000. Clearly, the region's economy and its local governments were greatly impacted by these changes. A "Loring Development Authority" was established by the initiative of local leadership and made responsible for recruiting business to the former base. Public and private partnerships and intergovernmental cooperation were essential in the transitional period. Maine's northern-tier counties (Aroostook, Piscataquis, and northern Penobscot) engaged in specific ventures and initiatives, which included several huge Phish rock concerts, festivals, and establishing training centers for Olympic biathlon teams and cross country skiing in Fort Kent and Presque Isle. It also considered the possibility of a Maine North Woods National Park, but while outside support was high, and southern Maine seemed somewhat supportive, there was strong opposition from many residents of central and northern Maine.

In 2000 the Millinocket Growth Area and Investment Council (MAGIC) was established. This economic development council was started even before the eventual bankruptcy of the town's paper mill, and its stated mission was to help diversify Millinocket's economy. MAGIC was to be the driving force for change so that Millinocket's economy would not have to rely on only one industry. While MAGIC did help secure a small number of grants, the town also supported it with a $50,000 startup loan and $25,000 per year. Much controversy arose when the prospective new businesses bailed out, leaving the town in debt of at least $300,000 and MAGIC simply has not yet produced the jobs that it promised. A split developed between those citizens who prefer traditional economic development strategies (for example, recruiting new business and supporting local entrepreneurs) and those who want to turn Millinocket into a gateway community based on tourism and a pro-environmental stand. There were also requests by some politicians and landowners to annex territory outside of Millinocket's town limits for various economical development schemes, but most of these latter ventures have failed to materialize. There appears to be some consensus that ecotourism is one way to go, but actually getting there is still another dilemma for many state and local officials.

The Advent of Service Centers

Another new way of looking at Maine's fragmented political geographic landscape of numerous civil divisions was developed by the State Planning Office (SPO), within the context of both population change and economic growth. The SPO focused on defining the concept of Maine's "Service Center" municipalities and did so by designating sixty-nine of its communities. Collectively, these communities housed 71 percent of all state jobs, 74 percent of all services (for example, hospitals, social services, education institutions, cultural activities, and general government services), and 77 percent of all consumer retail sales. The Maine SPO identified service centers by using the following economic measures: level of retail sales, jobs to workers ratio, amount of federally assisting housing, and volume of service center jobs.[15]

In essence, the designated service centers were "engines of growth," for much of the state and also included smaller urban places where Maine people work, shop, and visit for a wide variety of services. Moreover, the following three sub-categories were devised: twenty-nine "primary centers," twenty-one "secondary centers," and nineteen "small centers." This new measure would further refine the use of a different geographic entity for analyzing and managing the state's growth. As time went on, these concepts would be further refined (for example, an addition of twenty-six specialized centers), and their possible use for helping to determine resource allocations for state funding was debated within the political arena. Service centers did represent a novel attempt by Maine State Government to influence public policy at the local level.

For example, approximately one-quarter of the recent job growth in the Greater Portland area has occurred in the town of Scarborough during the past fifteen years. The town increased its population from 12,518 residents in 1990 to an estimated 18,840 in 2005. Moreover, it is predicted to have a population of more than 22,000 by 2015. A study by the town revealed a transformation from a farming and fishing community to one of the stronger economic service centers in the state. The development of an industrial park near Interstate 95 should even further accelerate growth. One of its newest major problems is to provide affordable middle-class housing in the residential zones.[16]

Many of the designated service centers also joined together to form the "Maine Service Center Coalition" and helped to bolster the state's older ailing urban areas, both large and small, which have experienced shrinking populations and higher costs for their aging infrastructure. Many of those core communities support daytime populations that are twice the size of their nighttime populations. Ed Barrett, Bangor City manager, was elected as chair of this coalition group which soon approached the legislature for more revenue sharing funding for these highly taxed communities. The coalition also supported revising the school-funding formula and a local option for an additional sales tax. Although this experiment of an urban/suburban service center coalition faces an uphill battle for its proposed agenda, it does illustrate a potential power base through group actions, demographic change, and its potential future impact on Maine's political geography.

Suburbanization and Sprawl

Social scientists and journalists alike have long identified many of the evils of suburbia and its inhabitants as a flight of the white middle class to the suburbs to purchase a home on a three-acre lot and obtain better education for their children, while still working in the city and commuting back and forth each day.[17] "Brain-drain" and abandonment of the central city meant an eventual decline in the revenue capacity of the core city and its ability to deliver services. Meanwhile, suburban refugees still milked the city's core for its amenities and took advantage of city's art, cultural events, sports, and other entertainment.

Moreover, development of the "edge cities" soon provided them with another choice—an expanding alternative commercial and industrial base closer to their residency—which further validated the multiple (economic) nuclei theories of metropolitan growth.[18] These edge cities are often found near the intersection of interstate highways and may bisect traditional city boundaries. As economist Charles Colgan states: "This may be observed in Maine, where the Maine Mall region in South Portland has developed as a major edge city, cutting across the boundaries of Portland, South Portland, Westbrook and Scarborough." Other examples in Maine may be found in and around the Bangor Mall and the expanding commercial development in proximity to the Augusta I-95 Belgrade exit.[19]

Suburbanization came late to Maine, compared to many other states, but it has flourished around Maine's major cities and coastal communities. Planners and attorneys who had done the "dirty work" of creating the suburban outer-ring design and infrastructure through their orthodox zoning ordinances, subdivision regulations (complete with low-density requirements) and highway and road planning, finally began to challenge the status quo of unmanaged suburban growth. It was time to change, but most of the U.S. suburban model was already firmly in place for housing, and during the past few decades, much of the economic base had been transplanted as well. Neoclassical planner Andres Duany argues that the suburbs have most of the correct elements or pods of a community, but they were simply planned wrong. Much of the blame goes to highway engineers and conventional planners, who do everything for the automobile and little for people, especially pedestrians, who are "rare birds" in most suburbs. Duany also chastises suburban designers for excessive separation of land uses (commercial, industrial, and residential) and devoting too much space to speedy roads that make people hostages in their cars and subject to frustrating gridlock. Because of the overuse of space, even short distances usually require one's private vehicle, especially to chauffeur children to school and recreational activities, and to transport the elderly virtually everywhere.

Thus, the new urbanism solutions involve incorporating traditional planning concepts that were largely rejected by five decades of modern suburban planning. For example, these neoclassical planners stress that the mixing of land uses in zones and transportation modes at a fine grain creates less traffic congestion and more healthy, regular interaction between people. It is reasonable to expect buildings in an area to be in scale with each other, but not that they all be for the same use or same type of resident. Subdivisions have been typically organized with a boring sameness, useless large front yards and often isolated from other parts of the community. In most areas the zoning and subdivision regulations of today would prohibit the building of the classic New England town of the past. Duany and his developer colleagues are passionate in their pleas that it is time to change these ordinances to allow for a more creative and efficient suburban lifestyle.[20]

In an effort to catch the attention of the national media and various political players (perhaps in order to highlight the negative impacts of suburbia and how its benefit has been at the expense of the core city), low density "sprawl" has become another villain—in predominately rural states where it needs to be stopped or at least contained. As an alarming 1997 report by the Maine State Planning Office, entitled "The Cost of Sprawl," explained about the spreading out of new suburbs 10–25 miles from the metropolitan areas:

The outward movement has increased local and state taxes in three ways. First it has required new and redundant infrastructure in remote areas; for example, state taxpayers have paid for over $300 million in new rural school capacity, even though the student population statewide has declined. Second, it has required the lengthening of service routes for police, fire, emergency road maintenance, and plowing; towns are losing economies of scale. Finally, it has left older city and town centers saddled with a declining population and an underused infrastructure. The ironic result is that even while rural taxpayers are pitching in to build new capacity, in-town residents are paying more (on a per-family basis) just to support the old capacity.[21]

Sprawl is a nationwide problem in virtually every state and its costs go well beyond the above calculations. Enlightened planners now argue that spreading out residential and commercial development also creates other unintended negative consequences such as more air pollution from private vehicles, more fragmentation of wildlife habitats, and more lake degradation from development runoff. Moreover, there are social costs, more difficult to measure, such as the isolation of the poor and elderly in cities, and the disruption of traditional farming and forestry uses in the country side.[22]

By the end of 2008, data collected by the *Portland Press Herald* and *Maine Sunday Telegram* revealed a decline of the sprawl trend—a gradual reversal of the long-standing development patterns that have contributed to sprawl. Low-density development has subsided in twenty-four of Maine's sixty-nine service center communities. It appears that Maine's aging population, as well as other factors, such as high energy prices, seem to be coming together to discourage more outer-ring sprawl. Since the late 1990s more planners have encouraged municipalities to enact zones that direct growth to various concentrated areas within Maine's communities, and preservation of open space is also becoming a priority. Therefore, these recent trends could represent a "sprawl stall" for the immediate future.

In Maine it seems certain that those geographic areas that have developed a meaningful sub-state regional perspective will be better equipped to deal with the urban and suburban problems of the present and future.

Case of the Plum Creek Development in Northern Maine

By 2005 a major challenge to enhance the possibility of sustained economic growth for the declining northern woods region emerged as one of the state's major "hot button" issues. Plum Creek Timber Company of Seattle, a real estate investment trust and the nation's largest private landowner, made a proposal for a development project in the Moosehead Lake area near the town of Greenville in Piscataquis County. Moosehead is Maine's largest lake and considered the heart of the largest undeveloped forest east of the Mississippi River. The service center community, Greenville, had failed to specify a vision for the future in its comprehensive plan, thereby making it easier for developers to propose their own plans, rather than the town. Moreover, most of Plum Creek's interest to rezone its more than 426,000 acres was in the surrounding unorganized territory outside of the municipality of Greenville, but including the forty-one townships around Moosehead Lake. For a decade, dozens of lots had been sold and $225,000 lots were the norm, with some being sold at $700,000. Nor had the State of Maine developed a long-range futuristic plan for its unorganized territories in this region. The original 570-page Plum Creek proposal called for 975 house lots (both waterfront and back lots), thirty subdivisions, two luxury resorts, eighty acres for four sporting camps, sixty-seven ponds, one golf course, and three recreational vehicle parks and a marina, which were placed within the 426,340 acres of forest land around Moosehead Lake. Plum Creek's conservation plan included a working forest easement that would protect more than 382,000 acres in a non-development zone, but only for a period of thirty years. It would set aside 89 percent of the total acreage as "working forest land" for the region's forest products industry.[23] In addition 10,890 acres of the shorefront land would be reserved under permanent conservation easements, as would seventy-one miles of snowmobile trails and fifty-five miles of hiking trails. Conservation lands included fifty-five ponds that would be protected from future development.[24]

While property rights need to be protected some would still argue that Plum Creek can do what it wants with its own land. It is also Maine's largest private landowner. However, the well-endowed private company asked for a rezoning of its 426,000 acres to change what it legally can do with its property. Therefore, this case entered the realm of public policy and debate about the public's interest in Maine's northern woods.

Plum Creek's petition was made to Maine's Land Use Regulation Commission (LURC), which is responsible for the limited governance of unorganized territories in the state and acts as a "super planning and zoning board" for the unincorporated townships. Early on, fourteen citizens—including several former LURC commissioners—signed a petition for the state to honor its 1997 promise of first doing a comprehensive plan to help guide development throughout the pristine region. They also urged that a moratorium be placed on all development of five lots or more. Jim Lund, a former state attorney, stated the significance of its scale, "The magnitude of this (Plum

Creek) proposal is perhaps ten times the size of anything that LURC has considered previously."[25] However, the commissioners unanimously voted against the moratorium, and began to prepare for an eventual formal process that would decide the outcome of the massive proposed changes to the area. Plum Creek had been acquiring land in Maine since 1997 and now its own concept plan for the area would be made public. LURC hired several key consultants to work with it, to help further refine Plum Creek's proposed development plan. Moreover, Evan Richert, former state planning office director during the Angus King administration, and attorney Ron Kreisman of Hallowell, would be paid $100,000 by Plum Creek for their services.

In response to the escalating state-wide controversy, the LURC commissioners took the unusual step to schedule a series of four informal "scoping sessions" across the state for the general public to discuss the controversial proposal in August 2005. Since the expanse of the Plum Creek project was "unprecedented," LURC opted to have these additional public meetings before it began the formal public hearings and decision-making process.

Karen Woodsum, Director of the Sierra Club Maine Woods Campaign posited that Plum Creek may have an advantage by going public with its plan, because "they managed to secure support from key town leaders and local business interests. So in step are local leaders with the Plum Creek public relations message that recent statements by local officials are virtually interchangeable with the statements of corporate spokespersons."[26] For example, when questioned about the lack of public input when the Plum Creek Plan went before the Greenville Board of Selectmen, their town manager stated, "I urged the board to support it. It's not uncommon for selectmen to adopt resolutions without going to townspeople."[27] At first, the Board of Selectmen supported the plan and then later reversed its decision in order to remain neutral.

Several prominent Green Party members scheduled a press conference to report on the formation of an opposition group, "Save Moosehead Campaign." Former Green Party gubernatorial candidate and environmental advocate Jonathan Carter, State Representative Jon Eder from Portland, and spokesperson Jym St. Pierre of "RESTORE: The Northern Woods," another opposition group, vowed to stop the project at all costs. They suggested the possibility of lawsuits or a citizen referendum and branded the plan as "wilderness sprawl."[28] Scott Fish of the Maine Heritage Policy Center also reported: "The Plum Creek Battle is happening on many fronts. In May, eco-terrorists vandalized Plum Creek's Fairfield Office with orange and black spray paint, covering the white clapboards and green roof with slogans like, '2nd Growth NOT 2nd Homes,' and 'GO AWAY.' In July its Greenville office was burglarized, with three computers and a hard drive stolen."[29]

This project concerns opponents in its scale alone, which is scattered across more than 426,000 acres. It is larger than the Big A Dam project that environmentalists defeated twenty years earlier, and is larger than any subdivision in Maine's history. There is also a strong feeling among the opponents that this project will encourage other developers to follow suit.[30]

If the project has any potential to boost the region's economy and contribute to sustainable growth, key political and economic elites typically favor staying the course. For instance, Greenville School superintendent Steven Pound urged residents not to select sides too early in the process because Plum Creek management seems willing to listen to concerns. Moreover, the vocal Greenville town manager, John Simko, and Piscataquis County commissioners made very early supportive statements about Plum Creek being an economic savior, but most residents were still not convinced. Simko went so far as to urge LURC to consider Plum Creek's proposal as a "potential comprehensive plan for the land it entails." Ironically numerous out-of-state residents have fled to this area in order to escape sprawl.

One interesting suggestion was made by Simko, who recommended to the Piscataquis County commissioners that half of the new property tax revenue generated in these unorganized territories should be shared with the service center communities. He added that half of the new revenue would come from subdivisions, renovations, or new construction, and should be placed in a regional infrastructure account to defray the capital costs of new or expanded infrastructure, because of the sustainable growth potential in Maine's unorganized territories.[31] The other half of the new taxes would continue to flow into the unorganized territories' account. While the county commissioners favored this new concept, it would have to be further refined and approved by the legislature.

There were huge differences in the area's tax rates—only $8 per $1,000 valuation in the unorganized townships, compared with the Town of Greenville's tax rate of almost $18 per $1,000 valuation. Cathy Johnson, North Woods project director of the Natural Resources Council of Maine, claimed that "none of these house lots are within organized towns so they would not contribute to the local tax base." Johnson also contends that "within this so-called 'no development zone,' Plum Creek is proposing to allow four new sporting camps, each twice the size allowed under LURC regulations and 116 rental cabins, four per township. So in fact, development would be spread all across the landscape, even within the 'no-development zone.'"[32] As growth has continued to flourish in the unorganized townships which surround Moosehead Lake, more pressure exists on the municipality of Greenville's infrastructure, which previously had been designated a "service center" for the region.

Other proponents, such as University of Southern Maine economist Charles Colgan, have supported the benefits of the Plum Creek concept plan. His own analysis suggested that "it could create 800 new jobs for a $41.5 million average annual contribution to Maine's economy." Consultant Colgan said overall the plan "would have significant positive effects on a regional economy that has been experiencing economic difficulty if Plum Creek could sell its rezoned land to developers and potential homeowners."[33] Indeed most of the early benefits would be from continuous residential construction, because Plum Creek limited the number of housing lots per year to 125, so home building would be active for at least a decade. The study also estimated a local construction industry dramatic increase from housing alone to be $10.5 million annually from 2006 to 2018, and $1 million annually thereafter from 2019–2023.[34]

Jonathan Carter, one of the key activists from the "Save Moosehead" coalition, which is an "ad-hoc veto group" that opposes the project, chided Colgan's analysis and reiterated that it was paid for by Plum Creek. Ken Spaulding of RESTORE: the North Woods group questioned his choice to predict benefits based on "purely speculative" descriptions of resorts and a saw mill.[35] Critics such as Carter and the Save Moosehead campaign argue that Plum Creek is concerned only with profit and cannot be trusted. Plum Creek has been in Maine for over a decade, and first said that it didn't have plans for commercial development. It owns approximately 950,000 acres of property in the state. While it is very likely that development would create jobs for a while, state policy also needs to consider the various alternatives such as the Maine Woods National Park, which the environmentalists argue would also be a more sound investment for the long run. The earlier contentious park proposal overlaps with much of Plum Creek's land. In 2001 economist Thomas Power projected that a national park could generate a minimum of 3,600 new jobs and between $109 million and $435 million in annual retail sales to Maine. (This analysis was paid for by the RESTORE group.)[36]

Ultimately the Land Use Regulation Commission would decide the issue of the Plum Creek proposal. However, the citizens of Maine, including some of those beyond the Moosehead Lake region, the Legislature, and the Governor all have roles in deciding the broader strategic issue of achieving proper balance between Maine's goals of sustainable growth and development and its concern for the environment. In 2003, Governor Baldacci noted that in the global economy, strong principles were needed to help conserve the Maine woods so that diverse economic opportunities would occur for Maine people; however, the national heritage of Maine woods would be protected through his "Maine Woods Legacy" statement of policy. "This shared vision of the future of Maine's forestlands is centered on the landscape scale, conservation of Maine's woods, waters and wildlife; the large underdeveloped tracts of forestland; the availability of the forest resources for sustainable forestry and public access for diverse outdoor recreation; the economic strength and vitality of gateway communities, such as Greenville, and a strong manufacturing base to meet the global market"[37]

Plum Creek is in the process of revising its initial plans to develop about nine thousand acres around Moosehead Lake after reviewing testimony from the scoping sessions, consultant reports, and having ongoing negotiations from the town of Greenville and dialogue with numerous interest groups. Ongoing considerations include the following:

locating more individual house lots closer to Greenville and other smaller developed areas;

finding more permanent ways to guarantee that approximately 400,000 acres remain forested, after the 30-year conservation easement expires;

moving the resort planned for Rockwood closer to Greenville;

scaling back the size of the original planned resort at Lily Bay.[38]

There were three agencies performing separate analyses (LURC's consultants, Eastern Maine Development Corporation, and Open Space). The Real Estate Investment Trust Company slightly revised its concept plan and eventually made its formal presentation to LURC. Plum Creek also has proposed to leave nearly 98 percent of its land in conservation and working forests.

For more than three years the LURC commissioners had wrestled with a concept plan from Plum Creek. Finally, LURC approved in principle the Plum Creek proposal in Fall 2008. However, the commissioners made several changes in the submitted plan. For example, they reduced the number of lakes affected from fifteen to six, eliminating all development on five pristine ponds, shrinking the major Lily Bay development from 4,300 acres to 1,800 (to mention only a few). Richard Barringer, former commissioner of conservation, director of state planning, and a research professor at the University of Southern Maine's Muskie School of Public Service said it best:

In this unfamiliar, new world of post-paper industry of the Unorganized Territory, we as residents of Maine could not have asked for more from the commissioners . . . We thank you (*Bangor Daily News*, October 4–5, 2008).

Time will tell how much the balance of values is adhered to in this salient public and private sector issue.

HEALTH POLICY: EVOLUTIONARY CHANGE

Like all other states, Maine has expanded its role in health policy enormously in recent decades.[39] Health-care expenditures grew from 5 percent of the nation's GDP in 1960 to 15 percent in 2000. The most important pieces of legislation shaping state activities have been the federal Medicare and Medicaid programs, established in the 1960s. While programs in Maine have generally paralleled those of other states, the state has been a leader in seeking ways to widen the availability of health insurance, and in trying to contain the costs of health care.

Until the mid-1960s, state government activities in the health field were mostly confined to three areas of responsibility: the protection of the public health (such as guaranteeing safe drinking water), regulating insurance companies that provided health policies, and managing the public institutions that cared for persons unable to care for themselves. Apart from a few federal grants-in-aid, such as the maternal and child health program, the entire field of medical services was a private-sector enterprise. The state Bureau of Health (part of the Department of Health and Welfare) was relatively small. By contrast, the current Maine Center for Disease Prevention and Control (in the Department of Health and Human Services) has approximately twenty programs located within eight separate divisions, including most recently a bioterrorism unit.

In the 1970s, the state government began to assist persons with certain kinds of health issues. In 1974, the legislature enacted a Catastrophic Illness Program to provide support for people with major illnesses who have exhausted their financial resources. It served about 2,500 individuals annually. A larger undertaking was the High Risk Insurance Program, which began in 1987, to offer insurance coverage to people who could not find private health insurance because of a pre-existing medical condition. Maine was one of several states to enact such a policy, but an unusual feature of Maine's program was that it subsidized premiums paid by low-income persons. The state also tried to increase the availability of insurance coverage by greater regulation of insurance policies. The legislature prohibited, for example, insurance companies from excluding individuals with certain health problems from coverage when they were part of a larger group of employees otherwise covered.

The efforts to expand insurance coverage were accompanied by attempts to contain health-care costs. The two objectives are closely related. Increases in medical costs causes the pool of policy holders to shrink (healthy persons and younger persons may no longer carry insurance), leaving a reduced population of insured persons characterized by a high incidence of health problems. In turn, that process puts further pressure on the cost of coverage. To limit costs, Maine has tried various forms of hospital regulation. Under a Certificate of Need requirement begun in 1979, the state can disapprove hospital expansions that are likely to create unnecessary duplications of services within a region. Under a commission established in 1984, the state regulated the revenues of hospitals, while assisting them in recouping debts from uncompensated services. Maine hospitals generally resisted those efforts, and most cost-control measures affecting them were abandoned by the end of the 1990s.

The state's participatory political culture has encouraged its innovations in health care. Maine consumer groups are strong and keep legislators informed on the consequences of rising health costs. Through public hearings in Augusta and their work in their districts, legislators are familiar with particular individuals whose medical costs have devastated their family budgets. The state government's habit of designing public policies to be as inclusive as possible has encouraged its trial- and-error efforts, over the past three decades, to find ways to expand citizens' access to health care at affordable prices.

New Rules, Chronic Problems, and Transformation

State governments have taken the lead in addressing concerns in health-care policy since the defeat of national health proposals in 1993–1994. The number of uninsured people, those depending on charity care in emergencies, has been a particular concern of Maine policymakers since the 1990s. In 2005 Maine had the highest rate of uninsured in New England.[40]

During the 1990s Maine implemented rules that required insurers to guarantee the issuance of coverage to all persons, with very strict rules that precluded lower rates for low-risk people.[41] This increased the cost of providing insurance, and ultimately decreased the number of health insurers in the state. Insurance is usually made up of three markets, individual, small group, and large group. With the new rules in place, the individual market fell from 88,548 individuals in 1992 to 37,618 in 2000 as the cost of insurance rose.[42] Between 1996 and 2002 the cost of a family health policy increased 77 percent while the median household income grew only 6 percent.[43] As the cost increased, many low-risk people decided to drop coverage, resulting in premium increases for the remaining individuals.

In Maine, Anthem Insurance purchased Maine's Blue Cross Blue Shield for $82 million in 1999. This was part of a national movement toward for-profit conversion of nonprofit hospitals and insurance plans. By 2003, Anthem Blue Cross Blue Shield had 475,000 members in Maine, and was overwhelmingly the major provider of insurance products across all segments of the market.[44]

The Maine Health Access Foundation, popularly know as MeHAF, was founded with the proceeds of the Blue Cross sale in April 2000. It became Maine's largest private health care foundation. The mission of the foundation is to promote affordable and timely access to comprehensive, quality health care and to improve the health of every Maine resident. Since 2002 it has awarded more than $17 million to organizations throughout the state.[45] The foundation provided support for the state's new program, Dirigo Health.

Birth of Dirigo Health

On his first day in office in 2003 Gov. John Baldacci, a proponent of comprehensive health-care reform, created the Governor's Office of Health Policy and Finance. Its staff, working with a group of stakeholders, designed the legislation that became Dirigo Health, the most far-reaching policy initiative in Baldacci's first term. The legislation addressed three areas: containing costs, ensuring access, and improving the quality of health care. The goal of the program was to provide all Maine citizens with access to health care by 2009. The state presents a particular challenge because it has unusually large rural, elderly, and poor populations with important health issues.

The enabling legislation established the Dirigo Health Agency as an independent entity. It is administered by a five-person board of directors, which is responsible for establishing and administering Dirigo Health, hiring an executive director, collecting savings offset payments, developing benefits and subsidies, and establishing the Maine Quality Forum to monitor the program. The governor nominates the directors.

To increase access, an insurance product called DirigoChoice was developed. It covers groups with fewer than fifty employees, including both self-employed and unemployed individuals, subsidizing costs for low-income members. It started enrolling members on January 1, 2005, and began with subsidies for members with incomes less than 150 percent of the federal poverty level. The advantage of DirigoChoice over other insurance products is its ability to lower costs for employees and small businesses when providing coverage for households meeting the federal poverty level guidelines. This is accomplished by blending MaineCare—Maine's Medicaid program—and DirigoChoice for employees who are MaineCare eligible. Eligible employees receive discounts on monthly payments and reductions in deductibles and out-of-pocket expenses. MaineCare, with its federal matching dollars, will purchase the DirigoChoice plan for eligible employees.

Provider's services are paid reimbursement rates that are higher for MaineCare members who join Dirigo Choice than those who do not. Health care providers have long called attention to the fact that MaineCare pays below market rates for its services. Having more members paying the private insurance negotiated rates will benefit providers. The second area of benefit for providers is the opportunity to decrease uncompensated care. In 2006 Maine hospitals provided $190 million in bad debt and charity care.[46] By lowering the number of uninsured, DirigoChoice has decreased the amount of uncompensated care offered by health care providers by an estimated $10 million.

The Board of Dirigo Health chose to bid to solicit an insurance company to administer and market its DirigoChoice plan. There had been much speculation over whether it would be administered by private insurers or be self-administered. Anthem Blue Cross Blue Shield was the sole bidder of five companies that had expressed interest. The state was authorized to start its own nonprofit company to provide the insurance if the bid was rejected. In 2005 Anthem was awarded the contract to administer DirigoChoice. The contract turned out to be short-lived; in late 2007 Harvard Pilgrim became the plan's administrator.

Protracted Conflict and Tough Solutions

An area that has proven to be controversial about Dirigo Health is the surcharge to recapture savings to Maine's health care system that is redirected back to DirigoChoice to provide subsidies for low-income members. The surcharge is called the savings offset payment (SOP). In October 2005 the Superintendent of Insurance certified that the Dirigo Health first year initiatives saved Maine $43.7 million. This was far less than the initial Dirigo Health filing of $136.8 million, later revised to $110.6 million.[47] The Board of the Dirigo Health then levied a 2.4 percent savings offset payment (SOP) on health care premiums. This has been fought by both those who provide insurance and those who purchase it, especially employers. The governor's office expected the savings offset payments would be realized by capturing the savings being created in the health care system. However, insurers perceived it as a tax levied on purchasers of health care policies.

The intent of DirigoChoice was to increase access by covering between thirty-one thousand uninsured and underinsured in the first year of operation and reaching between 110,000 and 189,500 over the first five years. The enrollment did not grow as quickly as planned; the first year participation was 15,400 members.[48] Based on the 2007 State's Health Plan, mandated by the Dirigo Health Reform Act, a much larger enrollment of uninsured and underinsured Mainers will be covered.[49] This will be met by developing and implementing a lower cost alternative health care product and a comprehensive marketing and outreach plan.

Even though its enrollment goals have not been met, DirigoHealth has made substantial progress. The benefits are fairly generous: it covers preventive care and, unlike many programs, it pays for treatment for mental illness. Further, it does not exclude persons with preexisting medical conditions. While about 60 percent of its enrollees already had insurance, most of them were paying an excessively high proportion of their income for that coverage.

In spring 2006 Governor Baldacci introduced legislation to self-insure DirigoChoice instead of contracting with a private insurance company. The bill appeared to have a broad majority of Democratic support but was defeated late in the legislative session when support waned. One goal of self-insuring was to lower costs to consumers by eliminating the need for profit. With the bill's failure, a private company (Harvard Pilgrim) will continue to administer the program.

Responding to the various controversies over Dirigo Health, Governor Baldacci created a blue-ribbon commission to make recommendations on a long-term funding plan to expand coverage and save health-care dollars. The commission recommended funding largely through an increase in "sin" taxes, on such items as tobacco, beer, wine, bottled soft drinks, and snacks. Although the legislature approved certain of those taxes in 2008, voters rejected them in a referendum. The Maine Supreme Judicial Court upheld, in 2007, the methodology used by the DirigoHealth Board of Directors and the Superintendent of Insurance. The Board announced that savings in the program in 2007 amounted to about $190 million—a major increase over earlier years.

Although this brief overview does not cover many of the issues involved in Maine's innovative approach to health care policy and its costs, its comprehensiveness and breadth are evident. Maine's government, like all other state governments, has been pushed into the health care business without much experience to draw on. A long, complex history has created the fractured health care system our nation struggles with, and Maine is arguably a leader in (if one forgives the pun) curing the illness rather than merely treating the symptoms. By 2007 DirigoHealth, which once commanded a national spotlight, was being eclipsed by Massachusetts's new plan that required health insurance for all residents. Like DirigoHealth, the Massachusetts program builds on Medicaid, but it departs from Maine's arrangement in that various insurance companies offer state-approved plans. Innovation is often a painful process fraught with "only ifs," and Maine is in the beginning of the process. Dirigo Health will most certainly not end up as it was initially envisioned. However, it does have the potential to develop into a workable solution to the skyrocketing costs of health care in Maine.

PUBLIC EDUCATION, ASPIRATIONS, AND REALITIES

A fifth policy issue speaks to a psychological and educational problem among many of Maine's young people: low aspirations regarding their own education and self-development. The issue has been identified with increasing concern by influential academics in Maine, such as Richard Barringer, a faculty member at University of Southern Maine's Muskie School of Public Service and a former cabinet officer in the administrations of governors James Longley and Joseph Brennan, and Robert Cobb, longtime dean of the College of Education at the University of Maine.

Since it first emerged as a major public issue in the mid-1980s, the state's "aspirations movement" has become a diverse group of education theorists and practitioners, feminists, business leaders, alternative school advocates, and promoters of programs for the gifted and talented. A widely attended conference in 1987, "Aspirations of Maine Youth," signaled the "coming-out party" of this coalition of activists. They hoped to broaden their political base by attracting the attention of Maine's public and private sectors, as well as the general public.

Familiar themes propagated by Maine's education leadership about the dangerous trends in high school dropouts, low college attendance rates, and the involvement of youth in such activities as drugs and sex had been reported for over several decades. However, the education establishment's plan for involving others in the community—business, social institutions, and parents, as a statewide action group—did represent a novel departure from previous strategies. This collaborative effort translated what had been seen mainly as a cultural problem—low self-esteem and the lack of educational advancement among Mainers—into a crucial economic issue. As Henry Bourgeois, president of the Maine Development Foundation, commented: "The single most important fact in business decisions in the twenty-first century will be quality of the work force." Select members of Maine's business community had become very concerned that there would not be enough workers trained in high technology available in the future.[50]

Maine's high school graduation rate in the late 1980s was about 78 percent, which is slightly above the national average. Of the 22 percent of ninth graders who do not graduate with their class, about 40 percent of these dropouts eventually obtain their diploma through adult programs. Another concern was that even though the dropout rate has remained rather stable, students were detected to be dropping out earlier than ever. Frank Antonucci, dropout and truancy consultant for the Maine Department of Education, argued that this phenomenon could be explained by such factors as higher graduation requirements, the perception of a strong job market, drug abuse, and family disintegration. The earlier that students drop out, the fewer skills they possess. Thus, it costs more to train them later, or to support them in a cycle of poverty. State studies also revealed that there were unexplained differences in the dropout rates between similar-sized communities. In the mid-1980s, Eastport and Jackman had dropout rates approaching 10 percent, whereas Rangeley and Falmouth had virtually no dropouts. Eve Bither, a former teacher and the state's commissioner of education at the time, established what she regarded as acceptable targets for raising student aspirations. She believed that a school should seek a graduation rate of 90 percent by 1993 and a college-bound rate equivalent at least to the national average of 58 percent.

By 2004, approximately half of Maine's high school graduates moved on to postsecondary education and about half of these students left Maine to attend colleges elsewhere. A survey of college graduates in 2006 sponsored by the Finance Authority of Maine (FAME, a business and financial aid agency) found that half of all Maine eighteen-year-olds, who had attended a college outside of Maine, eventually transferred back to a Maine institution to complete their degrees. The study revealed that 75 percent of the graduates from 1997–1999 ultimately earned their degree at a Maine college or university.[51]

Maine's problems of low aspirations, at least as measured by college attendance, may be partially explained by the rural and geographically isolated nature of the state. Because of out-migration that began after the Civil War, Maine had at one time the "most native" population in the United States. This trend did not begin to change until 1973. Maine ranked at about the midpoint among the states in the percentage of its population that is native-born. Further, approximately one-third of Maine's young people come from very small towns, where fewer than one adult in ten has completed college, and fewer than one in thirty-three has obtained a graduate or professional degree. The lack of role models to stimulate a desire to excel and achieve academic excellence strongly affects students' socialization process. Earlier evidence from the 1980 census suggested an unevenness in the work force as follows: "While 73 percent of the state's labor force was born in Maine, only 60 percent of the owners, managers, professionals, and technicians are natives. Moreover, of the people with graduate and professional degrees beyond college, about one-third were native Mainers."[52]

To increase student aspirations and opportunities, the McKernan administration undertook several initiatives. Under one program, schools received grants as incentives to make changes that are known to affect the learning pattern of students. The specific elements included financial incentives for schools that improve the promotion of stronger families and support from the business community. Some education theorists posited that "unless the dynamics of the school, home and community relations change and become mutually supportive of each other, it will be difficult to achieve the goal of a 90 percent graduation rate (which has been achieved in both Minnesota and North Dakota)."[53]

The McKernan administration also studied the connection between financial need and college attendance. Maine had one of the most poorly funded state grant programs for students in the nation, according to the Maine Association of Student Financial Aid Directors. Fewer than half of those eligible received any aid because of the lack of money available.[54] The state then took several initial steps to remedy that situation. In 1988 Governor McKernan signed a bill that created a Maine Loan Authority, which makes more money available to students at relatively low interest rates. In 1989 the legislature enacted a measure to consolidate student financial assistance services within the Maine Finance Authority. The intent of that measure was to improve the delivery of financial assistance to Maine students attending postsecondary educational institutions and to their families. But this has been a chronic problem over many years that had defied an easy solution.

In 2003 Maine received and "F" for affordability for students by a nonpartisan organization, the National Center for Public Policy and Higher Education. According to former (UM System) Chancellor Terry MacTaggert, "Maine does so poorly in this area because financial aid doesn't make up for high tuition and low per capita income. Compared to the best performing states . . . Mainers pay a greater percentage of their income for college costs,

Maine offers limited state aid for its residents, and students cross the graduation stage with higher debt."[55] Therefore, under this scenario, the aid never really catches up completely with the tuition increases.

More attention has also been directed at the traditional role of guidance counselors in the schools. Thirty-eight percent of 1850 Maine high school juniors surveyed by the Department of Education in 1986 claimed they had received little or no help in selecting a college or vocational school. Guidance counselors reported that they are reacting to the demands of their job and, unfortunately, had little time for one-to-one counseling. Successful counselors have used value-clarification approaches, field trips, guest speakers, and other techniques, even in middle school.

Finally, the Maine Aspirations Compact itself was a collaborative approach between the Department of Education and the Maine Development Foundation to assure that the school systems and businesses work together to help solve the aspirations riddle. During 1988–90 twelve competitive grants were awarded for model projects in local schools. Education and business leadership hoped that these strategies would all contribute to raising the aspirations of Maine youth. Realistically, the problem is quite extensive, with the prospect of change occurring only in the long run. Most of the solutions were experimental, and they were by no means comprehensive.

A report put together by faculty members from the state's public and private colleges in the early 1980s, *Maine: Fifty Years of Change 1940–1990*, identified the key policy questions in this area: How should educational systems respond to the education and training needs of the private sector? Since economic development in Maine depends on the quality of education available, will the quality of elementary, secondary, and postsecondary education in Maine encourage in-migration and business relocation? Will there be adequate educational opportunity for all children in the state? The report concluded, "Maine people have always been the state's most valuable resource . . . it will be the people and their values, and their individual and collective development, that will form the basis for Maine's state government of the future." Fifteen years later, a similar study, *Changing Maine 1960–2010*, concluded:

> "If . . . we do get it right, we may look forward to an era of a more decentralized and responsive state government; more effective and efficient (if a little more distant) local government; an economy built upon high standards of quality and high-end products and services; new, compact villages in which to raise our children and renew community life . . . a community college system that eases the passage of every high school graduate and adult learner to the world of opportunity and responsibility."[56]

Clearly, the State of Maine has a major agenda for its education policies of the future, which may be tempered by the state's limited financial
resources.

Changing Patterns of Public School Education

"No Child Left Behind" (NCLB) became federal law in 2001 and eventually
requires the states to implement standardized testing and performance measures for all students in K-12 by 2014. The law also challenges the states to
identify and sanction schools that fail to meet the federal guidelines. During
the academic year 2004–2005 69 percent of the state's public schools either
met or exceeded the federal government's educational standards. Higher-
target levels were utilized, which may have accounted for an increase in
Maine schools that didn't meet their yearly targets in reading and/or math
for the first time. One hundred schools were negatively impacted, as opposed to eighty-two in the previous year. The classification of schools was
based on the Maine Education Assessment (in math and reading), which
has been administered in the fourth, eighth, and eleventh grades. According
to Commissioner of Education Susan Gendron, 706 public schools were
tested, 489 received an adequate progress rating, while forty-eight schools
didn't meet the standards in math or reading for the second or third consecutive year. Moreover, another cohort of sixty-nine schools required further
review to determine if they too had made adequate progress.[57]

Federal law also requires the states to monitor the performance of specific
subgroups such as students who are low-income, minority, or disabled. The
rationale for this policy is to prevent states from reporting only the overall
performance of its best-achieving cohorts, while omitting some students
and leaving still others behind. Every state must establish a timeline with
progressively higher education standards, which must eventually be met.
The state's ambitious goal is that all students will obtain 100 percent pro-
ficiency rating at grade level in reading and math. A sample of 2004–2005
data revealed that there were forty-eight "continuous improvement priority
schools," which was two less than the previous year. Maine's designated
priority schools must work with Department of Education personnel to develop an improvement plan and implement new strategies. The state is then
granted federal money to help these under achieving schools improve their
ratings. For example, with additional funding a Swanville school obtained
monies to purchase a new reading program, sponsor workshops for parents
that enabled them to utilize strategies at home for their students; and also
develop plans for every child and hold additional seminars for teachers. As
David Silvernail explains,

Currently, the federal government pays just 7.5 percent of the yearly cost to educate Maine's children, but NCLB is having and, in all likelihood will continue to have a major influence on Maine's schools . . . at the core of the 1,100-page piece of legislation are new assessment and accountability requirements. It calls for yearly testing for ensuring that standards are being met by all children; and it calls for sanctions on schools that are not demonstrating adequate, yearly progress.[58]

While the NCLB statute has many commendable goals and objectives that could help promote a more equitable public education system, it becomes problematically more rigid and very inflexible when one considers the numerous details of the law. Professor Silvernail itemizes these as follows: "There is no accepted body of scientific knowledge that supports the concept of adequate yearly progress, as it is defined in the law; yet, there are over eighty-five ways a school may qualify as not meeting yearly progress, and the number of ways will double next year . . . by some estimates, 75–80 percent of our schools nationwide will score poorly on the tests, and so will fail to demonstrate adequate yearly progress and be subject to possible sanctions."[59] Severe penalties on schools could result, if they fail to meet "adequate yearly progress." Administrators and teachers alike could be terminated if students fail to improve on their test scores.

Therefore, because of NCLB, each state must show that its students are making continuous and consistent progress toward reaching a proficient level of achievement in reading and math. The states do have some flexibility in defining their own goals and measurements.[60] A required report revealed that the Maine school system as a whole did not make adequate yearly progress for the second straight year, because math proved to be very difficult for both the students-with-disabilities subgroup and the economically disadvantaged subgroup. While still in the implementation stages, numerous states have complained that much of the additional federal funding has not been distributed.

Commissioner of Education Susan Gendron proposed that the Maine Education Assessment exam be replaced by the SAT for high school juniors because it could allow many Maine students to attend college virtually free of charge. It had strong backing from the legislature and was first implemented in 2006.

Laptop Program and National Prominence

One of Gov. Angus King's most futuristic projects was a new direction—the Maine Learning Technology Initiative—which developed from his strong desire to prepare Maine's youth for a rapidly changing global economy. The Maine Legislature, supporting King's visionary strategy, formed a task force and charged it with making key recommendations about how to best prepare Maine youth for dramatic changes that were fast occurring worldwide. The task force concluded the following:

> . . . we must prepare young people to thrive in a world that doesn't exist yet, to grapple with problems and construct new knowledge which is barely visible to us today . . . To move all students to high levels of learning and technological literacy, all students will need access to technology when and where it can be most effectively incorporated into learning.[61]

By early 2001 the task force strongly recommended that Maine develop a plan to distribute learning technology to all of Maine's students and teachers in the seventh and eighth grades; eventually the program could include other grades as well.[62] While there was much debate in the legislature about this major initiative (some legislators opposed the costs, while others were fearful of possible easy access to pornography, and an overemphasis on addictive games; while still others argued against the potential destruction of fragile laptops). After a protracted policy debate, Independent Governor King's most notable accomplishment was approved by the legislature. By 2004 more than thirty-four thousand laptop computers had been distributed to 240 Maine middle schools. Early evidence suggested that this bold new program had been very effective in promoting technology to help further improve its literacy across virtually all students, regardless of their social and economic status. More than eighty percent of middle school teachers reported that their students were more engaged in their learning and that they produced better quality work. Moreover, teachers reported that all types of students seem more involved in their learning process, especially at-risk and special-needs children.[63]

Because of this program's benefits, Gov. John Baldacci supported its continuation and hoped to expand upon Angus King's vision. Most importantly, Maine's public education system soon ranked second in the nation for the numbers of students who have access to an Internet-connected computer, according to a survey by the research section of an independent newspaper, *Education Week*. Maine also ranked third in the number of students per instructional computer; fourteenth in the percentage of schools where at least half of the teachers are using computer technology; and nineteenth for the percentage of schools where at least half the teachers used the Internet for their instruction. Maine spent $12.7 million on technology in fiscal year 2004 and $15.2 million in fiscal 2005.[64] In 2005 Maine, Michigan, and New

Mexico were the only states that provided individual laptop computers for their students.

However, the results of a fifty-state phone survey on school technology spending found an unsettling trend that the states were being forced to commit millions of dollars to information technology to keep up with the requirements of the federal No Child Left Behind Law. As project director Kevin Bushweller explained, "Data management systems are beginning to overshadow the priorities of the past years where schools focused on putting computers in the classrooms."[65] The new emphasis of technology as a tool for tracking achievement data is strongly supported by the Bush Administration and the states appear to be going along with this priority at the expense of computer classroom learning technologies. However, in some states budget constraints, caused by economic regional downturns, also appear to be a factor slowing the expansion of technology within the public school classrooms. Maine's first-in-the-nation laptop program for its thirty-six thousand seventh-grade and eighth-grade students has been successful, and its Apple contract was evaluated in 2006 and renewed for four more years.

Seamless Public Education

Another way of improving Maine's public school system was to create a totally integrated public system from kindergarten through college. Governor John Baldacci had previously established a committee, which would help plan Maine's future direction with a more holistic approach to public education. The committee's report generated a number of new recommendations that would require significant policy changes to ensure that all students were prepared for kindergarten through higher education. The reports stated that "Maine needs a vision for an integrated and seamless system, which though it would take several years to achieve, will provide a context and direction for reform."[66] Dubbed by some as "PK-16" (pre-kindergarten through college) the state's educational institutions would collaborate to close the academic gap between high school and college.

The report also stated that the number of citizens with either an associate or baccalaureate degree must be dramatically "increased to ensure the state's economic health . . . A post secondary education is imperative to break the cycle of poverty and evaluate future incomes and quality of life." Remarkably, it goes on to recommend preparing a ten-year strategy so the state's higher education system can accommodate forty thousand additional students. The rationale for this optimistic enrollment was that as the number of students who aspire to college rises, "our educational systems must be poised to prepare all students for the academic and social demands they will encounter along the way."[67]

The report further specifies that "in order to ensure that students gain access to and succeed in higher education, colleges and the PK-twelve systems have to work together as partners to define areas of concern and make strategic interventions."[68] Unlike the earlier low-aspirations theory, this committee was in agreement that money was the major reason Maine students don't go to college, and thereby recommended creating a substantial scholarship program to assist all capable high school students from low-income families to pursue a college degree. Finding the means to support this worthy goal may turn out to be a daunting task.

The report also proposes the creation of a permanent PK-16 Council to institutionalize the collaborative work among the different educational levels in Maine. Accordingly, the council would have leadership representatives from the University of Maine System, the Maine Department of Education, the Maine Community College System, public schools, and adult education programs. However, the fact remains that only 37 percent of Maine residents age 25 or older possess a college degree, while the average for New England is 45 percent.

CONCLUSION

This chapter has briefly examined five key policy areas that currently engage state decision-makers. Although virtually every state is concerned with similar problems, many of the solutions that Maine seeks are distinctive. The state insists on maintaining and protecting its physical environment and will encourage the creation of jobs only if they are compatible with preserving the environment. Economic development raised the issue of the "two Maines," although by the late-1990s growth seemed to have alleviated some of the disparities between regions. However, the rapid increase in real estate development in some areas, especially around the coast and lakes, brought about state efforts to regulate growth, an important need because of the large number of small communities. More recently, the various sectors of the business community have been rather active in their efforts at different strategies for economic growth and also collaboration with other policy areas such as education and transportation. In its social policies, Maine can be considered fairly generous among the states, especially in light of its residents' traditionally low income. While the state has been effective in maintaining a floor under its citizens' living conditions, it has been less successful in instilling an attitude of achievement in its youth. For its economy to continue to expand, a heightened set of aspirations among its young people will be critical. In all these areas, the weakening of the Maine economy in the early 1990s, a mild recession in early 2000, and the severe economic crisis of late 2008 have presented extraordinarily difficult challenges to Maine policymakers.

CHAPTER ELEVEN

Maine in the Federal System

Maine's relationship to other governments—in particular, the New England states, the U.S. federal government, and the eastern provinces of Canada—has been conditioned by many of the state's special characteristics. Some are mostly physical, such as its large geographic size relative to the other New England states and its isolation from them. Others are cultural. The sense of Maine's being "a place apart" is important in understanding Maine politicians, including its national representatives. Likewise, Maine's rather low-key style of politics is cherished, even as the state's political interests are advanced in collaboration with the goals of other states with different political traditions.[1]

Maine's national politicians have to accommodate themselves to localistic norms when running for office. The strong identification that Maine's citizens have with their communities and their habit of expecting to meet politicians on a personal basis mean that candidates for federal office must travel widely and extensively during a campaign. Support is lined up on a person-to-person basis, and in very small groups. Once in office, members of Congress return most weekends to meet with groups of citizens, usually in different communities each weekend, and to answer questions and address problems in town-meeting fashion. Maine's two U.S. Senators maintained, in 2008, at total of twelve district offices (in Auburn, Augusta, Bangor, Biddeford, Caribou, Lewiston, Portland, and Presque Isle) to assist them in this work. Compared to other states, this was an unusually high number of local offices. Members of the delegation sometimes distribute their staffs differently. For example, in the mid-2000s, Sens. Olympia Snowe and Susan Collins and Representative Michael Michaud maintained about one-third of their staff in the Maine offices, and the rest in Washington. On the other hand, Representative Tom Allen kept about two-thirds of his staff in his Portland office—mostly to handle constituent requests—and focused his Washington staff primarily on policy matters.

MAINE IN THE CONGRESS

Maine's congressional delegation has long been strong and effective in bargaining with the federal government on critical issues affecting the state. The delegation has enjoyed a relatively prestigious position in the Congress. In 1986 Maine was the only state to have both of its U.S. Senators (William S. Cohen and George J. Mitchell) named as members of the joint Senate-House committee assigned to investigate the Iran-Contra affair. In 1989 Mitchell was elected Senate majority leader. He became the second leader of the Senate to come from Maine in the post–World War II period (Wallace White, a Republican, was the Senate leader in 1947–48). During that period, Sen. Margaret Chase Smith and Sen. Edmund S. Muskie were also national spokespersons for their respective parties on various issues.

There was a similar pattern of leadership in the nineteenth century. The state's most prominent politician during this period was probably James G. Blaine, who served in both the U.S. House and Senate and ran several times for his party's presidential nomination, securing the Republican nomination in 1884. In the 1890s, two Maine congressmen played a key role in the U.S. House. One was Thomas B. Reed, who was elected House Speaker; the other was Nelson P. Dingley, an expert on tariffs, who served as chairman of the House Ways and Means Committee, as well as the Republican Party floor leader.[2]

In accounting for Maine's tradition of influential members of Congress, certain features of the state's political system are relevant. One is that the state has no real career ladder of public offices that a politician can climb to win a congressional seat. There is no statewide elective office other than the governorship. Although many congressional candidates have had state legislative experience, legislative districts are too small to constitute an effective springboard for a congressional race. Moreover, the state offers few other types of structures that a candidate may use to gain support. The state has no large cities; its business organizations are predominantly small; and party organizations tend to be weak. The upshot is that candidates for Congress are unusually dependent on their personal talents and resources, and the most resourceful generally win. Once established in Congress, these members are in a strong position to rise in the congressional hierarchies if they desire a leadership role.

The current members of the delegation show the importance of personal skills and reputation in winning a seat in Congress. All four had extensive political experience before going to Washington, but their careers developed in different ways. Sen. Olympia Snowe was first elected to the Maine House of Representatives in a special election in 1973 following the death of her husband, Rep. Peter Snowe (R.-Auburn). Elected to a full term in 1974, she moved to the Maine Senate in 1976. Two years later she won the U.S. House seat in Maine's northern Second District when incumbent William Cohen was elected to the U.S. Senate. Snowe remained in the House until 1994, when she replaced retiring Sen. George Mitchell. Sen. Susan Collins did not enter electoral politics until 1994, when she won the Republican nomination for governor. In the general election she lost narrowly to Independent Angus King. Earlier, however, she had held political appointments as a federal regional official and as the Commissioner of Professional Licensure under Gov. John McKernan. She was elected to the U.S. Senate in 1996. Second District Representative Michael Michaud had served the Maine legislature for many years before his election in 2002. Michaud was president of the Maine Senate in 2000–02. The newest member of the delegation, First District Congresswoman Chellie Pingree, elected in 2008, was majority leader in the Maine House in 1997 and in 1999. She had run unsuccessfully against Sen. Susan Collins in 2002. She replaced former Democratic Congressman Tom Allen (1996–2008), who lost a race challenging Sen. Susan Collins in 2008.

Another aspect of Maine politics that influences its congressional delegation is respect for seniority. Although Maine has always reflected a view that politics is everyone's business, in keeping with its moralistic political culture, it has tended to keep successful politicians in Washington for recurring terms. In the 1890s, Maine's Republican delegation in the U.S. House of Representatives had substantial seniority in addition to being composed of skillful politicians. More recently, Sen. Margaret Chase Smith, who served four terms, and Sen. Edmund S. Muskie, who served nearly four terms, gained powerful committee assignments partly because of their seniority.

The tendency of Maine politicians to take a middle-of-the-road stance on pressing public issues, a fundamental characteristic of the state's politics, also influences the state's congressional delegation. While some other northern, moralistic states, such as Wisconsin and North Dakota, were experiencing third-party movements in the early decades of the twentieth century, Maine remained faithful to the Republican Party. Closer to home, New Hampshire, like Maine, lacks a "career ladder" of political offices. While New Hampshire regularly injects a great deal of conservative ideology into statewide campaigns, Maine politicians have stuck to "moderate" political appeals.

As the state developed a two-party system, successful candidates in both parties stayed fairly near the center of the political spectrum. The two current Republican senators (Olympia J. Snowe and Susan Collins) have compiled voting records that are distinctly more liberal than that of Senate Republicans as a whole. Both senators were part of a bipartisan coalition in 2005 that preserved the Senate filibuster in the face of efforts by conservative Republicans to overturn it. In 2009 Snowe and Collins were among only three Republicans in the Senate to support President Barack Obama's stimulus package, designed to deal with the severe economic downturn in 2008–09. The most faithfully conservative Maine Republican in recent years, Congressman David Emery (1970–82), was defeated overwhelmingly in 1982 by Democrat George Mitchell for a seat in the U.S. Senate. Maine's Democratic members of Congress have maintained liberal voting records, but their state campaigns have been moderate in tone, and on some issues—such as gun control—they have differed from their national counterparts. Probably the most avowedly liberal member in the delegation in recent decades was Sen. William Hathaway, who lost a reelection bid in 1978 to moderate Republican William Cohen.

The small role played by ideology can be partly attributed to the state's economic diversity. Maine's multiple concerns—including agricultural commodities, the fishing industry, tourism, defense installations, shipbuilding, pulp and paper companies, and manufacturing—have generally required its national spokespersons to balance locally competing interests. In addition, the tradition of high citizen participation and a town-meeting approach to politics have usually fostered politicians who relate well to voters on a personal, problem-solving basis. That need tends to force politicians to eschew ideology in favor of finding a solution to a specific concern.

In Washington, then, the members of the Maine delegation generally work well together on Maine issues, and are usually effective in coalition building. They also tend to manifest a strong concern—consistent with the moralistic culture—with the processes of government. In this latter respect, both Margaret Chase Smith and Edmund Muskie distinguished themselves nationally. Senator Smith is perhaps best remembered for her "Declaration of Conscience" speech in June 1950, when she spoke out against McCarthyism and encouraged the nation to find a more rational way to deal with the menace of international communism.[3] Senator Muskie was highly praised in the 1960s for his role in developing the Model Cities program and environmental legislation and in serving as the first chair of the Senate Budget Committee.[4] Between 2003 and 2007 Sen. Susan Collins was chairperson of the Homeland Security and Governmental Affairs Committee, which has jurisdiction over the Department of Homeland Security. In 2004 she won widespread praise for managing legislation reforming the nation's intelligence-gathering apparatus, and creating the position of national intelligence director. A member of the Senate Finance Committee, Sen. Olympia Snowe played a crucial role in negotiations over health-care reform in 2009.

In recent years, Maine has depended on its congressional delegation to handle certain major problems involving the federal government. The issues discussed here include the American Indian land-claims dispute, defense contracting, and grants-in-aid.

American Indian Land Claims

The most dramatic was probably the Native American land-claims controversy of the 1970s, which ended in 1980 with a settlement negotiated by White House representatives. The issue began when the Passamaquoddy Indian tribe, through the federal government, sued the State of Maine to recover lands taken from them in violation of the Non-Intercourse Act of 1790, which declared that no state could acquire any Native American lands unless such action was approved by Congress. Because of this law, a 1794 treaty between the Native Americans and Massachusetts (of which Maine was then a part) was rendered unconstitutional by the U.S. government because the treaty had not been ratified by the Congress. The land claims of the Passamaquoddies, and later the Penobscot tribes, eventually amounted to 12.5 million acres, or more than half of the territory of Maine. During the course of the legal dispute, land titles in much of the state were left in question, prompting the Maine Municipal Bank to cancel a $27 million bond sale.

The question facing Maine public officials was whether to seek a negotiated settlement or to contest the Native Americans' claims in court. State leaders at the time, principally Attorney General Joseph Brennan and Gov. James Longley, preferred to pursue the matter in court. Their strong stance undoubtedly helped Brennan in his successful 1978 gubernatorial campaign. The congressional delegation favored a negotiated settlement, and one was eventually worked out by a presidential task force. Under its terms, Maine was absolved of responsibility, and the federal government agreed to pay the Native Americans some $81.5 million. The critical step of securing Congress's approval for the funds was accomplished, many observers believed, in large part because of the efforts of Sen. Edmund Muskie. He was chair of the Senate Budget Committee and had a close working relationship with the Carter administration. Only a few months after the land-claims issue was settled, Muskie became President Carter's Secretary of State.

The state government has had an uneasy relationship with the Native American tribes over the past two decades. As they have in several other states, the tribes have tried to establish gambling casinos. Because of historical factors, the legal status of Maine's tribes differs from those in other states in that Maine tribes must obtain state permission to engage in activities available elsewhere without approval of the state government. In 2002 the tribes pursued through a referendum permission to build a casino in the town of Sanford in western Maine. The referendum caused a backlash in the form of a movement styled "Casinos No" which campaigned hard against the idea. Supporters of "Casinos No" included Gov. John Baldacci and former governor Angus King. The casino proposal was defeated by a nearly two to one margin, fostering considerable resentment in tribal communities. Other forms of gambling such as slot machines have, however, won approval in certain places.

More recently the tribes have focused economic development efforts in Washington County, the state's easternmost (and poorest) region. In early 2005 the town of Perry rejected their proposal to build a liquefied natural gas facility. The tribes have also faced Gov. Baldacci's strong opposition to their efforts to establish racino gambling in that county. Tribal members of the Maine Indian Tribal State Commission (MITSC), which was established to implement the 1980 settlement, boycotted its meetings in 2003 and 2004 in protest of Governor Baldacci's role in defeating the casino proposal. As a result the governor supported and the legislature approved the creation of a Tribal-State Work Group (TSWG). The TSWG has a broader membership than the MITSC (containing lawmakers, representatives of the state's five tribes, a governor's representative, and the chair of the MITSC), and is designed to help recommend solutions of disputes presented to the MITSC. A persistent issue centers on the meaning of the phrase "internal tribal matters," over which Native Americans have control. The state has sometimes contended that its powers are more extensive than the Native Americans will accept, especially over such issues as water quality, in their territories.

Defense Contracting

Maine is one of the New England states especially dependent on the income and jobs generated by federal defense spending. Defense contracting in Maine has been about as important as the pulp and paper industry. In recent decades each added about 8 percent to the state's annual gross product. Members of the congressional delegation watch over the state's defense-related industries in part by securing seats on the armed services

committees. Sen. Margaret Chase Smith (1949–73) was for years the ranking Republican on the Senate unit. Sen. William Cohen (1979–87) also held
a seat on the committee. His prominent role on military issues in the Senate,
especially in shaping his party's strategy, led to his appointment as Secretary of Defense during President Clinton's second term. In the current
delegation, Sen. Olympia Snowe served on the Armed Services Committee
from 1995 to 2001, when she moved to the Finance Committee and Sen. Susan Collins took her place. In the House, Congresswoman Chellie Pingree
was named to the Armed Services Committee in 2009.

The state has had to fight hard to protect its military installations. It has
suffered some losses, but on the whole has achieved considerable success in
retaining existing facilities. Most of the battles have been waged in front of
the four Base Realignment and Closure Commissions (BRACs) that the federal government has established since 1988. The first blow came when the
Defense Department closed Loring Air Force Base in Limestone in northern Maine in 1993. Due to the efforts of Sen. George Mitchell, a Defense
Finance and Accounting Service was established in the area, offering about
350 jobs and somewhat easing the unemployment caused by the base closure. In 1993 fears grew in southern Maine that the Portsmouth Naval Shipyard (located in Kittery) might be a candidate for closure, but it was spared
in the BRAC recommendations of that year. In 2005, in contrast, Maine appeared to be in very serious trouble. In May Secretary of Defense Donald
Rumsfeld recommended the closure of the Portsmouth Naval Shipyard, the
Defense Finance and Accounting Service in Limestone and a major reduction in the Naval Air Station in Brunswick on the southern Maine coast.
The potential cost in direct and indirect jobs in the state was estimated to be
nearly fourteen thousand.

For the next three months, the state's congressional delegation, the Baldacci administration and their staffs sought to persuade the BRAC commission
to overturn the secretary's recommendations. Congressman Allen described
the process as "far and away the most intense and effective collaboration
among members of the delegation that I've seen in my nine years in Congress. We are united with each other all the time."[5] Maine's case rested on,
among other factors, the efficiency and cost-effectiveness of the facilities.
In August 2005 the commission appeared to accept much of the state's ar-
guments. BRAC removed the Portsmouth yard and the Defense Services
Agency from the list, actually expanding that agency's workforce. However, it did recommend closure of the Brunswick Naval Air Station. That
Maine was able to save two of the three facilities at risk was a considerable
achievement as the BRAC commission accepted 86 percent of the Defense

Department's overall recommendations. Very strong community support for the installations and the congressional delegation's ability to enlist military expertise for its case contributed to the outcome.

Federal Assistance

Another task of the congressional delegation is to help the state acquire federal grants-in-aid and other forms of federal assistance. The rapid increase in the size of the federal grant system in the decade of 1960s took place at the same time as Maine politics shifted from one-party to two-party politics. The newly empowered Democratic Party brought about an expansion of state government spending and public policy initiatives. Gov. Kenneth Curtis (1967–75) actively sought federal assistance to help fund new programs. By the 1980s Maine, traditionally laggard in acquiring federal aid, ranked among the top ten states in the proportion of state and local revenues it derived from federal grants.[6]

The Reagan administration's budgetary cutbacks slowed the expansion of grants, forcing Maine policymakers to fight hard to defend programs such as the low-income energy assistance, food stamp and weatherization programs that were of particular importance to the state. Fortunately an unusually robust state economy helped to minimize the effects of budget reductions on state activities at that time. However, the decade marked the time when national grants-in-aid policy turned away from aiding places to assisting primarily people. As a result, programs for cities such as the Community Development Block Grant diminished in size. The loss of federal "place" assistance made localities in Maine more dependent on state support for their developmental needs, and intensified discussions over the proper role of each in funding local services, especially public education. The leading example of a "people" program is Medicaid, which currently accounts for about a fifth of the state's expenditures and more than half of its federal aid dollars. Even so, the state was reported in June 2005, to be experiencing a $342 million federal Medicaid shortfall over the next ten years.[7]

In 2003 Maine ranked eleventh among states in federal per capita spending on grants to state and local governments and was fifteenth in overall federal spending per capita. Federal grants have increased somewhat faster in recent years—as a proportion of the state revenues—than the state's own sources, including sales, gasoline, and income taxes. State officials currently try to maximize federal grant funding as the state confronts budgetary shortfalls. Maine's terms of trade with the federal government, meaning the amount of money it received in relation to dollars its citizens paid in federal taxes, stood at $1.36 in 2003—the highest among the New England states.

While the state maintains a generally harmonious relationship with national officials, conflicts have arisen over the application of certain federal statutes. In 2008 Maine became the last state to come into compliance with a federal identification law concerning drivers' licenses. Earlier the state legislature had passed a nonbinding resolution against participating in the Real ID program, the national identity card system that Congress enacted in 2004 in the aftermath of 9/11. State officials had argued that the programs was too costly and would have placed state drivers at greater risk of identify theft. Had Maine not acquiesced, its licenses might not have been usable as valid identifications at airports and other facilities. In another controversy, state education administrators in 2006 wanted to substitute the Scholastic Aptitude Test (SAT) for the Maine Educational Assessment Test to measure the mathematics achievement of eleventh grade students, a step required under the federal "No Child Left Behind" (NCLB) law enacted in 2002. Maine administrators believed broad use of the SAT test would encourage high school students to pursue higher education—a major goal in the state. U.S. Department of Education officials objected, stating that the SAT measure would be inadequate for their purposes. For several months it appeared Maine's insistence would result in the state's losing federal educational dollars. The conflict was resolved when the state commissioner of education agreed to add several questions to the SAT test when it was used as part of the NCLB evaluation.

MAINE AND THE PRESIDENCY

As a state with only four electoral votes, Maine does not have a large impact on presidential contests. However, for many years it enjoyed a reputation as something of an electoral forecaster, suggested by the slogan "As Maine goes, so goes the nation." Until 1960 Maine held its gubernatorial elections in September of even-numbered years, and its vote was thus known two months prior to a presidential election. The slogan came from the 1840 campaign when Maine, until that time a Democratic-Republican state, surprised most people by supporting the Whig candidate for governor.[8] The vote proved to be prophetic when, two months later, the Whig presidential ticket won nationally. Despite the 1840 elections, the slogan was never very accurate historically.

Between the Civil War and the late 1950s, Maine was an almost solidly Republican state. The state gubernatorial outcome and the national presidential result were in agreement (in party terms) about two-thirds of the time. That fairly high percentage existed only because the nation, as well as the state, was predominantly Republican during the period. In the years since Maine has become a two-party state, its gubernatorial vote has had even less predictive value. In the five closest presidential contests since World War II—1948, 1960, 1968, 1976, and 2000—Maine voted for the losing candidate every time (the only state to do so).

The state, nonetheless, has had several of its politicians on national tickets. Hannibal Hamlin was elected vice president in 1860 with Abraham Lincoln, and in 1884, James G. Blaine ran unsuccessfully for president on the Republican ticket. Arthur Sewall, in 1896, and Edmund Muskie, in 1968, ran for vice president on unsuccessful Democratic tickets. In the cases of Hamlin, Blaine, and Muskie, the route to the national ticket ran through the U.S. Senate, where each man had distinguished himself as a national politician. Muskie, for instance, was well known for his expertise on big-city and environmental problems, and was popular with urban and minority groups both in and outside Washington. Even so, Muskie's 1972 campaign to win the Democratic presidential nomination was not effective.

Three of Maine's recent governors have held positions in the executive branch. President Lyndon Johnson named John Reed (governor, 1959–67) to the National Transportation Safety Board. Through his support of the administration's Vietnam policies, Reed had gained the president's favorable attention. Kenneth Curtis (governor, 1967–75) was an early supporter of President Jimmy Carter, who later appointed him U.S. ambassador to Canada. After failing in 1990 and in 1994 to regain the governorship, Joseph Brennan (governor, 1979–87) was named by President Bill Clinton to the Federal Maritime Commission. Reed, Curtis, and Brennan were all considered political moderates and undoubtedly added to Maine's prestige during their respective years of service in national administrations. However, the state's primary point of access to the White House is through the Congress.

MAINE AND THE U.S. SUPREME COURT

Another link between Maine and the federal government lies within the court system. For many years, the state had relatively little involvement with the federal courts. In three decades following World War II, the U.S. Supreme Court did not review in full opinion any case appealed from the Maine Supreme Judicial Court. In contrast, since 1980 the Court has examined nine cases from the state's highest court, several of which have raised issues of national constitutional importance. A look at the cases helps indicate the extent to which Maine's policy concerns comport with those of the nation, at least in the area of constitutional law.

Several cases involved the interpretation of federal laws. *Fort Halifax Packing Co. Inc. v. Coyne* (1987) asked whether a state law affecting plant closings was unconstitutional by virtue of its having been preempted by federal law.[9] The Maine measure, enacted in the 1970s, stipulated that when a company closes a plant in order to relocate, workers not already covered by a severance pay contract should receive a one-time severance payment. The Maine high court found no conflict between that law and the national Employee Retirement Income Security Act of 1974. Specifically, it found that the federal law did not extend to state-mandated plans. The U.S. Supreme Court, in a 5 to 4 decision, upheld the Maine ruling on somewhat different grounds. It held that the federal law did cover state-mandated severance plans, but that in Maine's statute no such plan had been set forth, only benefits "triggered by a single event."

Another case involved interpretation of the word "discharge" in the federal Clean Water Act. The act required the owners of dams producing hydroelectricity to obtain state certification (as well as a federal license) when a dam might "result in any discharge into the navigable waters" of the United States. Maine's Board of Environmental Protection had denied certification to the S. J. Warren Company, holding that state laws might be violated by the company's dams on the Presumptcot River. The company appealed in the Maine courts, arguing the term "discharge" meant solely the discharge of pollutants. The Maine Supreme Judicial Court disagreed, asserting that the word included the limiting and releasing of water generally around a dam. In May 2006 the U.S. Supreme Court unanimously upheld the Maine court's ruling.[10]

Two other cases concerned with the effect of federal law on state policy were *Ridgway v. Ridgway* (1981) and *Conroy v. Aniskoff* (1993). The *Ridgway* case, which involved the Serviceman's Group Life Insurance Act of 1965, asked whether a state court could abrogate a beneficiary's right in federal law when the beneficiary's actions violated a state court decree. In this instance, Sergeant Ridgway had left an insurance policy funded with federal assistance to his second wife, not to the children of his first marriage as the state court had stipulated. The Supreme Court in a 5 to 3 decision held that the federal law prevailed.[11] In *Conroy v. Aniskoff*, the courts interpreted the Soldiers' and Sailors' Civil Relief Act of 1940, which provided additional time for military personnel to pay local tax bills. When Conroy failed for several years to pay his property taxes in Danforth, Maine, the town took possession and sold his property. The primary issue was whether an individual in the military had to make a showing of hardship to benefit from the law. The Maine courts decided that such a demonstration was necessary. The U.S. Supreme Court reversed the decision.[12]

The interstate commerce clause was the basis of two nationally important cases from Maine during the 1980–2006 period. In *Alden v. Maine* (1999), a Maine probation officer filed a complaint in Maine superior court seeking overtime pay under the terms of the national Fair Labor Standards Act of 1938. That court and the Maine Supreme Judicial Court held that the Eleventh Amendment to the U.S. Constitution forbade private suits against states in their own courts. The U.S. Supreme Court affirmed by a 5 to 4 margin, stating that the Article I powers Congress has over interstate commerce (under which the FLSA was enacted) cannot override the Eleventh Amendment.[13] *Camps Newfound/Owatonna v. Town of Harrison* (1997) tested a Maine law that permitted towns to grant property tax exemptions to charitable enterprises that predominately benefited Maine citizens. Camps Newfound/Owatonna operated a facility for children most of whom came from out of state, and it did not enjoy the tax exemption. The Maine courts rejected its plea for a tax refund, maintaining that the state showed no discrimination against interstate commerce because the camp was not placed at a competitive disadvantage in recruiting campers. The U.S. Supreme Court disagreed, employing a different line of reasoning. It held that states were prohibited from favoring resident consumers over nonresident consumers. In this instance, the consumption involved the enjoyment of natural surroundings.[14]

The remaining three cases engaged questions of civil rights. In a landmark ruling in 1980, the U.S. Supreme Court (in *Maine v. Thiboutot*) upheld a Maine Supreme Court's decision that individuals who won a lawsuit against the state Department of Human Services involving a program authorized by the federal Social Security Act have a right to be reimbursed for attorney's fees.[15] The case turned on an interpretation of the Civil Rights Act of 1871. Under the holding, the reimbursement policy applied to all federal laws, not only to civil rights matters. In *Maine v. Thornton*, the U.S. Supreme Court altered an existing rule of interpretation when it reversed a Maine Supreme Court decision that was based on established law.[16] The rule in question was the "open fields" doctrine—long enunciated by the court to permit warrantless searches in open fields. The Maine court believed that Thorton's arrest was invalid because the "open fields" standard did not apply to the first search of his property (Thorton was accused of growing marijuana). The U.S. Supreme Court held that the rule was broader than the Maine court believed, extending to all activities conducted out of doors except for a narrow area around the house. Finally, in *Maine v. Moulton* (1985), the Maine Supreme Court was upheld when it determined that statements made by a person indicted for a crime to another suspect, which were recorded by the police, could not be used against him in trial.[17] The U.S. Supreme Court reaffirmed an earlier ruling that the Sixth Amendment right to counsel attaches once an individual is indicted.

The nine cases considered here shared some interesting characteristics. First, they generated a high level of controversy in the U.S. Supreme Court. In four of them, the Court divided 5 to 4; in another case, they split 5 to 3; in two other cases, the alignment was 6 to 3. In resolving only two cases was the Court unanimous. Second, as suggested by those divisions, the cases presented issues of national significance. The events fostering the cases all occurred in Maine, but the questions they raised could have stemmed from activities in almost any state. Evidence of the importance of the cases was seen in a large number of *amicus curiae* briefs that various national interest groups filed in several of the cases. The briefs numbered more than twenty, for example, in *Camp Newfound/Owatonna v. Town of Harrison*. Third, despite the contentious nature of the cases, the Maine Supreme Judicial Court was not generally in disagreement with the U.S. Supreme Court. The high Court affirmed the Maine court in five cases and reversed its rulings in four others. To place those figures in context, in recent decades the U.S. Supreme Court has reversed about two-thirds of the cases it has examined from the state supreme courts. In one instance (*Maine v. Thornton*), the U.S. Supreme Court chose to modify an established precedent, an action the Maine Supreme Court could hardly have anticipated.

Two tentative conclusions can be suggested about the work of Maine courts in relation to federal courts. One is that while Maine's political culture and history are distinctive in the federal system, they do not appear to have given rise to policies that bring the state into much conflict with national courts. During the 1980–2006 period, the U.S. Supreme Court denied certiorari to approximately 200 cases appealed from the Maine Supreme Judicial Court, accepting for full opinion only the nine cases considered here. Among the two hundred cases were many that questioned whether Maine courts had upheld the guarantees in the federal Bill of Rights. Also among the cases were disputes involving major state laws in such policy areas as electric power, games of chance, and consumer credit. In those instances, the Court appeared satisfied that Maine had handled the issues appropriately.

Another conclusion is that where state law or practice does on occasion conflict with federal law or the U.S. Constitution, the Maine Supreme Judicial Court tries carefully to follow U.S. Supreme Court guidelines. In three of the nine cases described above, the Maine court rejected the claim of a state agency, finding that national jurisprudence compelled a different decision. Finally, it is worth noting that in several very controversial cases the U.S. Supreme Court translated Maine's rulings into national policy.

MAINE AND NEW HAMPSHIRE

Although Maine and New Hampshire were one jurisdiction in very early colonial history, they have separated in more ways than geographically. Because of an increasing number of disputes and differences between the two states, an article in *Newsweek* described them as "neighbors, not friends."[18] One area of competition has been over winter tourism. Another has involved fishing rights. A "lobster war" grew so intense in the 1970s that the U.S. Supreme Court was called in to settle it.

A particularly difficult area of conflict has to do with state revenues. Since 1969 Maine has taxed the income of nonresidents who work in the state, many of them from New Hampshire who are employed at the Portsmouth Naval Shipyard in Kittery. The tax is especially unpopular in New Hampshire, which does not have an income tax. In retaliation, New Hampshire enacted a commuter tax, which was found unconstitutional in 1975 by the U.S. Supreme Court because it taxed nonresidents differently from residents. The tax disputes between the two states erupted again when Maine added a nonresident spousal tax in 1986. This measure sets the rate of the nonresident tax, ranging from 1 to 10 percent of a family's total income. Although Maine does not specifically tax the earnings of a spouse who does not work in the state, it now calculates the income tax based on total family income. In 1988 over three hundred residents of New Hampshire demonstrated against this policy. Later in the year, New Hampshire's attorney general requested a refund of the Maine tax for a New Hampshire couple, resulting in New Hampshire challenging Maine's tax policy in court. In March 1990 the Maine Supreme Judicial Court rejected New Hampshire's claim. Subsequently, the U.S. Supreme Court refused to grant certiorari in the case, allowing that decision to stand.

In 2001 the U.S. Supreme Court was called on to settle another conflict when New Hampshire tried to set its southern boundary with Maine along the Maine shoreline of the Piscataqua River, which flows between New Hampshire and Maine to the Atlantic Ocean. The court found that New Hampshire had taken a different position in a closely related boundary dispute in 1977. Under the doctrine of judicial estoppel, it banned the new claim and established the boundary line in the middle of the Piscataqua River's navigable channel.[19]

Reinforcing the competition between Maine and New Hampshire are

important differences of ideology and political style. While Maine is char-
acteristically moderate in politics, New Hampshire's politics are more po-
larized and combative. In recent decades conservative Republicans have
mostly held sway in New Hampshire, in contrast to Maine, where a two-
party system has been in place since the 1960s. Officials in the two states,
especially members of their congressional delegations, usually cooperate on
issues pitting northern New England against other regions. That cooperation
was noticeably present in the successful drive in 2005 to remove the Portsmouth Naval Shipyard from the Defense Department's base closure list.
However, competition between the two states over economic development
and tax issues is likely to persist.

MAINE AND CANADA

Of the three jurisdictions bordering on Maine, only one—New Hampshire—
is part of the United States. The other two—Quebec and New Brunswick—
are provinces of Canada. Ties to Canada are further strengthened by the
ethnic composition of Maine's population. During the latter half of the nineteenth century, about one-quarter of all the French Canadians who migrated
to the United States settled in Maine.

In the 1970s, Gov. Kenneth Curtis tried to develop formal relations with
the Canadian provinces.[20] Under his direction, a state Office of Canadian
Relations was established in 1973. In the same year, the state also signed
agreements with several Canadian provinces promoting cooperation in such
areas as environmental protection, energy, trade, tourism, fisheries, forestry,
and recreation. A study of formal interactions between the American states
and Canada showed that, in 1974, Maine had concluded by far the largest
number of understandings and agreements of any state, accounting for 110
of the 766 understandings and agreements (14.4 percent) in existence that
year between the fifty states and Canadian provinces.[21]

Curtis believed that effective ties with Canada assisted the state in avoiding certain problems during his administration. As an example, during the
OPEC oil-embargo crisis of 1973, Canada sought to protect its supplies by
halting exports through a federal order from Ottawa binding on all provinces. A Great Northern Paper Company mill, which at that time obtained
its oil from a refinery in New Brunswick, would have had to shut down had
not Curtis persuaded the provincial premier, Richard Hatfield, to intervene.
Through Hatfield's work, an exception to the order was obtained.

After Curtis left office in 1975 his successor, independent James Longley, showed less interest in Canadian affairs. The state legislature thereupon

established its own office of Canadian affairs. The existence of many Democratic legislators from French-speaking constituencies was an important factor in the creation of the legislative office, which was unique to Maine. One of its tasks was to assist legislators whose districts border on Canada in working out constituent problems involving Canada. During the budget crisis of 1991, however, the office was eliminated. In 1996 the management of Canadian relations was assigned the Department of Economic Development, under the direction of the Maine International Trade Center. The center handles commercial relations with all nations involved with Maine businesses. In 1998 the center added a Canada desk to assist Maine companies, especially small firms, doing business across the border. In 2004 the legislature sought to reestablish links with its Canadian counterparts, creating the Maine-Canadian Legislative Advisory Commission, composed of eight legislators, four selected by the senate president and four by the Speaker of the house. According to the statute, one member must be fluent in the French language.

The most troublesome issue between Maine and Canada has focused on trade. Maine has sought to prevent Canada from flooding the United States market with such products as fish, lumber, and potatoes that compete at lower prices with Maine products. The state has not enjoyed a great deal of success thus far. The North American Free Trade Agreement of 1993 was opposed by both Maine senators, and is blamed for the loss of jobs in the paper and wood products industries. In 2004 Maine's lumber problem was exacerbated when the World Trade Organization determined that some U.S. duties on Canadian lumber were illegal under international rules. The decision was based on an appeal from a ruling of the U.S. International Trade Commission, which had determined that Canadian government subsidies allowed the sale of the Canadian lumber below the market price. Despite the difficulties attending certain products, the volume of commerce between Maine and Canada remains extensive. Canada buys one-third of all products Maine sells internationally. The value of all goods exchanged between Maine and Canada in 2005 was estimated to be between $3 and $4 billion.

Since the terrorist attacks on the United States in September 2001, Maine and Canada have faced a different kind of issue: how to secure their borders and still retain the ease of travel that has long existed between border towns in Maine and in New Brunswick and Quebec. That cooperation has been substantial. To illustrate, the high school in Calais, Maine, which is separated from St. Stevens, New Brunswick, by a short bridge, used the football field in St. Stevens in the early 2000s because it did not have its own field. The two towns have also had a mutual-aid agreement covering their fire departments.[22] The state hopes such cooperation will continue as the borders become more tightly regulated, and more elaborate forms of identification and documentation are required.

CONCLUSION

Maine has long depended on the federal government to protect its economic interests, even as it has sought to maintain its distinctive way of life. To a large extent, it has been successful. Its greatest battles have been fought in Congress, and its success there has been due to the presence of a very strong congressional delegation, which the state's political system seems able to produce quite regularly. The state is too small to engage in much bargaining in presidential politics, and it has not tried to challenge the U.S. Supreme Court. Competition seems to characterize the relations between Maine and its only U.S. neighbor, the state of New Hampshire. While this competition is largely based on the economic similarities of the states, it is probably strengthened by their ideological differences. On the other hand, Maine has undertaken to foster close ties with the bordering Canadian provinces, partly because its problems are not always of major interest to the federal government, and perhaps partly because it wishes to strengthen its hand in dealings with the federal government.

CHAPTER TWELVE

Local Government

Maine has a rather large territory (31,886 square miles) for a relatively sparsely populated eastern state. Although its total population in 2005 was only 1,324,690, the state contains a large number of local governmental units, including the following: 432 towns, 22 cities, 34 plantations, three Native American nations, 16 counties, and more than 300 special districts.

A newcomer who travels the state may be struck by the large number of small adjacent communities, and their distance both in miles and in habits from the state and national capitals. There are 827 governmental units and in addition 422 unorganized townships, which comprise more than 40 percent of the state's territory, and illustrate the underlying governmental diversity and noncentralization at the grassroots. Under Maine law, only cities and towns are considered municipal corporations. There are approximately 88,000 local units of government in the United States and Maine continues to rank high in the number of local governments. In fact, Maine is ranked second among the New England States (units per 10,000 population). Its 827 units are substantial, but not nearly the largest total among the states (Illinois has almost 7,000 units).[1]

Some long-time critics of Maine's vast landscape of local governments have even classified it as a "jungle" that inevitably forces more centralization. They argue that the weaker units of local government cannot perform adequately, and eventually lose control over some of their service functions.[2] These small governments were challenged in earlier periods as they lost direct control over education services to newly formed school administrative districts in the 1950s and to the State Department of Education (see Chapter 13 for a more detailed discussion). During the 1980s, the state government also became more active in local affairs by imposing more mandates in such areas as solid waste disposal, protection of natural resources, and land-use planning. Even more state mandates and additional demands for local tax dollars were expected because of the withdrawal of funding for key federal programs during the Reagan administration. Maine's system of local government and substate units will surely be tested as the state moves further into the twenty-first century.

TOWNS, PLANTATIONS, AND CITIES

Some authorities have contended that the early English parish meeting was the origin of New England town government, while others argue that it evolved from farm meetings in ancient Germany. In New England, town government began only a few years after the initial settlements in the Boston area. The New England town itself averaged twenty to forty square miles in size and usually followed the natural terrain while proceeding with straight lines. However, only a fraction of that area was actually inhabited. Colonists lived in the meeting house, schoolhouse, and town center. By the end of the seventeenth century, new settlements were created within the towns as the population often had dispersed. Residents began to insist upon and acquire local rights, as towns were divided into religious parishes, and road, militia, and tax assessment and collection subareas.

Due to an expanding population, the Massachusetts legislature decided that each settlement should be authorized to organize and govern as a town, in the same manner as the English parishes. Weekly or monthly meetings were held to conduct town business. Eventually, the agendas became unwieldy, attendance declined, and decision-making was delegated to a committee of "selectmen" who would act between meetings. Gradually this interim committee made it possible to lengthen the periods between meetings.[3]

Maine has been called a union of towns. Even today, towns remain the most numerous unit, and in terms of area, they continue to dominate the state. There are 432 towns, but about half of them have less than one thousand residents. When formally "incorporated" by a special act of the legislature, a community becomes a "town" under Maine law. As a municipality, it is given certain privileges; it also assumes obligations to perform duties that would not be required of an unorganized township, but that are required of all Maine towns. As a corporation, it may sue and be sued, and it has responsibilities for collecting taxes and supporting a school system. Maine municipalities range from ten to ninety-three square miles in size.

Within some Maine towns, "village corporations" were also authorized by special acts of the legislature. Historically, most village corporations were established to provide a specific service (e.g., fire protection for the town center) that applied to residents of the village, but not to the more rural residents, who did not use the service and were not taxed for it. The legislature established 124 village corporations from the 1830s to the 1930s, but only a few remain in operation. Most of them exist in a few coastal communities that need additional services for the numerous seasonal residents who may be clustered in a particular part of the town.[4] These village corporations may also he viewed as precursors of special districts, which are discussed in Chapter 13.

Plantations originated in the Massachusetts Bay Colony, and are unique to Maine among all the states. First envisioned as a temporary "halfway house" between an unorganized township and an incorporated township, they have continued to flourish as local government units. In 2005 there were still thirty-four plantations in the state. They may even again be considered as an option where town government has become too expensive for the smaller communities.[5] Most are rural and sparsely populated northern and northwestern communities where there is little demand for the variety of services enjoyed in the larger towns. Plantations are similar to towns in size and are, therefore, much smaller than counties.

Plantation government also resembles town government, with the traditional annual meeting constituting the legislative function. Assessors, rather than selectmen, are elected to carry on the day-to-day operation of government. However, there are several key differences: (1) plantations must be organized by a vote of the county commissioners, while towns are incorporated by a vote of the Maine legislature; and (2) they do not have the powers granted to towns and cities under Maine's home-rule statute. Thus, the chief disadvantage is that they lack discretionary authority in certain governmental matters.[6]

One municipal expert, James Haag, explains their perceived advantages for some communities:

> Plantations are small in population size but tend to be relatively well off in terms of high per capita tax commitment and low effective rates of property taxation—indeed, much better off financially than the average Maine town or city . . . plantations appear to have available all the state aid which is available to Maine towns and cities. In the instance of welfare, plantations receive state aid which is not available to Maine towns and cities.[7]

Maine has twenty-two cities that are incorporated through a charter form of government. The city charter or "local constitution" is a written document that outlines the city's general philosophy and form of local government.

Table 7: Distribution of powers between primary forms of local government in the
Northeast

	County	Municipal City	Municipal Township	Districts Special	Districts School
Connecticut	Neg	Hyp	Hyp	BA	Neg
Maine	Neg	Hyp	Hyp	BA	AA
Massachusetts	Neg	Hyp	Hyp	AA	Neg
New Hampshire	Low	AA	AA	Neg	AA
New Jersey	A	A	Hyp	BA	AA
New York	BA	Hyp	AA	BA	BA
Pennsylvania	BA	BA	BA	AA	Hyp
Rhode Island	Neg	Hyp	Hyp	Low	Neg
Vermont	Neg	A	AA	Neg	Hyp

Key: *Neg*—negligible; *Low*—low; *BA*—below average; *A*—average; *AA*—above average; *Hyp*—hyperactive

Sources: Adapted from G. R. Stephens and N. Wikstrom. *Metropolitan Government and Governance: Theoretical Perspectives, Empirical Analysis and the Future* (New York: Oxford University Press, 1999), 124–46, and displayed in David Y. Miller. *The Regional Governing of Metropolitan America* (Boulder CO: Westview Press, 2002), 63–64.

Cities are required by state law to adopt a charter stating how local self-government will be established, while towns are not. There are no minimum population requirements for cities, which often confuses newcomers to Maine about their status vis-à-vis towns. Eastport, for example, is a city of 1,646, while Brunswick is a town of 21,234. Still, cities tend to be the largest communities in the state, but are small by national standards.

In cities, representative government replaces the town meeting. City residents elect their representatives to serve on councils and establish the overall policies of the community. Medium-size and larger Maine cities—Portland is the largest with a population of 64,249—tend to be well-run communities with a capacity to administer and deliver a wide array of services. This is due in part to the use of council-manager government in Maine. According to the 2000 U.S. Census, 344,414 Mainers resided in its twenty-two cities.[8]

Table 7.0 provides some analysis for the nine northeast states, where the most active governments are the cities and towns. With New Hampshire, Pennsylvania and Vermont being the exception, the remaining six states have very active municipal governments. According to David Miller's study, "only Pennsylvania has a relatively modest role for its municipal governments," and Maine is classified as "hyperactive active."[9] Common to all states in the northeast region is the limited role of county government. In the six New England states alone, county government plays a negligible role. With the exception of Massachusetts and Pennsylvania, special districts' roles are generally limited.[10]

FORMS OF LOCAL GOVERNMENT

Maine's 491 plantations, towns, and cities have adopted a variety of different governmental structures. However, there are four basic forms of municipal government: (1) town meeting—selectmen, (2) town meeting—selectmen-manager/council-manager, (3) council-manager, and (4) mayor-council/mayor-council/administrator.

Town Meeting—Selectmen

For more than three hundred years, the town meeting has existed in New England, including Maine, and has been praised as a pure form of direct democracy. It is an assembly of the town's eligible voters, usually held in March, where the citizens themselves discuss and act on the issues facing the town.[11] Special town meetings may be held during the year and are called by either the selectmen or a specified number of voters in the town. Issues must be listed in the form of articles on a warrant that announces the time and place of the town meeting. Moderators traditionally have enjoyed broad discretionary powers to run a meeting.[12] At the actual meeting, votes may be taken only on the specific articles placed on the warrant.

The town meeting expresses the legislative function of local government. The townspeople pass the laws needed for town governance, approve a budget, levy taxes, authorize borrowing, and elect the various town officers. A plural executive body of three to seven members, historically called the board of selectmen (and often referred to as "selectpersons"), is elected for one-year terms and charged with administering town business, enforcing laws, and implementing the decisions made at the town meeting. Under state statutes, selectmen have specific administrative responsibilities that relate to town meetings, elections, finances, personnel, streets and highways, public safety, human services, public works, planning, and economic development. Maine state law also grants them some limited powers to enact laws or ordinances regulating vehicles, public ways, and public property.[13]

Other officials elected at a pure town meeting may include the town clerk, tax collector, road commissioner, board of assessors, and overseers of the poor. All of these officials have duties and responsibilities specified by state law. (If no such officials are elected by the voters or appointed by the selectmen, their duties are assumed by the board.) State law also requires the people to elect a school board (or representatives to a School Administrative District), which appoints the school superintendent.

The town meeting has been praised as the outstanding example of direct democracy. Thomas Jefferson called it "the wisest invention ever devised by the wit of man for the perfect exercise of self government."[14] In the late nineteenth century, James Bryce commented:

> Of the three or four types of systems of local government, which I have described, that of the town or township with its primary assembly is admittedly the best. It is the cheapest and the most efficient; it is the most educative of the citizens who bear a part in it. The town meeting has been not only the source but the school of democracy.[15]

While the town meeting has been glorified in the past, it has also been criticized for the following reasons:

1. Citizen apathy and poor turnout, which in turn have often allowed a few well- organized special interests (i.e., volunteer firefighters, teachers, relatives, and extended families) to control policymaking.

2. The physical problem in some towns of housing a large turnout of citizens for a meeting.

3. Problems increase as the size of the town population increases, especially beyond 2,500.

4. Problems of whether a part-time executive body (selectmen) can effectively administer town affairs (e.g., in some cases, selectmen lack clear-cut authority over other elected town officials, who have duties and responsibilities specified in state law).

5. The question of whether a citizen forum is capable of adequately deliberating very complex matters in one day (e.g., financial issues).

Indeed, some studies of the New England town meeting have provided evidence of poor attendance and relative lack of debate at times for even salient issues. For a number of reasons, a large percentage of townsfolk have given up their privilege of participating in this unique institution. However, as Joseph A. Zimmerman concluded about the citizens:

> Their lack of attendance at an open town meeting may be interpreted as a vote of confidence in a de facto representative town meeting. Fortunately,

attendance appears to be a function of the importance of the unresolved issues, and voter apathy tends to disappear when a major issue is brought to the open town meeting for resolution.[16]

One significant finding from a longitudinal study in Vermont by Professor Frank Bryan was that "on average only 20 percent of a town's registered voters attended their yearly town meeting . . . and only 7 percent of them spoke out."[17] Collecting useful data from hundreds of Vermont towns over three decades was difficult because New England town meetings often occur simultaneously in March.

For Bryan, size really matters: "When we take into account curvilinear properties, the size variable is extremely powerful, explaining 58 percent of the variance in attendance at town meetings. As far as citizen presence is concerned, real democracy works best in small towns. Of this there is no doubt."[18] Bryan's seminal work on town meetings concludes that "beyond meeting size, issues are the most important determinant of discussion at town meeting."[19]

During the twentieth century, the pure town meeting form was modified in a number of communities to help cope with socioeconomic changes. Under the various names of Finance, Warrant, or Budget, a special committee composed of elected or appointed citizens has been used by a number of Maine communities. First adopted by the town of Brunswick in 1902, this committee either participates in the preparation of the budget or investigates a proposed town budget. After a thorough review, the committee makes its recommendations on the budget to the town meeting.

Another possible modification in the town meeting establishes the "Limited or Representative Town Meeting." However, this reform drastically alters the town meeting as the citizen's legislative body and as an example of pure democracy. Persons are elected from each of several districts to attend the town meeting. Any voter may still speak, but only the elected representatives may vote. This form has been used by three Maine towns: Sanford, Old Orchard Beach, and Caribou. Today, only Sanford uses this town-meeting format with its seven wards and 134 town meeting representatives, but it remains very popular in other parts of New England. In 2004 Sanford voters approved a charter change that established a town council form of government, where the representative town meeting approves the budget and the council makes other decisions.[20]

Town Meeting—Selectmen-Manager/Council-Manager

Under this form of government, the board of selectmen hires a qualified full-time manager to carry out the various administrative duties of the board.

The manager may be given authority to appoint other personnel in the town and serves at the pleasure of the board of selectmen. In theory, the person should be professionally trained in public administration, but in practice, this does not always occur.

This modification of town government became a widely acceptable device in Maine, which effectively maintained the Yankee tradition of the town meeting while incorporating the values of professionalism expressed in the national movement to reform local government by means of the city-manager form of government. By 1970 more than 25 percent of town-meeting municipalities had added town managers; in general, most towns over 2,000 in population have adopted this form, while those under 1,000 have not. Most Maine towns adopted the selectmen-manager plan through provisions of the general law—an enabling act passed in 1939 that specifies the manager's duties, responsibilities, and powers. In the late 1960s, the town-manager enabling act was revised to help clarify the roles and duties of selectmen and managers, and to provide broader administrative authority to the manager for appointing department heads, subject to confirmation by the selectmen. Several traditionally elected offices, such as town clerk, tax collector, and treasurer, can be discontinued and their roles assumed by the manager or a designee.

In practice small-town managers have acquired a number of difficult roles and responsibilities, which may vary somewhat from one community to another. Official "hats" of the manager may include serving as purchasing agent, treasurer, tax collector, road commissioner, overseer of the poor, clerk, civil defense director, and building inspector. In general, the manager is responsible for administering all of the operations of town government with the exception of the schools. In Maine managers cannot serve as assessors, a practice that can occur in neighboring New Hampshire.

Since the passage of Maine's home-rule statute in 1969, towns and cities have had the authority, under a local charter, to adopt and frame any form of government that employs a town or city manager. Thus, a town or city may select either the "Statutory Town Manager Plan," or create its own list of duties and responsibilities for the manager and a framework for governance within the context of its own home-rule charter. Even before the town-manager enabling act, some communities received special authorization from the legislature to hire an appointed administrator. In 1925 Camden became the first Maine town to adopt this form of government, followed by Fort Fairfield, Mount Desert, Washburn, Rumford, and Dexter.

A number of hybrid forms of this plan dot the Maine landscape. More than seventy Maine towns, like Farmingdale, adjacent to Augusta, and the island community of North Haven, have hired full-time or part-time "administrative assistants." These assistants are hired by the selectmen to advise them on specified matters, often financial. There is no state law providing for administrative assistants. Therefore, they serve at the pleasure of the selectmen and derive their authority as delegated by the board. During the past twenty years, the town meeting–selectmen–Administrative Assistant option has been the fastest growing organizational structure, primarily in the smaller towns.[21]

Some of the smaller communities have cooperated to hire a "circuit-riding" manager to save on costs and obtain the services of a professional administrator, which they probably could not afford individually. An example of this cooperative arrangement exists in the towns of Castle Hill, Mapleton, and Chapman, located in northern Maine.

A slightly different variation used in twenty communities is the "town meeting–council-manager" form, whereby legislative functions are typically shared by the town meeting and the council. For example, most legislative functions regarding the budget are reserved for the town meeting, but selected legislative functions regarding ordinances (and sometimes executive duties such as appointments) are exercised by the council. Thus, the "council" acts at times in a plural executive capacity as "selectpersons" do, and, in addition, exercises legislative functions. In summary about one-half of all Maine towns (233) employ town managers, administrators, or administrative assistants.

Council-Manager

The tide of municipal reform of the early twentieth century swept into Maine and has had a very large impact, especially in the adoption of the council-manager plan and the previously discussed town manager plan. At one point, Maine was ranked fifth nationally in the number of managers, trailing only California, Texas, Michigan, and Pennsylvania. However, because of the large number of small towns and the town-meeting tradition, adoption of the pure council-manager plan has been limited.

In 1917 Auburn became the first Maine city to adopt the city-manager form of government. Portland followed suit in 1920. As was often the case nationwide, corruption and inefficiency under the previous weak mayor-council structure accelerated the trend. By 1970 there were twenty-eight council-manager municipalities (cities or towns). By 2005 the number had increased to approximately fifty communities, and thus the council-manager has become the most popular form of local government for those communities that have seen fit to eliminate the town meeting. It tends to be most prevalent in communities with a population more than five thousand. Unlike the town meeting—selectmen form, this form of government must be adopted through a local charter.

The council-manager form was first adopted by the small town of Staunton, Virginia, in 1906, when a professional was hired to conduct all the executive work of the community. By 1914 Dayton, Ohio, became the first major American city to adopt the plan, which gained rapidly in popularity. By 2004 the International City Management Association listed 2,721 communities with populations over five thousand that had adopted the plan. By the turn of the twenty-first century, the council-manager plan has become the most popular form of American local government. The basic features of the plan include (1) a small council, usually elected at large (each member of the council is elected from the entire community) and on a nonpartisan basis; (2) a mayor, usually elected from among the members of a council, who serves as chair and the ceremonial head of the city; and (3) an expert administrator—the city manager—hired by the council to manage the city's business.

This appointed professional can serve for an indefinite length of time. On the other hand, he or she may have a mutually agreed-upon contract with the council for a specific time period. The individual need not be a local person. Indeed, in most cases, an outside expert is hired because of his or her experience and educational background. Typically, the city charter specifies the manager's legal duties and responsibilities to include:

1. preparing the budget for the council

2. appointing and removing department heads

3. overseeing the execution of policy

4. making recommendations to the council

The manager has no vote, but does have influence because of his or her expertise, control of information, and full-time appointed executive status.

In Maine there are some deviations from the general model. For example, about one-third of the municipal councils are oriented toward a district or combination system (ward and at large), rather than being purely at large. Moreover, council appointment of city officials is fairly widespread. Some Maine managers are even precluded by charter or by historical practice from appointing or dismissing municipal officials (e.g., clerks, tax collectors, treasurers, assessors) whom, in theory, they are supervising.[22] Thus, in the area of personnel management, some of Maine local executives are often characterized as "weak managers."

The original theory of the city manager plan was patterned after the corporate business model used in the private sector. The council would decide on policy, the manager would execute the policy, and neither would interfere with the function of the other. Thus, the advocates of this plan believed the manager was to be a "nonpolitical" position, while the council would determine policy and remain as the political body.[23] This dichotomy has been debated and largely debunked elsewhere. The primary difficulty is trying to separate politics and administration.[24] This "gray area" of the plan remains controversial even among proponents of the council-manager plan. A major question is the extent to which the manager should be a leader in shaping municipal policies. Indeed, it seems that city managers often evaluate their own success and that of their colleagues on their ability to promote change, initiate policy, and build support mechanisms in the community, and not merely by just carrying out the council's will.[25]

Mayor-Council/Mayor-Council-Administrator

Although the mayor-council form is the second most popular local government structure among all U.S. communities, it has very limited application in Maine. As recently as 1970 there were only five mayor-council communities, which together served about 11 percent of all the state's population: Biddeford, Lewiston, Saco, Waterville, and Westbrook. All had adopted mayor-council charters in the latter half of the nineteenth century, which provided for the election of bicameral legislative bodies by wards and a mayor elected at large. Although the mayor was designated the "chief executive," administrative and financial powers also were vested in the legislative body. Waterville was the last to abandon bicameralism in 1967. Mayors and council members serve concurrent terms; voters can therefore change all elected officials during each election. With the exception of Lewiston and Biddeford, these all have a partisan nomination and election process. They also have substantial Franco-American populations.

Since the variations of the mayor-council form are rather wide in these five communities in Maine, each city's governmental structure will be described separately. For example, Westbrook created an ordinance for the position of "Administrative Assistant to the Mayor." It retained the concept of a "strong" mayor system, since the mayor has broad powers of appointment, administration, and handling legislation. The Westbrook mayor's initial appointments of the administrative assistant and department heads are subject to the approval of the council, but all reappointments to these positions are decided solely by the mayor. The mayor still has the power of veto on decisions by the council, which includes budgetary matters; and also the mayor was granted power over certain legislative functions of the council.

For more than four decades, Waterville maintained a strong mayor system of government, and its charter designated the mayor as chief executive officer and head of the administration for city government operations. Its charter also gave the mayor broad powers of appointment of city officers, with council approval, and authorized the mayor to remove city employees, with some exceptions, without council approval. Waterville mayors used their veto power over council decisions, including the line-item veto of the budget. The charter also established the office of "city administrator" who was described as the "mayor's principal assistant," and reported directly to the mayor. While the power to appoint or remove a department head was recommended by the administrator, the final decision was made solely by the mayor.

In November 2005 the voters of Waterville approved a new city charter by a 4-to-1 margin that would dramatically change their form of government to the council-manager plan. Under the charter revision the city manager becomes the chief executive, while the mayor and city council determine policy. Thus, the mayor's role will be weakened, and a strengthened position of city manager would replace the city administrator. Accordingly, the mayor's salary was decreased by 50 percent.[26] The shift of day-to-day administration has evolved from a part-time mayor to a full-time professional.

In Biddeford, a city manager is nominated by the mayor and confirmed by the city council. The manager is responsible for the day-to-day administration of the city, such as implementing policies established by the city council. According to the city charter, the manager "must report to and receive policy guidance from the mayor and the city council" (this dual-reporting mechanism illustrates why Biddeford is still technically classified under the mayor-council form, rather than the pure council-manager form). Moreover, the mayor is still the "chief executive magistrate," and retains some significant legal authority in such areas as appointments, finance, and veto power. However, Biddeford continued to revise its charter in the 1990s and has gradually moved toward an executive-level reform. The manager prepares the budget for the finance committee and evaluates designated employees. In this case the city uses the same level of financial and management skills that a professional administrator can bring to Biddeford.

The neighboring city of Saco also displays many of the same characteristics of Biddeford's addition of an appointed professional city administrator to the traditional mayor-council option. Policy making and legislative authority are vested in the seven-member city council. The council is elected on a non-partisan basis. The mayor and all council members are elected to two-year terms from seven district wards. The city council is responsible for passing ordinances, adopting the budget, confirming mayoral nominations of committees, and the city administrator. The city administrator is responsible for carrying out the policies and ordinances of the city council, for overseeing the day- to-day operations of the city, and for appointing the heads of the city's departments, some with required city council confirmation.

Local Government Reform in Lewiston

The City of Lewiston, which had a unique mayor-council system, was once designated by University of Maine political scientist Edward F. Dow as "a government of 37 legs and no head." Its administrative and finance authority was fragmented among six boards and commissions, each with five members, a seven-member board of aldermen, and a mayor. Like many other "weak mayor-council" cities, Lewiston eventually altered its government structure. It now has a new city charter and a city administrator, who reports to an elected council and acts as the appointed executive.

During the latter part of the twentieth century some changes (i.e., closing a textile mill) altered economic, political, and social patterns. The result was more support for professionalism in local government. In addition, a significant rise of the second and third generations of the Franco-American middle class demanded more efficiency and staff expertise in city government.

Since 1980 Lewiston's city government has been a mayor/council-city administrator form of government. The new charter, approved in 1979 by Lewiston voters, brought in a "weak mayor, council-administrator government." In this structural reform, a professional administrator is responsible for supervising departments, and producing and executing the budget. The administrator reports to the city council, whose members are elected for two-year terms. The council looks to the administrative staff for assistance in creating policies, voicing budget concerns, and other business before formally conducting an open session twice a month. The council consists of seven voting ward representatives, the city administrator, and the mayor. The mayor's responsibilities include officiating council meetings, acting as "the head of the city government for all ceremonial purposes" (City Charter 2.03). The mayor has some additional authority in that he or she can break a tie vote, and appoint individuals to various boards (and some require council approval). The mayor and council are barred from interfering with the administrator's subordinates. The council, however, does reserve the power to terminate an administrator's employment.

The only other elected Lewiston board is the school board. The superintendent sits on the board as secretary and nonvoting member. Seven board members are elected to serve for two-year terms. One at-large representative is also elected from each ward. The city council president also appoints one city councilor to the board to serve as a voting member. The board chair is selected among the members. This board is somewhat unique in that it must report to the city council. Even though it functions as a fairly autonomous school board in most of its deliberations, every budget must be approved by the council, which reserves its right to make changes.

The city elections are legally nonpartisan, in an attempt to break from the traditional party domination of city politics. However, Lewiston remains a very political community. There are seven wards, five with two precincts and two wards with three precincts; council terms are for two years. Councilors and school board members can be elected to an unlimited number of terms, while mayors are restricted to two successive terms, totaling four years. Mayoral candidates must win elections by more than 50 percent, and if that number is not achieved, a runoff election is required.

Lewiston dramatically changed its city charter in 1980, and now seems to be much more closely aligned with many of the characteristics of the council-manager form, yet it still retains some aspects of the mayor-council form. It all goes to illustrate that after home rule (1969) became instituted and an accepted practice, more and more communities acted as their own "architect" and designed many different plans and organizational structures. Therein the term "hybrid" form of government began to be used more frequently, because of the new found freedom at the community level to design local governments from the bottom up.

In practice, there are and have been numerous variations over time in the specific structure of Maine's new mayor-council communities and in the actual division of power between the legislative body and elected political executive, the mayor.[27] In general, these communities followed an evolutionary pattern in urban politics associated with larger cities in the United States. Ethnic politics, which in Maine's case involve mainly Franco-American and Irish-American participants, often influenced both the structure and behavior of city governments. These communities resisted the early major prescriptions of twentieth century reformers, such as nonpartisan elections, the city manager plan, short ballots, smaller councils, home rule, and professionalism in general. While these parts of the "reform package" became operational in many other Maine cities and towns, the ethnic composition within the urban culture of these small cities continued to dominate and often restrict more drastic structural change.

However, these communities began to change incrementally by hiring professionals, even if their form of government remained the same. Pressure for competition with other communities and regions, the impact of economic growth, and the influx of new ideas from newcomers all had an effect. In the 1970s, Lewiston hired a Harvard-educated planner, and Westbrook employed a professionally trained city administrator to provide new leadership, even though not all of the "reform package" was acceptable in those cities. The middle-class reform ideology did not always go over well in these heterogeneous cities, as was also the case in Boston. The reformers wanted to take politics out of local government and eliminate the boss and machine, which were branded as corrupt, or at best inefficient. Party structure, class, and ethnicity acted as brakes on reform in these cities.

POLITICS FROM SMALL TOWN TO SMALL CITY

As earlier chapters have explained, Maine's history is one of a rural state that has recently experienced selective urban growth along Interstate 95, on the coast, and in its southern sector of York and Cumberland counties. The three Metropolitan Statistical Areas (MSAs) of Portland, Lewiston-Auburn, and Bangor; as well as the interstate MSA of Portsmouth-Rochester-Dover, New Hampshire, which extends into Southern York County and contain 40 percent of Maine's population in 2000. The four MSAs have collectively experienced moderate to rapid growth during the past three decades. Eighty percent of the U.S. population now resides in metropolitan areas. Thus, local politics in Maine takes on several basic forms—that of small-town politics, which is characterized by the large number of communities in the state under 2,500 in population, and the urban and suburban politics of Maine's four relatively small metropolitan areas.

Economist Charles Colgan explains the changing Maine landscape as follows: "with the expansions of the metro areas following the 2000 Census, which was released only in June 2003, a more accurate picture of the role of urban areas becomes clear, and the actual proportion of population in metro areas is seen to have grown, not declined."[28] Certainly, the expansion of Maine's metropolitan areas can be partially explained by the federal government's changing definition of metropolitan areas; however, another major driving force has been the geographic expansion of Maine's urban areas (since more of the economy has been concentrated in urban areas), and more people have moved to the outer metropolitan rings, away from

Table 8: Population of Maine's metropolitan statistical areas (MSAS)

MSA	1960 Census	1970 Census	1980 Census	1990 Census	2000 Census
Bangor			83,919	121,964	124,906
Lewiston-Auburn	70,295	72,474	84,864	102,889	101,778
Portland	139,122	141,625	193,831	299,765	333,624
Portsmouth, NH-ME			42,011	69,716	71,232

Sources: Based on the U.S. Bureau of Census. *Current Population Reports*, Series P-26, No. 85-ME-C, Estimates of the Population of Maine Counties and Metropolitan Areas: July 1, 1981 to 1985, (Washington DC: U.S. Government Printing Office, 1988), 7; U.S. Bureau of Census. *1990 Census of the Population and Housing*, Summary Tape File 1A, New England Divisions: Maine, issues August 1991, Data Users Services Division, Washington DC; and www.Census.gov/Population/Cen2000/phc-+29/tab09.pdf.

the central city. The end-result of recent suburbanization growth has been condemned by many as sprawl.[29]

Oliver Williams and Charles Adrian have developed a typology for different images of the proper role of government, which is especially useful in analyzing Maine's local governments. They believe that a government's role can be one of an agent of growth (active economic development strategy), a provider of amenities (additional services for a good living environment), a caretaker (basic services, low taxes), or an arbiter (managing conflict among competing interests). These possible roles may help us better understand the relationship between social and economic change, and political changes.[30] In most Maine towns, there has been a longstanding tradition of caretaker government. Only a few cities have fit the role of provider of amenities or, at times, arbiter. More recently, a number of cities and some towns have used their municipal government in an agent-of-growth role.

Small-town politics is usually practiced in relatively homogeneous and stable communities, where relationships are personal and informal. Townsfolk assume that the various community interests are more or less in harmony with each other. As Clarence Stone comments,

> Perhaps because small towns and villages tend to he socially close knit, conflict and open competition are frowned upon. So, village politics is a politics of consensus. Petty squabbling and personal rivalry may be inevitable, but they are nevertheless regarded as improper. Historically small

town life has not accommodated competition and dissent, nor have things changed much in the contemporary village.[31]

Small-town politics is usually a matter of obliging friends rather than choosing policy alternatives.[32] All too often salient issues are avoided, and politics revolves around personalities and small irritants. Limited government may be found in the town of Acton, which in the early 1990s had a year-round population of 1,900 and one police officer, eighty-three-year-old Frank Gemelli. Still other towns have no local police and must rely on the county sheriff and the state police.

Rural local government has been characterized as being run by part-time actors, as having an amateur style rather than a professional style, and as being perceived by the citizens as "nonpolitical." However, as Roscoe Martin warned in his classic statement on "The Physiology of Little Government":

> Little government, being personal, intimate, and informal is supposed by some to be free of politics. In simple truth, no concept concerning local government has less merit. The image of politics as an evil art practiced somewhere else by somebody else is, of course, quite unrealistic, for politics is found wherever people debate issues of public import.[33]

In Maine the small town has dominated because of the historical dispersion of a small population throughout a relatively large area, political non-centralization, a lack of numerous medium-size and large cities, and the early absence of substate regional administrative alternatives. However, population growth in Maine's four metropolitan areas, and along the coast and Interstate 95, is changing political traditions and landscapes. Urbanization as a movement of people into cities and their suburbs is dramatically affecting southern Maine. The greater Portland area has rapidly expanded to well over one-third of a million persons (see Tables 7 and 8).

Quite naturally, growth can be a powerful force that overruns the more primitive local governments and their caretaker outlook. New schools have to be built and services expedited. Coastal communities, especially, have experienced soaring property values and taxes that were previously associated only with urban areas to the south. Growth has meant more diversity in town government as natives and newcomers often "square off" for more extended debate on town councils or at traditional town meetings.

In 1960 Maine had almost 20 percent fewer full-time local government employees per 10,000 population than did other states (188 employees versus the national figure for states of 232 employees). This pattern was consistent with its previous historical emphasis on citizen participation, and amateur leadership and governance. While Maine had significant governmental structure, much of it was in the hands of part-time employees and volunteer citizens.[34]

By 2001 a comparative state analysis revealed that Maine local government personnel had mushroomed to 413 full-time employees per 10,000 population. Moreover, during the forty-one-year period, Maine's number of local government full-time employees had more than doubled! In 2001 Maine had exceeded the average for all states—393 employees at the local level. In fact, the rate of growth in Maine revealed an increase in municipal employment in the decade of the 1990s of almost 20 percent, compared with an overall 6 percent increase for the states nationally.[35]

University of Maine economist Philip Trostel concurs with the abundance of administration in Maine's state and local governments: ". . . recent Census Bureau data indicate that Maine has one FTE employee in state and local government administration for every 294 people. This is the fifth lowest ratio in the country (where the national average is one per 439)."[36]

GROUPS AND INDIVIDUALS: MOVERS AND SHAKERS

Influentials in Maine community politics are diverse, and range from the interest groups of the larger cities and towns to the churches and service clubs that are sometimes active in smaller towns. In a mail survey, city and town administrators (N = 219) were asked to assess the degree of influence that a list of twenty-seven groups or individuals had on local issues. The administrators answered at an 84 percent response rate.[37] Those groups receiving more than 50 percent in the three highest categories of "moderate, "high," or "very high" influence were as follows:

Key Individual Citizens	72%
Local School Board	67%
Businessmen and Merchants	67%
Maine Municipal Association	63%
Fire Department	63%
Taxpayers, Homeowners Associations	54%

Businesspeople/merchants and taxpayers/homeowners associations are perceived by the Maine managers as being influential, as is the case in other states. In Maine, fire departments rate high in influence because they are staffed with volunteers in many of the smaller communities. These volunteers are very active in the town meetings. The Maine Municipal Association has been one of the most influential interest groups representing communities in Augusta. Because of its substantial staff and credibility with local government administrators, it ranks as one of the most potent and influential organizations.

Groups which were classified by three-fourths or more of the respondents as being in the lowest categories of "none" and "low" influence were the following:

Civic Groups	85%
Republican Party Officials	83%
Democratic Party Officials	83%
Private Sector Labor Leaders	83%
Neighborhood Associations	82%
Lawyers, Legal Associations	82%
Public Utility Officials	81%
Groups of Low Income People	80%
Bankers	79%
Other Mass Media	78%
Churches or Religious Groups	77%
Chamber of Commerce	75%

However, many of the above groups are very influential in select communities, but they registered low scores on this statewide survey because some groups tend not to exist in many small communities. Some have been very active and effective in Maine's larger and medium-sized communities. Interestingly, political parties were seen as being influential in only approximately 17 percent of the communities—mainly in those cities in which the traditional form of urban politics occurs.

Groups that registered some moderate influence on local issues were newspaper editors, police departments, municipal employees or their union or association, contractors and real estate developers, environmental groups, regional planning commissions and councils of government, farmers, and high-income people.

Group Coalition in Action

An interesting development of interest group coalition building on a regional basis may be found in the Penobscot River Restoration Project, which advocates returning the river to its original free-flowing state. The objective of this significant plan is to purchase and remove several dams (in Old Town and Veazie), and then create a fish bypass at the Howland Dam. In addition, the project plans to increase power generation at six other dams from the town of Medway to Graham Lake, so approximately 96 percent of its present power generation would still continue.

One section of the coalition is composed of the following active environmental and other groups: American Rivers, the Atlantic Salmon Federation, Maine Audubon, The Natural Resources Council of Maine, and Trout Unlimited. A very important and significant member of the coalition is the Penobscot Indian Nation. These groups argue that communities need to embrace this river initiative as an economic development concept, which has positive environmental, recreational, and tourism implications. Removal of the dams would allow fish—especially salmon and sturgeon—to once again swim up and down stream without being hindered. It is estimated that the restoration of the ecology section of the project would cost around $50 million, which is supported by the U.S. Department of Interior.[38]

The Penobscot River is Maine's largest watershed and has 113 dams, twenty of which generate hydroelectric power. Another significant component to the River Restoration coalition group is Eastern Maine Development Corporation (EMDC), which works with thirteen river municipalities (from the city of Bangor to the town of Lincoln) and the Penobscot Indian Nation. There is not much economic activity for most of the smaller towns along the Penobscot River and most of the towns' visible structures are boat launches, river-front parks, and small businesses.

These impacted river communities were eager to consult the recent successful model of the Kennebec River, which had been cleared in 1999 and opened up with the removal of a key dam in Augusta. The "new river" has attracted both an influx of wildlife and numerous fishermen and boaters (also see the section on Plum Creek development in Chapter 13).

Decision-making in Maine's local governments has ranged from elitism to pluralism, where many different groups compete on different issues.[39] Domination of political institutions by a few economic elites, or by the private-sector leadership of a one-industry town, was much easier to accomplish in earlier periods of history than in the present. However, there are still fears of rich out-of-state seasonal owners and developers dominating the politics of Maine's "golden coast" and its inland lakes.

With the gradual diversification of the economic base in some areas, coupled with the strong acceptance of the town meeting and amateur government, it has been possible for the average citizen to participate in his or her local government. Findings from the earlier Maine managers' survey somewhat strengthen the argument of the pluralists. In most communities, decision making involves different alignments of power, due to the various interests of the different groups that occur within the community on different issues.

CONCLUSION

Since the 1920s, some constructive tension has existed in Maine between the need for modern management of local government and small-town and small-city cultures and politics. Many groups and individuals do become involved in the political process from time to time and can be influential. Access to the political process is usually high, but participation is high or low depending on the saliency of the issue. Where elitism exists, it tends to be in unorganized townships, small towns, and plantations that operate under the influence of a few paper companies and numerous out-of-state developers.[40] Often, however, it is some of these influential individuals (for example, philanthropist Roxanne Quimby) building or buying property for themselves.

Most important, much of Maine's growth today is suburban and southern. The outlying towns in both Cumberland and York counties experienced major growth in the 1970s and 1980s, while the growth of the major core cities (Portland, Lewiston, and Bangor) remained stable or declined slightly. Smaller coastal communities also experienced continuous growth from the 1980s to the present because of "newcomers from away" who perceive an opportunity for a high quality of life in Maine. The impact of these demographic trends on Maine's local governments will continue to be felt for years to come.

CHAPTER THIRTEEN

Substate Regionalism and State-Local Relations

Filling the gap between local and state government services has been a major concern for the State of Maine. The tension between the desire for local participation and control, and a sense of fairness in service delivery and its financial burden, has produced an impasse of sorts. This chapter examines the traditional role of county government, the establishment of a regional council system during the past three decades, the prototype initiatives for new regionalism, the programmatic use of special districts, and a growing number of other specific examples of cooperation between municipalities. North-south rivalries, as well as rivalries between communities of different population size, have heightened conflict between the state's geographic sections and metropolitan areas.

By and large, Maine has chosen not to pursue the type of drastic institutional mechanisms for solving regional problems that have been attempted in other states, such as city-county consolidation, the urban county (either the Lakewood Plan of California or the two-level approach of Miami-Dade County), or the more developed metropolitan councils formed in Minneapolis–St. Paul and in Portland, Oregon, where a great deal of authority and responsibility have been delegated to regional decision makers. Yet both recent governors King and Baldacci attempted to analyze these difficult political issues. Some communities have experimented with cooperative and voluntary ventures in working with each other. County government still remains, and many see it as another "project" with which to tinker. However, the threat to the status quo posed by the perceived need for both economic growth and protection of the environment may cause greater change in the future.

COUNTY GOVERNMENT

In his classic reform text of 1917, *The County: The 'Dark Continent' of American Politics*, H. S. Gilbertson called counties creatures of tradition that "once established, acquired a tendency to 'stick' tenaciously to their original form."[1] In some respects this conclusion remains valid for many aspects of county government in Maine.

County government has posed a particular dilemma to policymakers and analysts for many years. In New England in general, and in Maine specifically, county government has been a weak institution. In Maine reformers have coalesced into two camps—those who want to abolish counties (as was done in Connecticut), and those who want to strengthen them (as has been done in California and Florida). No one seems pleased with the status quo.

County government came to New England as a part of the English tradition in the British shire model.[2] Massachusetts created four districts in Maine for its courts in 1636. These eventually evolved into nine counties by 1820. The remaining seven counties were added after statehood. The Maine legislature of 1820 maintained the county system it inherited from Massachusetts, and most officials were appointed by the governor and council. The major role of the county was to administer justice rather than provide general services or enforce local policies. Most political responsibilities rested with the executive branch of state government.[3]

In New England, municipalities (towns and cities) emerged as the prime form of local government in the 1700s. Since that time, towns throughout New England have retained their dominant position as service providers, with counties administering only those few services required of them in their respective state constitutions. Traditionally, these mandated services have included the recording of deeds and other real estate transfers, regional law enforcement, and judicial administration.[4] Outside of New England, county government has a history of providing a stronger base that has aided in its evolution toward a general-purpose type government with significant regional responsibilities.[5]

In 1855 the appointive county officers became elective. However, there was relatively little change in the structure of Maine county government between the mid-1800s and the 1970s. The duties of county officials have remained largely administrative and narrowly defined because the county is a subunit of the state that operates under state laws. Therefore, local voters have very limited control over county affairs. Unlike towns and cities, counties were not incorporated, and until recently did not have the opportunity to create charters or utilize legislative powers.

Counties do enjoy considerably more responsibilities in the unorganized territory, where there is an absence of town or city government, and where counties provide all services not provided by the state, such as fire protection and road maintenance. Maine counties do not operate schools, welfare programs, or hospitals, as do counties in other states.

Maine county governments were responsible in the early 1900s for constructing and maintaining bridges and roads. However, since the early 1970s, these responsibilities have shifted to the state and municipal governments. Maine counties also controlled the superior courts until they were reorganized in 1975 and replaced by a more streamlined superior court system (see Chapter 8). Thus, during the 1970s, while many counties nationwide were doing more because of demographic and other pressures, Maine counties were doing less. Their major role was maintaining the sheriff's department, probate court, and the county jails. They remained one of the last bastions of partisan politics in local government, where a certain amount of patronage and favoritism could still be found.

In general, Maine's counties are rather typical of counties in other New England states because they never developed, or in some cases have abandoned, the wide array of local services (i.e., roads, schools, welfare administration) found in many counties nationwide. This was due largely to the earlier strength of the town governments and the political culture of New England communities. The town governance structure itself has been made legitimate by Maine statute.[6]

Maine's sixteen counties reflect a diversity of geographic size and population (see Table 9 and Map 1). The smallest county, Sagadahoc, covers only 254 square miles, while the largest county, Aroostook, is the size of a small state at 6,672 square miles; it is larger than Connecticut and Rhode Island combined. Ten counties have populations of 60,000 or less. In general, about half of Maine's counties are probably too small in population to become an effective sub-state regional unit of government under their present geographic boundaries, while others may be too large geographically to function effectively.

Maine counties have shared with other New England counties a long history of the absence of a strong chief executive. They also lack any real basis as a unit of self-government. Maine citizens in each county elect three commissioners to be their chief administrators. Moreover, state law has designated the offices of treasurer, sheriff, judge of probate, register of probate, and register of deeds. John Forster, a former regional planning commission executive director, argued that Maine counties derive no powers from the people, but are entirely creatures of the legislature: "They were created by the Legislature and their powers are controlled by the Legislature."[7]

Map 1. Maine counties (Source: *Annual Register of Maine*, p. 78)

Table 9: Population and land area of Maine counties

Counties	Square* miles	1980 (U.S. Census)	1990 (U.S. Census)**	2000 (U.S. Census)***
Androscoggin	470	99,509	105,259	103,793
Aroostook	6,672	91,344	86,936	73,938
Cumberland	836	215,789	243,135	265,612
Franklin	1,698	27,447	29,008	29,467
Hancock	1,589	41,781	46,948	51,791
Kennebec	868	109,889	115,904	117,114
Knox	366	32,941	36,310	39,618
Lincoln	456	26,691	30,357	33,616
Oxford	2,078	49,043	56,602	54,755
Penobscot	3,396	137,015	146,601	144,919
Piscataquis	3,966	17,634	18,653	17,235
Sagadahoc	254	28,795	33,535	35,214
Somerset	3,927	45,049	49,767	50,888
Waldo	730	28,414	33,018	38,280
Washington	2,569	34,963	35,308	33,941
York	991	139,739	164,587	186,742

Sources: *www.quickfactcensus.gov/qfd/states, 4/11/2005. **"Maine's Population Growth Grew 9.2% from 1980 to 1990," *Bangor Daily News*, January 28, 1991. ***U.S. Census Bureau and the National Association of Counties, "Census 2000: Two Maines Chasms Growing," *Bangor Daily News*, June 16, 2001.

While counties elsewhere, as in Maine, have been characterized by a plural executive (i.e., county commissioners or supervisors), most other counties nonetheless began to address the pressures of demographic shifts, population increases, cultural change, and the accompanying demands for urban services.[8] Ralph Widner has pointed out that the presence of strong county governments may explain why it has been easier for the southern states to adopt consolidated and metropolitan forms of government than other states.[9]

During the 1970s Maine counties faced the prospect of abolition at each legislative session.[10] At the same time, in some instances, they selectively assumed more functions in law enforcement, civil defense, transportation, and social services. For example, Androscoggin County provided a free bus service for elderly, handicapped, and low-income residents because of federal subsidies and local needs. County governments also took advantage of federal monies and contracts under the Comprehensive Employment and Training Act (CETA) to provide training and jobs for thousands of Mainers. These regional services were developed during the 1980s and supported by the federal government, and provided some needed adrenalin for citizen identification with Maine counties. Because of the geographic diffusion of the population and the state's relative isolation, these pressures came late. Moreover, they were diverted by the strength of small-town culture, traditional town government, and the legal limits placed on the county as a potentially self-governing body.

However, some changes did come to county government during the 1980s. A 1980 act (L.D. 1038) to provide county self-government amended existing county charter provisions (under 30 M.R.S.A., sec. 1501) and added new provisions to the state statutes. Prior to this act, counties had to submit their budgets to the legislature for approval before they could appropriate funds. Indeed, this cumbersome budget requirement was made more stringent in 1973, when a section (30 M.R.S.A., sec. 253-A) was added to give the legislature the power to "change or alter specific line categories within county estimates." Thus, two of the more significant provisions of the 1980 act provided for a method of appropriating money for county expenditures other than the past statutory method (in 30 M.R.S.A., sections 2, 252, and 253), and provided for the establishment of a finance committee as an alternative method for approving the county budget.[11]

Even with these incremental changes, Maine counties do not possess a pure home-rule option. The legislation enables counties to adopt charters, but unlike under municipal home rule, counties may not adopt a charter granting any power that the legislature has not already granted them. For example, the legislature has not granted counties the power to levy taxes on citizens; therefore, they cannot adopt a charter that would allow them to do so.[12]

There has been a perception among many state and municipal officials that county government is rather expensive for the limited services received. In 1988 counties received slightly less than $30 million in property tax revenues, whereas the municipalities collected more than $700 million. Counties in Maine continue to be "weak" when compared with towns and cities (as is the case in the other New England states). Counties receive about 30 percent of their funds from fees and charges. For example, in Maine all persons convicted of Class D and E crimes (mostly misdemeanors) and persons sentenced to prison for nine months or less must be housed in county jails. The state reimburses the counties for these costs. Counties also share in the state tax on the transfer of real estate and these funds help support the office of recorder of deeds.[13]

After the 1996 legislative session, all but two counties were empowered to enact their own budgets. In some cases, the commissioners enacted the budget; while in others it was the responsibility of a special budget committee, which usually included some municipal officials.

Even though gradual change has occurred regarding county self-government, few Maine counties actually have tried to adopt charters. York, Androscoggin, and Hancock tried unsuccessfully to adopt county charters through referendums. Cumberland County was successful in establishing a charter commission, but when the newly drafted charter proposal went to the voters in 1985 and 2002, it was defeated.[14] Only voters in Aroostook and Knox have adopted a county charter.

By the 1990s gradual experimentation provided for the option of a professional county administrator, a reform prescription that has long been suggested by those who have urged the adoption of the county manager form of government.[15] The new Maine statute reads as follows:

> The county administrator shall be the chief administrative official of the county and shall be responsible for the administration of all departments and offices over which the county commissioners have control. He shall act as the clerk of the county. He shall act as purchasing agent for all departments and offices of the county, provided that the county commissioners may require that all purchases greater than a designated amount shall be submitted to sealed bid. He shall attend all meetings of the county commissioners, except when his removal or suspension is being considered. He shall keep the county commissioners and the legislative delegation of the county informed as to the financial condition of the county and shall collect all data necessary for the preparation of the budget.

Currently twelve of Maine's sixteen counties have adopted the county administrator form. The initial lack of support may be explained in part by earlier restrictions placed on continuing the salaries of the county commissioners: if a county adopted the plan, commissioners would lose most of their salary base. In May 1988 the legislature chose to exempt only York and Aroostook counties from the restrictions because the proponents of change argued that their solution would encourage those counties that have already shown some previous initiative, while continuing to compensate the elected commissioners for their participation. As an example of this gradual trend toward appointed leadership, Roland "Danny" Martin, a former town manager and legislator, was appointed county administrator by the Aroostook County commissioners in 1987, while David Adjutant assumed the same position in York County in 1984. In November 1989 the voters of Aroostook

County approved a charter that established a nine-member finance committee to help implement the "home-rule" procedure of approving the county budget.

By 2007 about three-fourths of the Maine counties had added a county administrator to their governmental structure, including fairly recently several rural counties with relatively small populations. Knox County hired a manager in 2005 and Waldo County may eventually join this group. Maine has been long known as a state that produces numerous town and city managers and now it appears that a majority of the counties will have appointed chief executives, with varying degrees of authority and responsibility. These administrators will oversee day-to-day finance, personnel, and the "housekeeping business" of county government. Maine's political culture supports the notion of an appointed, professional chief executive to help manage its towns and cities, so in some respects, this is a natural process of change that has been long overdue.

There are many different variations in how each county's set of commissioners have decided to govern. At one end of the continuum is Cumberland County, which comprises much of the greater Portland area, where the manager became the state's "strongest" county manager. By 2007 experienced County Manager Peter Crichton oversaw eleven departments with a $35 million budget, which included four hundred employees and a $1.5 million capital improvement plan. Crichton previously spent a decade in the City of Lewiston as a public works administrator and an assistant manager, received an MPA degree from the University of Maine in 1998, and earned $82,000 as the Cumberland County manager.

At the other end of the continuum is the very rural Piscataquis County, which is Maine's second largest county geographically and very sparsely populated by approximately seventeen thousand people. Michael Henderson, formerly an experienced Marine Corps administrator, who received an MPA at the University of Maine, became this county's first manager in 2004. The "rookie" manager was paid a starting salary of $47,500, and is responsible for a $3.7 million budget and ninety employees. He also administers an unorganized township budget of $961,000, which is funded by the state. When a long-time employee retired as clerk, the commissioners voted to make the structural changes and hire a professional administrator.[16] It is clear that this manager has limited authority and assists the three commissioners in implementing their policies. The commissioners still view themselves as a plural executive.

Some counties have incrementally expanded their programs beyond the traditional service areas (law enforcement services for the sheriff's department, jails, and probate judges). Lincoln County, for example, operates a recycling center and has a planning and economic development office. Penobscot County has been heavily involved in developing a Regional Communications Center (911 system) that now includes most all of the county's municipalities. There is the prospect of saving taxpayers money by avoiding duplication of services and helping more than fifty communities fulfill the stringent state emergency dispatching requirements. For some years the City of Bangor had withheld its support for this major initiative due to a fear of the loss of its local control, a reduction of quality service, and the probability of false savings.[17]

Another example of regional cooperation at the county level occurred when the state police and the Penobscot County Sheriff's Department signed a formal "Resource Coordination Agreement" to cooperate and improve the overall law enforcement coverage in the county area. The agreement states that "work shifts from each agency would be mirrored, with one crew from the state police working the same hours as one from the Sheriff's Department."[18] Sharing these shifts should make it easier for deputies and troopers to exchange information, and coordinate investigations. Previously, officers might have to wait long hours before communicating with the investigator they needed.[19] The agreement also divided the county into two geographic sectors, with each agency covering half of the county. Each group may also cover the other's section, where needed. Thus, the goal of more seamless, sub-state regional coverage becomes possible.

Another example of new county initiatives occurred when the Washington County commissioners and the county budget committee provided the catalyst to facilitate the creation of a new quasi-municipal ambulance authority. Eastport's city manager and the chair of the Washington County Emergency Medical Service Authority said the county's financial contributions would help establish a regional ambulance operation, which served seventeen communities with seven to nine ambulances.[20]

REGIONAL PLANNING DISTRICTS
AND COUNCILS OF GOVERNMENT

In response to a 1969 Office of Management and Budget (OMB) circular that called for greater federal coordination within substate regions, Gov. Kenneth Curtis issued an executive order to establish a uniform system of planning and development districts:

1. Districts should be made large enough to encompass as many state and federal programs as possible, but small enough in geographic

size to permit travel from peripheries of the district to the district's service center within a desired one-hour driving time.

2. Each district should have a population base sufficient to finance an adequate regional planning and development technical staff. A population base of 100,000 was considered sufficient for adequate local financial support based on present local support of regional planning commissions augmented by federal and state grants.

3. The districts should cover the entire state. Each district should include organized and unorganized territory. Districts should also be balanced in regard to real estate valuation and urban and rural population.

4. In no instance should a district boundary cut through a local governing unit (not applicable to counties or unorganized towns or plantations).

5. Districts should encompass total economic, environmental, and human resource areas where possible.[21]

The original eight planning districts were based on the geography of Maine's major river basins. Regional planning districts could not levy taxes or buy or sell property; and in general they were not delegated the legal authority of cities or towns. Instead they were to develop comprehensive plans for their regions and provide technical assistance to help communities deal with regulations and obtain grants for programs in air and water pollution, solid waste projects, growth management, and shoreland zoning. Their role was to advise municipalities. In general the regional councils hire staff and focus on activities where they find a demand for services.

In Maine there are currently eleven regional planning and development districts served by eleven regional councils, which consist of five councils of governments (COGs) (located in Portland, Lewiston-Auburn, Bangor, Augusta, and Calais) and six regional planning commissions (RPCs) (see Map 2). One regional council area, previously represented by the Southern MidCoast Regional Planning Commission, was once without a regional planning agency for several years. The State Planning Office filled this gap by using some of its own staff, and by reserving some monies normally allocated to the regional councils for use in the southern mid-coast region. Eventually, a restructured Municipal Regional Planning Organization of Lincoln County was formed and later renamed Lincoln County Planning Area.

Regional councils serve more than 350 dues-paying municipalities within

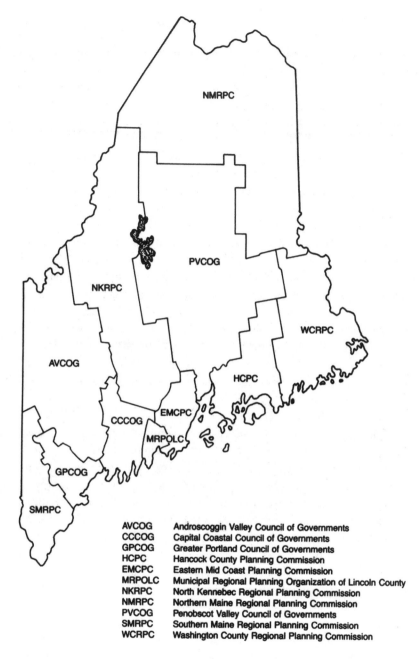

AVCOG	Androscoggin Valley Council of Governments
CCCOG	Capital Coastal Council of Governments
GPCOG	Greater Portland Council of Governments
HCPC	Hancock County Planning Commission
EMCPC	Eastern Mid Coast Planning Commission
MRPOLC	Municipal Regional Planning Organization of Lincoln County
NKRPC	North Kennebec Regional Planning Commission
NMRPC	Northern Maine Regional Planning Commission
PVCOG	Penobscot Valley Council of Governments
SMRPC	Southern Maine Regional Planning Commission
WCRPC	Washington County Regional Planning Commission

Map 2. Regional councils and their boundaries (*Source*: Penobscot Valley Council of Governments)

their jurisdictions. It is interesting to note that approximately 140 towns are not active members of a regional council. These towns indirectly receive certain benefits from the regional councils because some funding sources require services that provide benefits to the entire region. Nonmember communities may also derive spillover benefits from transportation and economic development activities in neighboring communities.[22]

Maine's regional councils received their funding from a variety of sources, including local and regional governments, the state, state-administered federal grants, direct federal grants, and miscellaneous sources. Funding for all regional councils exceeded $3 million in 1987–88, or about $300,000 for each council. This average was skewed toward the two largest units, the Greater Portland Council of Governments (more than $1 million) and Androscoggin Valley Council of Governments (almost $1 million). The eight smallest regional councils had average revenues only in the thousands of dollars. However, there was a growing consensus among regional council directors that it became more difficult to break down funding for just the regional councils/COGs because most of these are not really a single entity anymore. Most regional councils and COGs now function along with some type of planning entity; and although funding sources from regional councils/COGs differ from the planning entities, their financial "bottom line" comes down to combined funding.[23]

After the 1983 Blaine House Conference on State and Local Relations concluded that regional approaches to delivering public services should be encouraged, and that intergovernmental communications needed to be improved, Gov. Joseph E. Brennan issued an executive order encouraging state-local partnerships through regional COGs.[24] Regional councils were viewed as providing a useful forum for local officials to exchange ideas, express opinions, and work with state and federal officials to improve intergovernmental responsibilities and set priorities for public investments. Regional councils were seen as providers of assistance to local officials and as mechanisms for implementing state programs. The latter reason was debated by many town officials, who valued their local autonomy. In addition, the governor's order stated that the regional councils can assist state and local governments in identifying effective cost-saving measures.

It was further ordered that state agencies would use regional councils, as appropriate, to assist them in planning programs, setting priorities, and delivering services to local governments. Moreover, the regional councils would be defined as "Councils of Governments,"[25] which in Maine means that at least half of the representatives of each member municipality in a regional council must be elected municipal officials. RPCs had been composed of mainly appointed officials. The Penobscot Valley Council of Governments (Greater Bangor Region) moved quickly to take advantage of the COG status.

Thus, in the face of pending and actual federal cutbacks during the 1980s, the governor's order attempted to link the state government to the RPC delivery system more effectively and to strengthen it by further promoting the COG concept. Previously, only the Greater Portland Council of Governments had evolved beyond the RPC status.[26]

THE ROUGH ROAD TO NEW REGIONALISM

Faced with the loss of regular federal funding during the 1980s (Reagan-Bush I years), Maine's Regional Councils were forced to be much more entrepreneurial in order to survive as effective sub-state regional districts and, at the same time fill the gaps (between the municipalities and state government). In some respects they played the role of "consulting companies" to help implement some of the state's policies in planning and growth management, solid waste management, conservation, and transportation. As PVCOG Director Dean Bennett explained:

> "Maine RPCs and COGs receive their funding from a variety of sources. These sources include municipal dues, State Agencies and through contract generation. There is a great disparity among RPCs and COGs in terms of funding sources and functions. This is due primarily to the inconsistent funding of these organizations and other measures to ensure their survival. These organizations share common elements as they are municipally created for and on behalf of municipal governments. They perform primarily planning services directed toward assisting municipal governments (with their home rule powers to create and enact comprehensive plans and land use regulations). In addition, RPCs and COGs are utilized by various state agencies in their efforts to educate and promote state-initiated programs."[27]

However, many of their new activities had little direct regional impact, but were oriented to their clientele at the town and city level, such as providing technical services to subdivision and site plan reviews, comprehensive plans, and zoning ordinances.

More than 70 percent of Maine's population resides in a corridor twenty miles wide on each side of the interstate highway from Kittery to Houlton. This density contrasts dramatically with approximately 40 percent of Maine's land mass of unorganized territory in primarily the northwestern part of the state, which according to the 2000 Census has only 7,600 residents. This area is characterized largely by its 423 unorganized townships, but includes no municipalities. It is supervised and taxed directly by the state. Maine's Land Use Regulation Commission is responsible for the planning and implementation of numerous policies within this huge area of 10.3 million acres.

In 1997 during the Angus King Administration, there was a renewed interest in regional approaches that could possibly have led to greater efficiencies at the local government level. A twenty-one-member task force on Intergovernmental Structure was formed with representatives from all public sectors (state, municipalities, counties, school districts, and select academic advisors). This "inner-circle," led by Evan Richert, director of the State Planning Office, studied the maze of Maine's governmental units and recommended a number of constructive changes (e.g., reorganizing and streamlining county government, especially the elimination of elections for sheriffs and promoting changes in their reporting authority). According to Richert, the unanimous recommendation of the committee's "Proposal to Reduce the Cost of Government through Reform of Governmental Relations," would have reduced property taxes collected by the counties by 62 percent. It would have greatly expanded the opportunity for joint municipal services, using county government as the vehicle.[28] However, by 1998 there was little consensus among the various stakeholders when the task force's recommendations went public, and eventually the King Administration moved on to other more pressing concerns. Earlier legislative studies in 1989 and 1997 had also suggested major changes, especially to county government, but their recommendations were largely ignored.

The task force's report also would have modernized Maine county government and brought it closer to the national county government models outside of New England. To accomplish this restructuring there would be adjustment of county boundaries, substitution of state-county revenue sharing for local property taxes (to fund the delivery of such state services as jails) and limits on property taxes that could be charged for county services. Finally, the report touted the reduction of duplications and promised improvement in cooperation between all types of governmental units—towns, cities, counties, and the state.[29]

When Gov. John Baldacci assumed his office in 2003, the financial burdens of state and local government had continued to swell. Maine's three largest cities (Portland, Lewiston, and Bangor) were still gradually losing population, and the cost of providing the rapidly growing outlying communities with schools, roads, and appropriate personnel to manage them had dramatically increased. In fact, it was reported that "Maine state government alone spent approximately $338 million on new school construction, predominantly in the fast-growing towns, even though the state's school population dropped by 27,000 between 1970 and 1995."[30]

In early 2004 Governor Baldacci proposed new legislation that soon became law, which encouraged partnerships and consolidations for both municipalities and school systems. Previously in the first session of the 121st Legislature (2003) he had proposed a blueprint for municipal service districts, which would have had rather extensive authority. Towns and cities in these districts would receive additional funds, but in turn would relinquish some of their homerule powers. Facing strong opposition from the Maine Municipal Association, the legislature did not endorse this concept. Thereafter, the governor moved to more moderate and cooperative, voluntary approaches.[31]

LD. 1930 "An Act to Promote Intergovernmental Cooperation, Costs Savings and Efficiencies," included competitive planning grants, which would create regional plans and additional funding for implementation of up to $200,000. In March 2005 the grants were made available through the "Fund for Efficient Development of Local and Regional Services." What followed was an active "feeding frenzy" of grant proposals from groups of communities, who hoped to take advantage of the new law. The "new regionalism" era in Maine would now be characterized by a number of experiments in various regional approaches where groups of cities and towns would be encouraged to cooperate.

For example, the Penobscot Valley Council of Governments (PVCOG) proposed to obtain a state grant that would lower local government costs through pooling its communities' purchasing power. PVCOG's membership includes eighty-nine communities in Penobscot and Piscataquis counties. Approximately half of these member municipalities have previously taken part in a cooperative program each year. For twenty-five years PVCOG had coordinated a successful bulk purchasing program, which included salt for roads and heating fuel.[32] However, the advent of this newest grant system would facilitate a process whereby its well-tested model could also be shared with other regions. Once the model became operational it could even be replicated within a six county service area (of the Eastern Maine Development Corporation's parent organization). Most importantly, PVCOG would formally serve as the district's purchasing agent. By using the district's buying power to obtain lower prices, major savings could be passed on to the taxpayer.[33]

The state first agreed to provide $1 million in its program to encourage communities to plan for consolidating some of their services. Governor Bal-dacci said that these funds would be used, "as a means of exploring the joint delivery of services, as one way to reduce local government spending and counteract escalating property taxes."[34] The money was awarded to twenty-six collaborating groups of local governments, which comprise some 121 municipalities and other participants such as school districts and counties.

Typical examples for approved state grants were: Regionalization of Assessment Services, Regional Financial Accounting Center, Multi-town Curbside Recycling Project, Regional Assessing Program, Storm Water Working Group, and Regional Recycling Center. In summary, a total of $134,500 was dedicated to the planning grants, while $865,500 was direct-ed toward the implementation of cooperative service grants.

But the winds of political change were not powerful enough to harness both state and local support, and what was a central issue in 2003 and 2004 was given less attention in 2005. As reported by Mark Peters: "Gone are pro-posals to give more state dollars to communities that created new 'regional school districts' and 'municipal service districts.' Even a second-wave grant program to provide money for cooperation across town lines didn't survive the past legislative session."[35]

During the winter of 2005 Baldacci had proposed another grant fund that both schools and municipalities could use to help formulate and imple-ment cooperative agreements. But the governor and the legislature were soon forced to cut back these funds to increase spending on education and thereby close the gap in the state's two-year budget cycle.

SPECIAL DISTRICTS AND SCHOOL DISTRICTS

Special-purpose districts represent a type of government established by law to deliver a specific service. They are designed for a single purpose, as op-posed to the general-purpose units, such as towns and cities. Boundaries of special districts may encompass territory within jurisdictional lines of one community, conform to municipal boundaries, or include parts of more than one community. This type of governmental unit is considered here because of its potential and actual use in providing regional services.

Special districts have proliferated both nationwide and in Maine, yet the number of the state's special districts or single purpose governments is small when compared to many other states. There are between three and four hundred in Maine, depending on what particular type of substate dis-trict classification system is used and whether purely local or state districts are counted.[36] The first known special district in Maine was founded in 1903 when the Augusta Water District was established by special legislation. Until 1941 the "private and special" act was used to form all special districts. However, soil and conservation districts were shortly thereafter authorized by general law. Several other variations have been established since the 1940s, including school districts and housing authorities. These districts were created under general law and must be established by specified procedures for local or regional action, but without legislative participation. The legislature still retains its right to establish any type of special district.[37]

In Maine, these special-purpose districts are legally considered separate local governments with their own authority to levy taxes, deliver services, sign contracts, and sell property. Most have been established in Maine to govern light and power, sanitation, water, and education services. Sanitation and water districts must be established by a special legislative act. Their administrative body or board of directors may be either elected by the voters or appointed by the municipal officials within the boundaries of the district. Light and power districts are also established by legislative special acts, but must be formally approved by the district voters.[38] During the early 1950s there was a Bangor Recreation Center district, created with its own board of directors, to provide a mechanism for issuing bonds to fund construction of the Bangor Auditorium. In some cases, districts have even been established to satisfy particular interest groups.[39]

Special districts allow communities to charge user fees to those who benefit from the services, which helps to raise additional revenue. Some districts, such as those in the natural resources area, were successful in taking advantage of state and federal aid. Moreover, special district boundaries can often include more than one community, which presents local decision makers with still another option in regional problem solving. This often allows decision makers to bypass the perplexing limits of boundary and taxation problems for service areas. Thus, enabling laws facilitate the creation of the following multi-municipal special districts: lake watershed protection, sanitary, electric, municipal transportation, and refuse disposal.

There was growing evidence that regionalism in Maine had evolved into a new phase by the mid-1980s.[40] Pressure for landfill closures by the Department of Environmental Protection and the passage of Maine's Solid Waste Management Law, which established bold recycling goals, helped to stimulate the exploration of many forms of area-wide service delivery. Regional experimentation included establishing disposal districts (i.e., the Boothbay Regional Refuse Disposal District with four towns and the Penobscot Valley Refuse Disposal District with thirty-three participating member communities). There was an early infatuation with privatization in the latter, multimember special district in the greater Bangor area. However, tipping fees were eventually increased in midstream of an agreed-upon contract between the privately owned PERC plant and the participating communities. Political fallout included an uproar in most communities and public perceptions of some mistrust and rigidity with this regional approach.

It is important to note that special districts have been criticized on the following grounds:

1. They are often insulated from the citizens, who seldom understand them or have contacts or access to the district government.

2. The degree of citizen apathy is often high, which reduces voting for the directors where elected.

3. Overlapping powers of districts and municipalities can cause inaction, confusion, or delay.

4. Inefficiencies and waste may occur because of duplication of equipment and employees between districts and municipalities.

5. The boards of directors are often unresponsive to the community's elected officials and to citizen input when it does occur.

Why, then, have special districts been popular in Maine as well as the nation? They facilitate a very flexible response to local government problems with their variable boundaries. Where traditional general-purpose government cannot act, special districts have the capability to help fill this vacuum. Many districts have been established merely to avoid the debt and taxing limits placed on the municipality by the state. Thus, special districts can become a convenient mechanism to perform additional functions. For example, the City of Lewiston has continued to add numerous new districts and authorities over the last several decades to the point where some consultants and academics alike have questioned their cumulative impacts on citizen awareness and participation.

Others have challenged the basic assumptions of the opponents of special districts. As Robert Hawkins stated: "Our studies lead to two conclusions: (1) that there are few economies of scale to be realized for most governmental services, and (2) that where they can be realized it is through variously structured organizations, including special districts." Relying on public choice theory as a framework and reviewing special districts in California, Hawkins concluded that districts are a responsive form of local government. Moreover, a fragmented structure will increase the efficiency and responsiveness of local government because elected officials will compete for scarce public resources, community support, and new ideas about how government should operate.[41] For these proponents, special districts are not seen as illogical units of local government, but instead as organizational choices that may be used when traditional local government experiences operational limits.[42]

Nationwide, districts have been established for virtually every service: fire protection, sanitation, transit, highways, soil conservation, parks and recreation, insect abatement, cemetery, library, irrigation and water conservation, drainage, hospitals, and housing. Clearly natural resources, fire protection, and education have been among the most used districts. Special districts have provided Maine officials with a politically palatable alternative to address some of their growing service-delivery concerns. However, in taking advantage of this option, officials may have postponed the need to explore cooperative regional problem solving, unless there is a regional dimension to the district.

Special districts represent the growth industry of American local governments. From 1952 to 1997 they increased 182.5 percent (to 22,364), while cities increased by 15.5 percent and school districts declined by 75.6 percent. Overall, the role of special districts is somewhat limited in the New England region, except for the State of Massachusetts, when compared to other regions.[43]

School Administrative Districts and Community School Districts

School districts in Maine are really one more specific application of the special-district concept (although the U.S. Bureau of Census classifies them as a separate form of local government). The school district reorganization movement, which gathered momentum in the 1930s, reduced the number of school districts nationwide. While circumstances often varied from state to state, such contributing factors included changes in social and economic conditions that created demands for new and better services, developments in transportation and communication resulting in population changes, high per-pupil costs of the smaller schools and an inadequate tax base, and declining population in rural areas and movement to larger communities.[44] Subsequently, the number of school districts in the United States declined by about 40 percent over the decade from 1942 to 67,346 in 1952, and districts currently number around thirteen thousand.[45]

It seems likely that Maine's geographic isolation, sizable rural population, and small-town domination, contributed to postponing this national trend. However, throughout its history, the organization of Maine's local schools has been in constant flux. An evolutionary pattern developed from its early roots in the Massachusetts Bay Colony, to the district and town systems of the nineteenth century. Additional reorganization efforts occurred with the creation of supervisor unions in 1918 and community school districts in 1947.[46] In order to establish a district, the community school board within the proposed district must first vote to apply to the state Department of Education for permission to form a district. Majority votes in each community are required for final approval. School Administrative Districts, or SADS as they are commonly called, include all grade levels, while Community School Districts (CSDS) may limit the number of grades. The latter districts allow a town to retain its own elementary school and then send its youth to a regional high school. In both types of school districts the school board members are elected in proportion to the populations of the communities that form the district.

In many respects, the SAD legislation (Sinclair Act) approved during the Muskie administration in 1957 has been Maine's boldest effort at service delivery beyond town boundaries. As Stephen Bailey's study reported:

> Education may not have been Mr. Muskie's specialty, but Maine schools clearly needed help and the Sinclair Bill, unpalatable as some of its provisions might be to Yankee localists, was about the best help the State had in its power to give.[47]

Because of this significant act, many district mergers occurred between towns, ending the classic one-room school tradition in some towns and the school sports' rivalries that reflected a single town's culture. In 2005, Maine had 74 SADS, 15 community school districts, 34 unions, and 78 cities or towns with their own systems. There is also one school unit within the unorganized territory of Maine, which is identified as the "Division of State School in Unorganized Territory." This huge geographic division operates six schools with an enrollment of 202 students. Approximately one thousand other resident pupils attend the nearest public school system.

Much of the intergovernmental service debate by the turn of the twenty-first century focused on the perceived need to further consolidate Maine's school districts. Governor King had previously formed a task force and spoke out on the inefficiencies in the smaller school districts. Governor Baldacci also formed several task forces and had tried desperately to push new legislation that would require more school district consolidations.[48] However, opponents argued that the proposed legislation was incredibly complicated and would further escalate the incentive money, as a new district grew in size, not in efficiency; nor did it address the chronic problem of rising school costs. Baldacci first settled on a strategy to encourage groups of two or more school districts to merge into single governing bodies, where each combined district would have at least one thousand students. His ambitious blueprint also encouraged five or more school districts to join together in "regional cooperatives" that would jointly provide regional services and programs.[49] Based on their size, these districts would be promised 7.5 percent to 10 percent increases in state aid. The governor had long concluded that Maine had far too many school districts and noted that "eight districts have fewer than 250 students."[50] He felt that consolidation would provide more specialized courses (e.g., Advanced Placement and Programs) for more students, while at the same time returning more money to the taxpayers. The governor intimated that the state really needed a "Sinclair Act II" to reduce the number of school districts through further consolidations.

In 2005 Maine operated 711 schools, and 290 school administrative units, which provide education to over 208,000 students. Education Professor David Silvernail reports that this heavy load is "on average, one school district for every 730 students, one administrator for every 200 students, and one school board member for every 115 students."[51] A state task force report found evidence that many of these districts and schools were very costly—approximately $400 to $600 more per student than the larger districts.[52] A report on the School Administrative Unit Task Force Proponents of Change argued that their evidence proves larger school districts can achieve the same or better results than the smaller districts.

However, a growing coalition of various citizens, school board members, professional school administrators, and teachers are desperately trying to preserve Maine's numerous small rural school districts. They even offered strong opposition to the voluntary regionalism and consolidation alternatives. The demographics, however, project school enrollments to decrease by 10 percent by 2010, which would mean a further decline of approximately eighteen thousand students.[53]

The State Board of Education released an architectural and engineering-oriented study in 2005 that revealed major inefficiencies of schools with smaller enrollments, as they require more square footage per student. The student and staff-shared areas (e.g., gymnasiums, auditoriums, libraries, hallways, etc.) do not decrease at the same proportional rate as the number of students have done and are projected to do. The report concluded, "with limited state resources available for capital construction, encouraging consolidation in order to build larger schools is in the best interest of the state's expenditure for capital construction projects."[54] The report was touted as one more piece of evidence that sizeable efficiencies could be obtained by school consolidation. Currently 70 percent of all school construction is paid for by the state.

Opponents of the study, such as Keith Cook, coordinator for the Small Schools Coalition, were quick to respond, saying that "You need to look at the effectiveness side as well as the cost." He also noted that small schools have a lower dropout rate, which helped low-income families stay off of unemployment, welfare, and Medicaid programs.[55] The state government also examines the effectiveness of education programs and the distances between schools, when dividing up state funds for school construction. Because of Maine's large land mass and its many less-densely-populated areas, Maine's schools are generally "small" compared to most other states' averages and national standards.

Phil Trostel, professor of economics at the University of Maine, and research assistant Kate Reilly have argued that there are economies of scale to be found through various types of consolidation without a loss of student performance. Compared with other states, Maine has the eleventh most-expensive public schools per student, yet teachers salaries are still ranked thirteenth from the bottom; Maine schools average 290 students, when the national average is 506; Maine school districts average only 734 students, while the national average is 3,177. Some reformers even suggested expanding school district regions by making their boundaries parallel to the 35 state senate districts. They claim in theory that the $70 million now spent each year on administration could be reduced to $40 million with these changes.[56]

An impasse of sorts had developed between the state and local governments until Governor Baldacci found some needed support from the legislature to help move ahead on a significant plan for school district consolidations. The state's 290 school administrative units are managed by 190 school superintendents. Representative Emily Cain of Orono was the head of a four-member subcommittee of the Appropriations Committee that designed a plan which would reduce the state's 290 school administrative units to about eighty school districts with at least two thousand students per district. The new regional school districts would be governed by a regional board with a set number of members from the various municipalities. Districts of at least 1,200 students would be allowed (when geography or demographics made it nearly impossible to consolidate the schools into one large regional district). Some previous state demands were granted exceptions so that certain school districts (e.g., Native American Schools, those in isolated areas, or those on islands) could remain the same. The school consolidation bill was signed into law in June 2007 and is expected to be mostly implemented by late 2009. Currently in Maine about $2 billion a year is being spent by state and local governments on pre-kindergarten through twelfth grade. Projections by University of Southern Maine's Center for

Policy, Applied Research and Evaluation predicted savings with school districts greater than 2,500 students to be around $114 million for one year and $342 million in three years. Finally, part of the projected savings would go to needed tax relief from the areas of education and human services. The state's own estimates for the first fiscal year showed $36 million saved.

Other Cooperative Solutions

Maine citizens ultimately will have to balance the increased costs and demand for services with their traditional values of local participation and control. Informal cooperation between towns, such as regional meetings among professional administrators (town managers, planners, assessors, etc.), and formal cooperative arrangements for mutual assistance have a rich history in Maine. One voluntary, cooperative option that may see more use in the future is the right of local governments to enter into contracts with other towns and cities as well as counties and the private sector.[57] Under the Interlocal Cooperation Act of 1963, municipalities are allowed to contract for the joint handling of obligations, but relatively few cases were reported until the mid-1980s. In some instances, these arrangements have evolved from an informal mutual-aid pact (e.g., especially for police and fire services) to a formal contract between two or more local governments. Because of economies of scale, many very small communities may be forced to cooperate with larger units, such as towns and cities, COGs, and county governments, for full services. Coastal Lincoln County and the city of Presque Isle in northern Maine serve as different examples of a contracted-host option.

A mail survey of 219 city and town managers was conducted in 1987 and produced an 84 percent response rate.[58] Maine municipal managers (32 percent) felt that entering into joint service or purchasing agreements with other governments has been a "major or moderately used strategy" by their communities. Another 32 percent reported it as a minor strategy, while 35 percent reported it was "not used." Moreover, 27 percent of the managers verified that contracting out services to the private sector was a major or moderately used strategy in their communities, 29 percent reported it as a "minor" strategy, while 45 percent reported not using this technique. In the mid-1990s, a related study by the Maine Development Foundation reported fifty-eight respondents had listed 349 inter-local agreements and only three respondents failed to mention any agreement.[59]

Interlocal agreements such as the Camden/Lincolnville/Hope/Rockport Solid Waste Facility on Maine's coast and the Northern Aroostook Regional Incinerator Facility are earlier examples of the trend toward necessary

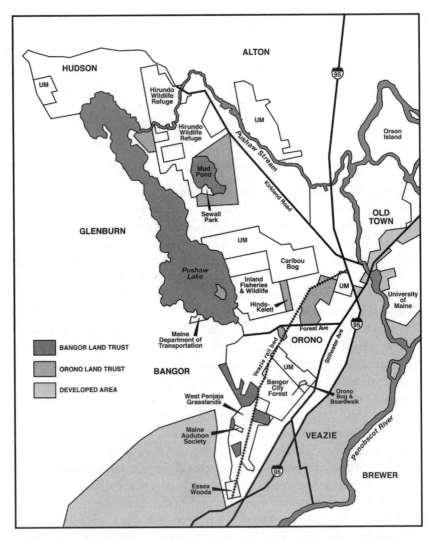

Map 3. Caribou Bog Penjajawoc Project (*Source*: MEGIS Data, Corridor Map by Chick Crockett; University of Maine Forest Service, Maine Office GIS; *Bangor Daily News*)

cooperation among communities. Under Maine law there are several possibilities. One basic interlocal agreement option does not create a separate
legal or administrative entity. Thus, major financial or property-related decisions must be approved by the various legislative bodies of the proposed
membership. Another more complex type of interlocal arrangement—the
"Interlocal Corporation"—creates a separate legal or administrative entity.
Regional Waste Systems, Inc. in Portland (twenty members), Mid-Maine
Waste Action Corporation in Auburn (twelve members), and Sandy River
Waste Recycling Association in Franklin County (seventeen members) fit
into this category.[60] While these entities lack the authority to tax, they do
provide for local control over the organizational design through a negotia-
tion process among the participants.

Another different budding form of regionalism became a reality when the
Bangor and Orono land trusts began planning and working together. By building rapport with numerous communities, they were able to create public access and new opportunities in the Bangor metropolitan area. More than 900
acres were purchased in this major land conservation and public recreation
project. Eventually, the plan was named the "Caribou Bog—Penjajawoc Project: A Conservation/Recreation Corridor." Several patrons of conservation had
already purchased 1,100 acres of the Caribou Bog in 2004 and agreed to sell
part of it to the land trusts for conservation purposes; and thereby hopefully
preserve this huge track of land for use as a regional recreation and wildlife
habitat. The two lead land trusts (Bangor and Orono) began "a collaborative
regional plan for a conservation and recreation corridor connecting Bangor to
Veazie, Orono, Old Town, Alton, Hudson, and other large blocks of wildlife
habitat further north."[61] The group bought land and negotiated conservation
easements on a ribbon-like strand of land that will connect Hirundo Wildlife
Refuge, Penjajawoc Marsh and the Bangor City Forest. Additional conserved
land straddles the Orono–Old Town border and includes a major portion of
the Caribou Bog, and a mile of shore land on Pushaw Lake. Many other supportive groups and agencies such as the Maine Chapter of the Nature Conservancy, Maine Audubon, Maine Department of Inland Fisheries, and Wildlife
and numerous private donors have been working to obtain funding from the
Land for Maine's Future's Program and Outdoor Heritage Fund. This represents a long-term, incremental project that will encourage regional planning
and further enhance the quality of life in this corridor.

CONCLUSION

Regional problem-solving continues to emerge around such salient issues
as pollution control, public transportation, solid waste management, and

health care services. While interlocal agreements seem more politically ac-ceptable for some problems, a substate regional approach (through either the regional councils or more active county governments) and state assump-tion of certain local services have been supported by some planners and academicians as more rational alternatives for some services.[62] Governors King and Baldacci each addressed these problems by forming task forces to study the issues and recommended various cooperative solutions.

Since Baldacci's past proposals for regionalism met strenuous opposition, he eventually concluded that communities didn't want these policies being promoted by the state. He then indicated that regional cooperation would be a bottom-up, rather than a top-down state-mandated process. Moreover, the $1 million in grants that was distributed to numerous town and cities could become a catalyst for successful regional pilot projects and produce useful models for communities to replicate.

In 2005 the governor also began envisioning local government spending caps as a means to stimulate regionalism and select consolidations. As a part of a tax reform package, the governor claimed that communities would have to search for new ways to save money and concluded, "There is no trickle down in Maine. It grows from the grass roots up."[63] By 2007 Governor Bal-dacci had gained support in the legislature to move forward with a plan for consolidating most school districts and creating Regional School Units.

The decision as to whether to make county governments truly general purpose in nature and providers of additional services remains as a major policy choice. Meanwhile, Maine continues to use other acceptable mecha-nisms, such as special districts, contracts, and interlocal corporations, which involve the private sector (e.g., solid-waste disposal plants in southern and central Maine).

CHAPTER FOURTEEN

Concluding Observations

One conclusion that emerges from this study of Maine politics is that the state has been something of a political pioneer. As we have seen, its many small communities contain an extraordinarily high number of appointed professional managers. The state has led the nation with certain innovative programs in health insurance and educational technology. The court system is one of the best organized in the country. For a small state, it has produced more than its share of national leaders, especially in Congress. Government and politics are important in Maine, even though its picturesque environment and rather isolated location may be its best-known characteristics.

Yet it is the relationship that Maine people have with their environment that has provided the state with so much of its political energy. The state has long been a leader in developing environmental law. By overwhelming margins, Maine citizens insist that the land must be protected even at the expense of economic development. Such a bond between the population and its natural environment probably could not have occurred in many other states. We think its presence is due in part to Maine's political culture. We have argued that the moralistic culture, which stresses a commonwealth view of public affairs and encourages widespread political participation, has helped foster in Maine a consensus about large issues that transcends demographic groupings.

We observed in chapters 2 and 3 that the social and economic changes that took place in Maine in the nineteenth and early twentieth centuries gave rise to some other political characteristics. Among those that have become especially prominent since the 1950s are a tendency toward moderation on the part of the two political parties, and a willingness by citizens to support an activist state government. Those changes have included a tremendous expansion of the service sector, which has accounted for nearly all of the job growth in the state since the 1980s and has aligned, for the first time, Maine's economy with that of the nation. Another major development has been the rapid increase in population in the southern coastal counties, which has sharpened economic differences between those areas and northern Maine.

There is little evidence that those shifts will significantly alter the trend of Maine politics in the near future. Despite substantial in-migration from southern New England and the middle-Atlantic states, newcomers to Maine seem mostly to be individuals seeking the kind of lifestyle that Mainers have traditionally cherished. They prefer to settle in small towns, not large cities. Their voting patterns reveal no particular challenge to the state's existing moderate political culture. Unlike Vermont and New Hampshire, Maine's newcomers have not shown an eagerness to run for statewide office, nor have they appeared to try to make a distinctive imprint on public policies.

Still, economic modernization has certain political consequences. One of the most significant has been the professionalization and institutionalization of the state government. The changes that have taken place in the past forty years in the three branches of state government are remarkable, and they reveal some of the tensions attending the changes in Maine's political system. For most of its history, the state had a citizen legislature with very high rates of turnover and an inclination to meet only occasionally during its two-year term. Beginning in the 1970s, legislative sessions became longer and legislators' tenure extended beyond the traditional one or two terms of office. Eventually a professional cadre of legislators emerged to direct the affairs of the institution, allowing the legislature to compete fairly evenly with the executive branch in shaping public policy. When combat between the two branches in 1991 resulted in a shutdown of state government, angry voters initiated a referendum that led to term limits on legislators. Their efforts might be seen as an attempt to reestablish the moralistic or participatory culture in a legislature that had become too distant from the citizens.

In the executive and judicial departments, the rise of professionalism has also taken place, but with less conflict. Many agencies were once directed by boards and commissions dominated by citizens named to those bodies on the basis of their interest in health, or welfare, or education. Maine departed from that system in the early 1970s, creating in its place a cabinet, within which particular functions became the responsibility of a commissioner, usually a career administrator or politician, named by the governor. The courts, too, have revised their arrangements to enhance professional management. In the early 1960s, Maine abolished its municipal courts, largely staffed by citizen judges, and replaced them with the district court and its career judges. Citizens still find ways to participate in court business, such as in juries and in committees assigned to handle certain functions, but they no longer preside over trials.

Professionalism has not been limited to state government. The number of Maine towns adding managers and other professionals grows steadily. Their work has enabled some communities to continue using town meetings and citizen boards for governance. Yet, an inexorable trend toward state centralization of some local functions seems to be underway. The complex problems that towns must face often impose financial demands that exceed the towns' financial capabilities. In the past two decades, several small Maine towns have given up their charters, leaving the state and weak counties to provide services ranging from tax collection to police protection.

The effects of professionalism are important to notice. All states have shared in the general growth of state and local governments recently experienced by Maine. However, few states have cherished as deeply as Maine the value of citizen governance. For most of its history, Maine did not just listen to its citizens; citizens directed the government. Now government seems to fall mostly into the hands of a political class of managers, technicians, bureaucrats, and politicians for whom government service is their livelihood.

What are the implications of this change? One probable implication is that political power will increasingly be found within governmental institutions. That statement sounds like a truism, but it speaks to a significant shift in Maine politics from the not-very-distant pattern of private interests having inordinate power over policy. In 1974 the *Maine Times*, a weekly reform-oriented newspaper, conducted a survey seeking to answer the question: Who Runs Maine? It identified the heads of five large companies, including Central Maine Power and the Maine Central Railroad, as constituting a kind of power elite. Their influence extended over a broad array of policies and decisions in the legislature and executive branch. In contrast, when the newspaper examined the same issue in 1988, it found the problem harder to resolve: "Today, the answer to the question is: no individual or small group runs the state. Maine has progressed from an individualistic to an institutional power structure."[1] In particular, the state bureaucracy was by then seen as a critical force in virtually all areas of public policy.

A second implication of professionalism is that the political class is growing larger and more elaborate. When Maine created the district court system in 1961 and, a decade later, established a cabinet in the executive department, the new arrangement meant primarily that cabinet officers and judges would be individuals with appropriate credentials who served on a full-time basis. Currently, a career ladder exists for many top posts. Officials have not only the educational backgrounds for the positions they hold, but often significant experience in subordinate posts as well. Justices on the Maine Supreme Judicial Court are now usually drawn from the Superior and District benches. Cabinet officers typically have a decade or more of service in subcabinet positions. Interestingly, the idea of political class also applies to the legislature, despite term limits. In 2005, for instance, nineteen members of the state senate had not served in that chamber in the preceding session but only five lacked previous legislative experience. Eight new senators had been termed out of the house in 2004; three others were former house members, and another three were former senators.

A third development associated with the rise of government professionalism is the expanded use of the initiative and the referendum. Although Maine has not relied on those devices as extensively as some states, referendums are now seen regularly on the November state election ballot. The surge in popular lawmaking began in the 1970s, a decade that marked the beginning of Maine's income tax and the expansion of state governmental responsibilities. The growth of the initiative and referendum is indicative of the efforts by some citizens to narrow the gap they perceive widening between themselves and public officials. The most dramatic uses of those devices have occurred when the legislature has failed to act on matters the public deems urgent, such as limiting the length of service in the legislature.

Between 1820, when Maine became a state, and 1969, when voters approved a significant home rule amendment to its state constitution, Maine's towns and cities were closely regulated by the state legislature. In addition its state courts had strictly interpreted municipal powers in the tradition of "Dillon's Rule," whereby they denied a municipality any power not specifically included in its charter. Accordingly, Maine courts did not alter that stance until 1987, when the legislature by statute interpreted home rule to encourage greater flexibility for its many different-sized local governments. Since the 1990s, Maine communities are finally enjoying an increased level of home rule authority, and thereby opportunities to initiate charter changes (e.g., the various hybrid forms of local government discussed in Chapter 12). Home rule does not equal total local autonomy, but it does create another opportunity for more bottom-up, citizen participation at the local level.

Many of the challenges Maine faces in the next decade will be ones of resolving tensions inherent in its political culture. The state has long prided itself on widespread public participation in its politics. Its governing institutions have, in fact, been crafted to facilitate citizen involvement. Its large legislature and its nearly five hundred localities all provide invitations for engagement in the decision-making process. Further, the culture insists that

policies formulated by that process should embrace the entire community—
not just a segment of it—because politics are not a specialized profession
but, instead, a responsibility and opportunity for all citizens.

The difficulties Maine faces in the policy arena are two-fold. One is that
the construction of complex public policies necessarily involves persons
with advanced training and knowledge. That need runs against the "town-
meeting" mode of decision-making in which everyone, in theory, can and
should be involved. The crisis the Maine legislature experienced in 1991
was a fight over two political values—participation or representation on
the one hand, and professionalism in policymaking on the other. In 1993
Maine voters decisively declared for representation by limiting the length
of service of their legislators. The same issue is now gaining prominence at
the local level, as the cost of funding hundreds of small jurisdictions raises
the possibility of consolidations of among towns in their service delivery.
As one official has said, "we cannot have a public facility at the end of every
driveway." Such reforms could, in turn, sharply limit the access of some
citizens to local governing officials.

The second dilemma involves the boundaries of public policy. Over the
past four decades, Maine has moved from a state with very modest public
services to one of the most energetic and innovative states in the country.
The transformation, though dramatic, has followed a path very consistent
with its participatory political culture: once the state establishes a policy,
such as health care, it urgently tries to enable as many citizens as possible
to take advantage of its services and benefits. The government in Augusta
rather meticulously seeks to spread its resources into every nook and cranny
of the state. It seeks to avoid the "silo" effect of addressing a policy to one
narrow ban of recipients. Additionally, the state has sought to sustain balance among its many programs, such that an initiative in one area does not
displace or downgrade activities in another. The leading example is the stout
refusal of Mainers to pursue the goal of economic development and job
growth at the expense of protecting the state's environmental resources.

The formation of comprehensive and balanced policies has been expensive,
and is revealed in the growth of Maine's public sector. Between 1960 and
2000, state and local spending moved from a little over 8 percent of the gross
state product (the value of all goods and services produced) to 13 percent.
State and local taxes that have fueled that growth are currently among the
highest in the nation. Consequently, financial and budget issues increasingly
take center stage in legislative debates. In the early years of the 2000s, those
questions tended to be defined in terms of the "proper" balance between state
and local governments in meeting their various responsibilities.

How well will Maine figure out new governmental structures and policy boundaries? Can it resolve those issues without inflicting damaging, long-term divisions on its politics? As the debate continues, two features of the state should be kept in mind. One is that Mainers are moderate in their political habits, and tend to avoid extremes in politics and ideology. They try to seek consensus on most major issues. The other is that Maine has long been a state willing to innovate and experiment in matters of both governance and public policy, as this book has shown. It has fashioned many unique features, which are mostly pragmatic adjustments to its special culture and politics. Those qualities bode well for the future. The state will, of course, continue to be influenced by the demographic, economic and political trends touching its New England neighbors. Still, as in the past, its evaluation of those trends will be distinctly on its own terms.

CHAPTER FIFTEEN

Maine Documents and Sources

RESEARCH CENTERS

Collections

Maine has a well-established institutional arrangement for maintaining and distributing state documents and records. The State Library, located in Augusta in the State of Maine Cultural Building, which is a short distance from the State House, is the principle depository for all state documents. State departments are required by law to submit copies of their publications to the State Library, which then distributes copies to thirteen depository libraries around the state. These depositories include libraries on campuses throughout the University of Maine System (Orono, Fort Kent, Machias, Presque Isle, Farmington, Gorham, and Portland), as well as libraries of three private colleges (Bates, Bowdoin, and Colby), the Portland Public Library, and the State Law and Legislative Reference Library (hereafter referred to as the State Law Library).

The State Law and Legislative Reference Library is located in the State House in Augusta. Its collections include statutory codes for all fifty states. The library also provides online access to state and federal codes, Canadian statues, and state and federal court cases. The Maine legislative documents are the most comprehensive, going back to 1865 for house documents. The library's collections are also geared to provide information on current legislative issues, such as health insurance and prescription drug benefits. As a selective U.S. government depository, the library provides access to congressional bills, reports, and debates. The library also maintains a file of state newspaper clippings listed under a wide range of governmental subject headings, such as "Ethics in Government" and "Municipal Government." The library Web page (http://www.state.me.us/legis/homepage.htm)

includes links to the URSUS online catalog, a form for asking a librarian a question, and pages with state and federal legal links.

The University of Maine system has two social science research institutes that are sources of governmental data. The larger of the two is the Edmund S. Muskie Institute for Public Service at the University of Southern Maine in Portland. The institute provides programs in teaching and applied research, and has particular strength in health and human services policy. The other institute is the Margaret Chase Smith Center for Policy Studies at the University of Maine in Orono. Its staff is especially engaged in interdisciplinary studies with faculties in several fields at the university and other institutions. The center publishes *The Maine Policy Review*, a research journal that examines a wide range of public issues facing the state, one to three times per year. Other research centers are the Maine Historical Society in Portland, which publishes the *Maine Historical Society Quarterly* and occasional bibliographies of various aspects of Maine life, and the Maine Municipal Association in Augusta, which publishes the *Maine Townsman* monthly, as well as other materials for local governments.

Other research institutes are the George J. Mitchell Department of Special Collections and Archives at Bowdoin College, and the Edmund S. Muskie Archives at Bates College. The Bowdoin unit contains the papers of former Senator Mitchell, together with the manuscripts of several nineteenth century Maine members of Congress, including Speaker of the house Thomas Brackett Reed, Sen. William Pitt Fessenden, and Sen. William Pierce Frye. The Muskie Archives contain, in addition to the papers of former Senator Muskie, approximately four hundred transcripts of interviews (in both oral and typed form) of individuals who worked with him during his years as Maine governor, U.S. senator, and U.S. Secretary of State. Colby College recently added its new Goldfarb Center, which promotes conferences and the related research work of its faculty.

During the last decade, several centers and think tanks have developed largely along advocacy and ideological lines. The liberal Maine Center for Economic Policy (www.mecep.org) is a major source for analysis for legislators, selectmen, city councilors, other progressive advocates and the press. The Maine Heritage Policy Center (www.MainePolicy.org) represents a conservative constituency and publishes the quarterly *Dirigo Watch* report on health and taxation reforms and *Maine View*. Other examples include the Maine Public Spending Research Group, which claims to be neither liberal nor conservative, and the Bangor-based Maine Public Policy Institute, which advocates reversing Maine trends in taxes, regulation, health care coverage, and education (see their Web site at www.Maineinsitute.com).

The pro-business Maine Economic Research Institute (MERI) operates in Augusta, providing research reports and analysis on Maine's economy and business interests. A mostly Republican- oriented organization, its Web site is www.fixmaine.com.

General Reference Works

James S. Henderson (ed), *The Maine Almanac & Book of Lists* (Topsham ME: Maine Times Co., 1994) contains much statistical information on the state's government and economy. Henderson also has a Maine resource on CD-ROM titled *Maine: An Encyclopedia*. Its Web site is http:people.maine .com/publius/almanac/encycweb/htm/enintro.htm. *The Maine State Library Government Publications Checklist*, published by the Maine State Library, lists Maine state agency reports and publications. The *Checklist* is now published on the Web (http://www.maine.gov/msl/about/govpub/). The *Index to Maine State Documents*, published annually, lists Maine state government items by subject. The primary source for locating Maine state government officers and their agencies' programs and organizational structures is the *Maine State Government Annual Report* (Augusta: Bureau of the Budget). The oldest state directory is *The Maine Register, State Yearbook and Legislative Manual* (Portland: Tower Publishing Co., 1820 to present). Published annually, this source lists the officials of every town in the state and all principal state officials, and provides much descriptive data on state and local agencies. It is the closest reference Maine has to a "Blue Book."

State Government Overview

The best overview of Maine politics in the one-party period remains the chapter on Maine in Duane Lockard, *New England State Politics* (Princeton NJ: Princeton University Press, 1959). An appraisal of the shifts in the state's political life in the 1970s is found in Neil Pierce, *The New England States: People, Power, and Politics* (New York: W.W. Norton, 1976). A current, richly detailed study is Richard Barringer (ed.), *Changing Maine: 1960–2010* (Gardiner ME: Tilbury Press, 2004), which contains twenty chapters written by specialists in the principal areas of Maine politics and policy.

The State Constitution

PRIMARY SOURCES Maine's constitution is codified every ten years by the state's chief justice, who incorporates amendments added during the preceding time period. The most recent codification was in 2003. The Constitution is also available on the Web (http://www.state.me.us/sos/arc/general/constit/conscont.htm). In the interim years, the Office of Secretary of State publishes newly enacted amendments separately. The amendments are inserted in a pocket inside the back cover of the constitution, which is made available in booklet form (free of charge) from the Office of the Secretary of State. When the legislature proposes amendments for ratification, the Secretary of State prepares a pamphlet, *Maine Citizen's Guide to the Referenda Election*, for distribution in advance of the election. Editions of the guide from 1997 to the present are available at the election results page (http://www.maine.gov/sos/cec/elec/priorlst.htm).

SECONDARY SOURCES The best and most detailed analysis is Marshall J. Tinkle, *The Maine State Constitution: A Reference Guide* (Westport CT: Greenwood, 1992), which discusses the history of each amendment. For a political appraisal of the document, see Kenneth T. Palmer and Marcus A. LiBrizzi, "Development of the Maine Constitution: The Long Tradition, 1819–1988," *Maine Historical Society Quarterly* 28 (Winter 1989), 126–45.

The State Legislature

PRIMARY SOURCES Maine's legislature maintains a fairly complete record of its proceedings. A verbatim record of all debates and floor proceedings is contained in the *Maine Legislative Record*, which starts from 1897. The day-to-day substantive actions of the legislature are found in the *Journal of the House* and the *Journal of the Senate*, which are available only in the State Law Library. All legislative documents in any form in which they have been considered are annually indexed in *State of Maine History and Final Disposition of Legislative Documents*. A related publication, *Laws of Maine*, publishes the texts of enacted measures. Links for all online editions of the *Legislative Record*, the text of bills and amendments, the *History and Final Disposition*, and the *Laws of Maine* are available at the State Law Library's Maine Law and Legislation page (http://www.state.me.us/legis/lawlib/melaw.htm).

Biographical material on state legislators, including their home and business telephone numbers and their standing committee assignments, is provided in the *Senate and House Registers*, a booklet published biennially by the clerk of the house and the secretary of the senate. Written testimony presented at public hearings since 1983 is available in paper from the State Law Library. The State Law Library holds paper copies of all committee study reports. Study reports produced since 1995 are also available online (http://www.maine.gov/legis/opla/reports2htm).

SECONDARY SOURCES For a description of the legislature, the most useful guide is a biennial publication: *A Guide for Maine Legislators: Procedures, Services & Facts*, also known as the Legislator's Handbook. The current edition is available online (http://mainegove-images.informe.org/legis/opla/ leghand04.pdf). See also *A Citizen's Guide to the 122nd Maine Legislature 2005–2006* (Portland ME: People's Resource Center, 2005). Finally, the Legislature maintains a comprehensive Web site that includes links to the house and senate, legislative offices, publications, audio broadcasts, bill status and schedule information (http://www.state.me.us/legis/home page.htm).

The State Executive

PRIMARY SOURCES A basic source on the state executive is the *Maine State Government Annual Report* (Augusta: Bureau of the Budget). This annual volume sets forth the administrative structure of each executive department and agency. It also contains a budget summary and a brief description of the functions of each unit, its activities over the preceding year, and publications available from the agency. Names and telephone numbers of senior agency personnel are included in each agency description. A source of detailed financial information is the *State of Maine Budget Document*, an annual booklet published by the governor's office. Links to all executive agencies are available on the general Web site (http://www.maine.gov/portal/ government). The Legislature's Office of Fiscal and Program Review publishes the *Compendium of Fiscal Information* (the site for the current edition is http://www.maine.gov/legis/ofpr/05compendium/c05toc.htm), which is especially useful for comparing financial data over a period of years. The State Law Library maintains a collection of studies and reports produced by gubernatorially appointed commissions and committees from 1867 to present. It also houses a substantial compilation of the advisory opinions of Maine's attorneys general since 1863. The state archives contain the papers and documents of recent governors. Established in 1968, the State Planning Office is a valuable source for researchers interested in particular policy areas.

SECONDARY SOURCES A brief description of Maine governors and their impact on the state, from William King in 1820 to Kenneth Curtis in the 1970s, is Jane Radcliff, *150 Years of Maine Governors* (Augusta ME: Maine

State Museum, 1972). Among works devoted to individual governors are Donald Nevin, *Muskie of Maine* (New York: Random House, 1972); Kermit Lipez, *Kenneth Curtis of Maine: Profile of a Governor* (Brunswick: Harpswell Press, 1974); and Willis Johnson, *The Year of the Longley* (Stonington: Penobscot Press, 1978). The State Law Library contains books of newspaper articles on the career of every governor since the early 1950s.

The State Courts

PRIMARY SOURCES   One source of information on Maine courts is *Maine Administrative Office of the Courts: Annual Report*. Published since the mid-1970s , this volume provides fiscal and caseload data, although in recent years it has reduced the amount of information it contains. Title 4 of *Maine Revised Statutes Annotated* has the best description of the structure and authority of the several courts. *Maine Rules of Court*, an annual publication of the Tower Publishing Company, provides the rules of civil and criminal procedure, rules of evidence, and the Maine Bar rules and the code of judicial conduct. *The Maine Reporter* contains cases decided by the Supreme Judicial Court. These cases, as well as superior court cases from 1979, may be searched online in the State Law Library. The judicial branch maintains a Web site (http://www.courts.state.me.us/index.html) with links to supreme court opinions from 1979, court rules, court orders, and legal forms.

SECONDARY SOURCES   A source of general information about the Maine court system is William H. Coogan, *A Citizen's Guide to the Maine Courts* (Portland ME: Administrative Office of the Courts, 1987), which describes court procedures and organization for the would-be litigant. It is also available online (http://www.courts.state.me.us/courtservices/citizen_guide/index.html). Discussion of a wide range of judicial issues can be found in the *Maine Bar Journal*, based in Augusta, which published six issues a year, and in the *Maine Law Review*, a quarterly journal published by the University of Maine Law School in Portland.

The State Parties

PRIMARY SOURCES   Maine's Republican state committee (in Hallowell) and Democratic state committee (in Augusta) contain state and congressional district bylaws, and some municipal bylaws. Convention programs and party platforms are also on file. The material is mostly current, going back only a decade or two. The State Law Library maintains a collection of party platforms adopted since 1920. For election figures, see *Official Vote for Republican and Democratic Primary Election Candidates and Non-Party Candidates Filing Petitions*, published regularly by the Election Division of the Office of Secretary of State. Information on recent elections is available at the Secretary of State's Web site (http://www.maine.gov/sos/cec/elec/priorlst.htm).

SECONDARY SOURCES Most of the works listed under "Maine Government Overview" (above) include sections devoted to Maine's political parties. For recent analyses of party politics, see Kenneth T. Palmer, "Maine," in *State Party Profiles: A 50-State Guide to Development, Organization, and Resources*, Andrew M. Appleton and Daniel S. Ward (eds.), (Washington DC: Congressional Quarterly, Inc., 1997), 132–138; Sandy Maisel and Elizabeth Ivy, "If you Don't Like Our Politics, Wait a Minute: Party Politics in Maine at Century's End" in Jerome Mileur (ed.), *Parties and Politics in the New England States* (Amherst MA: Polity Publications, 1997), 15–35; and Christian P. Potholm, *This Splendid Game: Maine Campaigns and Elections, 1940–2002* (Lanham MD: Lexington Books, 2004).

The Local Governments

PRIMARY SOURCES Maine's local governments are closely connected with the Maine Municipal Association (www.memum.org) in Augusta, which offers numerous services for its clientele of town and city officials; including publications. Examples include a town meeting *Moderator's Manual* and a helpful newcomer's guide book, *Local Government in Maine* (Augusta ME: Maine Municipal Association, 2005). Also useful in understanding the concept of home rule and comparing it among states is Dale Krane et. al. (eds.), *Home Rule in America: A Fifty State Handbook* (Washington DC: CQ Press, 2001); Maine is discussed at pp. 183–190. For understanding New England's unique form of town meeting government, see Frank M. Bryan, *Real Democracy: The New England Town Meeting and How It Works* (Chicago and London: University of Chicago Press, 2004). While most of its coverage deals with Vermont, readers will benefit from the empirical findings and methods of research. Also see an excellent study by Joseph Zimmerman, *The New England Town Meeting* (Westwood CT: Praeger, 1999).

SECONDARY SOURCES Former Maine town manager and current University of Pittsburgh Professor David Y. Miller has authored, *The Regional*

Governing of Metropolitan America (Boulder CO: Westfield Press, 2002). This innovative work provides a number of tables on comparative metropolitan areas within U.S. regions and states, with good comparative coverage of both New England and Maine. For a very useful source to help assess county government reform, see Beverly A. Cigler, "Administration in the Modern American County" in George Frederickson (ed.), *The Future of Local Government Administration* (Washington DC: 2002), pp. 157–174. For more background on the history of Maine, see Richard W. Judd, Edwin A. Churchill, and Joel W. Eastman, eds., *Maine: The Pine Tree State from Prehistory to the Present* (Orono: University of Maine Press, 1999).

Newspapers

Several newspapers provide extensive coverage of state government. *The Bangor Daily News*, the *Portland Press Herald*, and the *Maine Sunday Telegram* have the largest circulations. As Augusta's only newspaper, the *Kennebec Journal* has had a long association with Maine's politics and government. The State Law Library maintains subject and biographical files of newspaper clippings. Subjects emphasize topics of statewide interest rather than local news. Biographical articles relate to Maine legislators (and legislative candidates), attorneys, judges, congressional representatives, and governors. Most files begin in the early 1970s, but the collection includes some earlier articles, especially biographical pieces. The University of Maine's Fogler Library maintains a regularly updated series of state periodical indexes (*Newspapers and Periodicals Indexed*) through its Special Collections Department.

Notes

1. STATE OF THE STATE

1. Gerald C. Wright Jr., Robert S. Erickson, and John P. McIver, "Public Opinion and Policy Liberalism in the American States," *American Journal of Political Science* 31 (November 1987): 989.
2. Matthew C. Moen, Kenneth T. Palmer, and Richard J. Powell, *Changing Members: The Maine Legislature in an Era of Term Limits* (Lanham MD: Lexington Books, 2005), 26.
3. Wendy Griswold, "History Plus Resources Equals a Sense of Place," *Maine Policy Review* vol. 11 (Spring 2002): 78.
4. Griswold, "History Plus Resources," 78–79.
5. Market Decisions, *The People of Maine: A Psychographic Study*, vol. 2 (South Portland: Market Decisions, 1989).

2. MAINE'S POLITICAL CULTURE

1. See chapter 5, "The States and the Political Setting," in Daniel J. Elazar, *American Federalism: A View from the States*, 3d ed. (New York: Harper and Row, 1984) 109–49.
2. *State O'Maine Facts* (Camden ME: Down-East Books, 1982), 92.
3. Charles E. Clark, *Maine: A Bicentennial History* (New York: W. W. Norton, 1977), 91.
4. Governor Joshua Chamberlain, quoted in Edward Chase Kirkland, *Men, Cities, and Transportation: A Study of New England History, 1820–1900* (Cambridge MA: Harvard University Press, 1948), 1:466.
5. Neal Peirce, *The New England States: People, Politics, and Power in the Six New England States* (New York: W. W. Norton, 1976), 372.

6. Jim Brunelle, ed., *Maine Almanac* (Augusta ME: Guy Gannett Publishing Co., 1978–79), 11.

7. Ray Allen Billington, *The Protestant Crusade, 1800–1860: A Study of the Origins of American Nativism* (New York: Macmillan, 1938), 293–94.

8. Billington, *Protestant Crusade*, 310.

9. Billington, *Protestant Crusade*, 294.

10. Samuel Carleton Guptill, "The Grange in Maine from 1874 to 1940" (PhD diss., University of Maine, Orono, 1973), 26.

11. David B. Walker, *Politics and Ethnocentrism: The Case of the Franco-Americans* (Brunswick: Bureau for Research in Municipal Government, Bowdoin College, 1961), 7.

12. Walker, *Politics and Ethnocentrism*, 16.

13. Norman Sepenuk, "A Profile of Franco-American Political Attitudes in New England," in *A Franco-American Overview, New England* (part 1), edited by Madelein Gigiere (Cambridge MA: Evaluation, Dissemination, and Assessment Center, Lesley College, 1981), 3:221.

14. Sepenuk, "A Profile of Franco-American Political Attitudes," 219.

15. David B. Walker, "The Presidential Politics of Franco-Americans," in Gigiere, *Franco-American Overview*, 1:203.

16. Ronald Larry Bissonnette, "Political Parties as Products of Their Environments: A Case Study of Lewiston, Maine" (Honors thesis, University of Maine, Orono, 1977), 51.

17. See *Census Reports, 12th Census of the U.S., Taken in the Year 1900, Population*, part 1 (Washington DC: U.S. Census Office, 1901), 1:807.

18. David C. Smith, "Towards a Theory of Maine History," in *Maine: A History through Selected Readings*, edited by D. C. Smith and E. U. Shriver (Dubuque IA: Kendall/Hunt Publishing Co., 1985), 208.

19. Smith, "Towards a Theory of Maine History," 208.

20. Edward Bonner Whitney, "The Ku Klux Klan in Maine, 1922–1928: A Study with Particular Emphasis on the City of Portland" (BS thesis, Harvard College, Cambridge MA, 1966), 53.

21. James Hill Parker, *Ethnic Identity: The Case of the Franco-Americans* (Washington DC: University Press of America, 1983), 48–49.

22. *Maine Sunday Telegram*, August 21, 1988, 18A.

23. Parker, *Ethnic Identity*, 37.

24. Walker, "Presidential Politics," 204.

25. Demographic material for this section has been drawn from Richard Sherwood and Deirdre Mageean, "Demography and Maine's Destiny," in *Changing Maine, 1960–2010*, edited by Richard Barringer (Gardiner ME: Tilbury House Publishers, 2004), chap. 1.

26. See, for example, Louis A. Ploch, "The Reversal in Migration Patterns: Some Rural Developments," *Rural Sociology* 43 (Summer 1978): 293–303.

27. See Maine State Planning Office, *The Cost of Sprawl* (Augusta ME: Maine State Planning Office, 1997).

28. David Vail, "Tourism in Maine's Expanding Service Economy," in *Changing Maine*, ed. Barringer, 431.

29. The Brookings Institution, *Chartering Maine's Future: An Action Plan for Promoting Sustainable Prosperity and Quality Places* (Washington DC: The Brookings Institution Metropolitan Policy Program, 2006), 130.

3. MAINE'S TRADITIONAL POLITICS AND ITS TRANSFORMATION

1. Peirce, *New England States*, 379.

2. Peirce, *New England States*, 376.

3. David Clayton Smith, "Maine Politics, 1950–1956" (Master's thesis, University of Maine, Orono, 1958), 12.

4. Brunelle, *Maine Almanac*, 240.

5. Smith, "Maine Politics," 4.

6. Samuel Eliot Morison, *The Oxford History of the American People* (New York: Oxford University Press, 1965), 741.

7. Duane Lockard, *New England State Politics* (Princeton NJ: Princeton University Press, 1959), 108.

8. Smith, "Maine Politics," 3.

9. Lockard, *New England State Politics*, 95.

10. Lockard, *New England State Politics*, 99–100.

11. Smith, "Maine Politics," 89.

12. Smith, "Maine Politics," 123.

13. Peirce, *New England States*, 376.

14. Smith, "Maine Politics," 94–95.

15. Smith, "Maine Politics," 106.

16. Cherrill Anson, *Edmund Muskie: Democratic Senator from Maine* (Washington DC: Grossman Publishers, 1972), 15.

17. Peirce, *New England States,* 378.

18. Smith, "Maine Politics," 125.

19. Peirce, *New England States*, 378.

20. Peirce, *New England States*, 391.

21. James Horan et al., *Downeast Politics: The Government of the State of Maine* (Dubuque IA: Kendall/Hunt Publishing Co., 1975), 4.

4. CONTEMPORARY MAINE POLITICS

1. Election statistics in this chapter have been drawn from materials furnished by the Maine Office of Secretary of State.

2. Kenneth P. Hayes, "Maine Political Parties," in *New England Political Parties*, edited by Josephine F. Milburn and William Doyle (Cambridge MA: Schenkman Publishing Co., 1983), 191–203.

3. Howard L. Rieter, "Who Voted for Longley: Maine Elects an Independent Governor," *Polity* (Fall 1977): 65–85.

4. Kenneth T. Palmer, "Maine," in *State Party Profiles: A 50-State Guide to Development, Organization and Resources,* edited by Andrew M. Appleton and Daniel S. Ward (Washington DC: Congressional Quarterly, Inc., 1997), 132–83.

5. See *2007 Report on the Maine Clean Election Act* (Augusta ME: Maine Commission on Governmental Ethics and Election Practices, 2007).

6. Liz Chapman, "Linnehan Leader in Campaign Spending," *Bangor Daily News*, October 30, 2004.

7. Bonnie Washuk, "Bennett Leader of the PACs," *Lewiston Sun Journal*, December 8, 2002.

8. Duane Lockard, *New England State Politics* (Princeton NJ: Princeton University Press, 1959), 79.

9. Clive S. Thomas and Ronald J. Hrebenar, "Interest Groups in the States," in *Politics in the American States: A Comparative Analysis*, edited by Virginia Gray et. al (Washington DC: Congressional Quarterly Books, 2008), chap. 4.

10. Douglas Hodgkin, "Interest Group Politics in Maine: From Big-Three to Diversity," unpublished paper.

11. Christian P. Potholm II, "As Maine Goes: A Look at Politics in the Pine Tree State," *Bowdoin* (Winter 1990): 21–22.

12. Potholm, "As Maine Goes," 21–22.

13. Scott Allen, "The Utilities Probe," *Maine Times*, January 11, 1985.

14. "Conservative Think Tank Gets Mixed Reviews," *Portland Press Herald*, July 11, 2005.

15. Susan M. Cover, "Women's Lobby Gets New Boss," *Kennebec Journal*, August 6, 2003.

16. Paul Carrier, "Lobbyists Hit Racino Jackpot," *Portland Press Herald*, February 21, 2004.

17. George Smith, "Skin Like An Elephant," *Kennebec Journal*, April 14, 2004.

18. Susan M. Cover, "Beliveau Part of Lobbying Change," *Lewiston Morning Sentinel*, April 4, 2004.

19. Susan M. Cover, "Shaping Policy on the Sidelines," *Lewiston Morning Sentinel*, April 6, 2004.

20. Quoted in Scott Allen, "From Lobbyist to Candidate," *Maine Times*, May 23, 1986.
21. See Moen et al., *Changing Members*, 108–10.
22. Paul Carrier, "Maine Referendums: The Bolder They Are, The Harder They Fall," *Maine Sunday Telegram*, November 4, 2004.

5. THE CONSTITUTIONAL TRADITION

1. The drafting of the Maine Constitution in 1819 is discussed in Ronald F. Banks, *Maine Becomes a State: The Movement to Separate Maine from Massachusetts, 1785–1820* (Middletown CT: Wesleyan University Press, 1970), 167–79.
2. William Pitt Prebel, quoted in Banks, *Maine Becomes a State*, 153.
3. Ronald M. Peters Jr., *The Massachusetts Constitution 1780: A Social Compact* (Amherst MA: University of Massachusetts Press, 1978), 193–94.
4. Daniel J. Elazar, "The Principles and Traditions Underlying State Constitutions," *Publius: The Journal of Federalism* 12 (Winter 1982): 11–26.
5. Marshall J. Tinkle, *The Maine State Constitution: A Reference Guide* (Westport CT: Greenwood Press, 1992), 9.
6. Fred Eugene Jewett, *A Financial History of Maine* (New York: Columbia University Press, 1937), 30–34.
7. Lawrence Lee Pelletier, *The Initiative and Referendum in Maine* (Brunswick: Bureau for Research in Municipal Government, Bowdoin College, 1951), 8.
8. Peter Neil Barry, "Nineteenth Century Constitutional Amendments in Maine" (Master's thesis, University of Maine, Orono, 1965), 60–61.
9. Herbert M. Heath, *A Manual of Maine Corporation Law* (Portland: Loring, Short and Harmon, 1917), 13–14.
10. Hebert Kaufman, *Politics and Policies of State and Local Government* (Englewood Cliffs NJ: Prentice-Hall, 1963), chap. 2.
11. *Doe v. Rowe*, 156 F. Supp. 2d 35 (2001).

6. THE STATE LEGISLATURE

1. Moen et al., *Changing Members*, chap. 2.
2. *Maine Sunday Telegram*, March 6, 1988.
3. Citizens Conference on State Legislatures, *The Sometime Governments* (New York: Bantam Books, 1971), 52–53.
4. Banks, *Maine Becomes a State*, chap. 8.
5. Glendon Schubert, *Reapportionment* (New York: Charles Scribner's Sons, 1965), 65–82.

6. *Baker v. Carr*, 369 U.S. 186 (1962).

7. Allen Pease and Wilfred Richard, eds., *Maine: Fifty Years of Change 1940–1990* (Orono: University of Maine Press, 1983), 106.

8. Philip S. Wilder, *Maine Politics* (Cambridge MA: Harvard University, Unpublished PhD dissertation, 1951), chap. 2.

9. Moen et al., *Changing Members*, 66–68.

10. Maine legislative Web site (http://janus.state.me.us/legis/).

11. Scott Allen, "Speaker of the House," *Maine Times*, January 9, 1987.

12. Moen et al., *Changing Members*, 73.

13. Moen et al., *Changing Members*, 74.

14. Quoted in John Diamond, "Mr. Smith Goes to Augusta," *The Washington Monthly* 21 (July–August 1989): 36.

7. THE GOVERNOR AND THE ADMINISTRATION

1. Kenneth T. Palmer, "Governmental Reorganization in Maine: A Commentary," *Juncture* 2 (October 1971): 24–27. The arrangement of departments is contained in Legislative Research Committee, *Government Reorganization Phase II—Status Report* (Augusta: State of Maine Printing Office, 1970).

2. The survey considers the sixty-one governors who served six months or longer. These delimited periods, while fairly arbitrary, seem generally to correspond with those that other studies of Maine's government and politics have found useful. See, for example, Pease and Richard, *Maine*.

3. Data on Maine governors have been drawn primarily from Joseph E. Kallenbach and Jessamire S. Kallenbach, *American State Governors, 1776–1976*, vol. 2 (Dobbs Ferry NY: Oceana Publications, 1981).

4. Frank M. Bryan, "The New England Governorships: People, Position, and Power," in *New England Politics*, edited by Josephine F. Milburn and Victoria Shuck (Cambridge MA: Schenkman Publishing Co., 1981), 82.

5. Much of the discussion of the Baldacci administration is drawn from interviews with members of the governor's staff.

6. "Taking the Lead," *Maine Sunday Telegram*, June 22, 2003.

7. *Maine Sunday Telegram*, July 9, 1989.

8. Theo Lippman Jr. and Donald C. Hansen, *Muskie* (New York: W. W. Norton, 1971), 90.

9. Paul Carrier, "Baldacci Rejects Claims of Cronyism," *Maine Sunday Telegram*, July 20, 2003.

10. Governor's Task Force on Government Reorganization, *Toward a More Responsive and Effective State Government* (Augusta: State of Maine Printing Office, 1969), 2–9.

11. Market Decisions, *The People of Maine*, 1:17.

12. Data in this section are drawn from the state government Web site (www
    .maine.gov) and various editions of Maine State Government Annual Report.

8. THE COURT SYSTEM

1. A good discussion of the history of the Maine courts is found in Horan et al.,
   Downeast Politics, chap. 5.

2. Quoted in Horan et al., *Downeast Politics*, 168.

3. Statistical information and much of the discussion of this chapter has been
   drawn from the Maine courts' Web site, http://www.courts.state.me.us/, and
   materials supplied by the Administrative Office of the Courts, Portland ME.

4. *Portland v. DePaolo*, 531 A.2d 669 (1987).

5. Kathleen O'Leary Morgan and Scott Morgan, *State Rankings 2004: A Statistical View of the 50 United States* (Lawrence KS: Morgan Quitno Press, 2004),
   Section II.

6. Kermit V. Lipez, "Adventures and Reflections of a New Judge," *Maine Bar
   Journal* 2 (November 1987): 324–36.

7. *Maine Times*, November 30, 1984.

8. *Maine Times*, October 31, 1975.

9. *Alden v. Maine* 715 A. 2nd 172 (1998).

10. *Alden v. Maine* 527 U.S. 706 (1999).

11. Robert A. Kagan, Bobby D. Infelise, and Robert R. Detlefsen, "American State
    Supreme Court Justices, 1900–1970," *American Bar Foundation Research
    Journal* (1984): 371–407.

12. *Davies v. City of Bath*, 364 A.2d 1269 (1976).

13. *Bell v. Wells*, 510 A.2d 509 (1989). The remaining cases were drawn from
    newspaper files, Maine State Law Library.

14. 767 A.2d 310 (2001).

15. *State v. Events International, Inc.*, 528 A.2d 458 (1987).

16. *Association of Independent Professionals v. Maine Labor Relations Board*, 465
    A.2d 401 (1983).

17. *Central Maine Power Co. v. PUC*, 751, A.2d 448 (1999).

18. Cabanne Howard, "Civil Constitutional Law: Is the Law Court in the Maine
    Stream?" *Maine Bar Journal* 3 (May 1988): 133.

19. *Putnam v. Town of Hampden*, 495 A.2d 785 (1985).

20. Quoted in Edgar Allen Bean, "Invisible But Powerful: A Rare Look at Maine's
    Supreme Court," *Maine Times*, July 8, 1988, 9.

9. MAINE'S BUDGET AS POLICY

1. National Governors Association, National Association of State Budget Offi-cers, *The Fiscal Survey of the States*, June 2005. Washington DC.
2. "Government Performance Project: State Reports," *Governing*, February 2005.
3. Office of Fiscal and Program Review, *Budget Overview 122nd Legislature 1st Regular and 1st Special Sessions*, Maine State Legislature, July 2005.
4. "Maine Bond Rating Lowered," *Bangor Daily News*, May 25, 2005.
5. "Part 2's Warning," *Bangor Daily News*, June 8, 2005, 8.
6. Office of Fiscal and Program Review, *Budget Overview 122nd Legislature 1st Regular and 1st Special Sessions*, Maine State Legislature, July 2005, 9.
7. *Special Report: Federal Tax Burdens and Expenditures by State*, Tax Founda-tion, March 2006, No. 139, 3.
8. *2004 State Expenditure Report*, National Association of State Budget Offices, 2005.
9. *Maine State-Local Tax Burden Compared to U.S. Average (1970–2006)*, Tax Data, Tax Foundation, April 11, 2006.
10. Michael Allen, *Maine Tax Incidence Study: A Distributional Analysis of Maine's State & Local Taxes*, Presentation to the Maine Center for Economic Policy Tax Forum, January 14, 2005.
11. Quoted in Jewett, *Financial History of Maine*, 34.
12. Jewett, *Financial History of Maine*, 120–21.
13. Charles Colgan, "Tax Reform: A Long Walk Home" *Choices*, Maine Center for Economic Policy. Vol. 11 No. 1, January 21. 2005.
14. *State Spending Trends, Fiscal 2003*, National Association of State Budget Of-ficers, 2003 State Expenditure Report, 2.
15. *International Tax Comparisons*, 1965–2003, Citizens for Tax Justice, April 21, 2005.
16. *New Realities in State Finance*, National Conference of State Legislatures, ix.
17. *Summary of the Program and Budget Proposals for the Fiscal Years 1990–1991* (Augusta: Maine Office of the Governor), 7.
18. "Flat and Happy," *Forbes*, June 6, 2005, 60.
19. Edmund Cervone, *Maine Revenue Primer 2006*, Maine Center for Economic Policy, May 2006, 4.
20. Governor John Elias Baldacci, Press release, April 29, 2005.
21. Jean E. Lavigne and Patricia Hofmaster, "Policy Issues in Maine School Fi-nance Reform," *Maine Policy Review*, vol. 2, December 1993, 37.
22. Geoffrey Harman, "Why Tax Reform," *Maine Townsmen*, June 2002.
23. A. J. Higgins, "Tax reform measure passes Baldacci lauds 'historic moment,'" *Bangor Daily News*, January 21, 2005, 1.

24. Judy Harrison, "Tax Bill to go on fall ballot in Maine," *Bangor Daily News*, May 5, 2006, 1.

25. Jeff Tuttle, "Colorado Business Leaders Warn of TABOR," *Bangor Daily News*, July 28, 2006, 1.

26. Jewett, *Financial History of Maine*, see appendix, Table A.

27. Jewett, *Financial History of Maine*, 90–94.

28. *2003 State Expenditure Report*, National Association of State Budget Officers.

29. Eileen R. Ellis, Vernon K. Smith, and David Rousseau, *Medicaid Enrollment in 50 States: June 2004 Data Update.* The Kaiser Commission on Medicaid and the Uninsured, Kaiser Family Foundation, September 2005.

30. "State Expenditure Developments," *The Fiscal Survey of States, July 2005*, 6.

31. *State Government Finances in 1989*, U.S. Bureau of the Census (Washington DC: U.S. Government Printing Office, 1990).

32. Chris Hastedt, Mary Henderson, and Ana Hicks, *TANF at a Glance: Maine*, Maine Equal Justice, 2.

33. U.S. Census Bureau, Government Division, 2004 Annual Survey of Government Finances, January 2006, Revised May 2006 at www.census.gov/govs/www/state04.html.

34. National Association of State Budget Officers, Total Balances, *Fiscal Survey of the States, July 2005*, 16.

35. Maine State Treasurer's Office. Debt Bonds at www.maine.gov/treasurer/debt.htm.

36. "Higher Ed Comes Up Short," *Bangor Daily News*, November 15, 2005, 8.

37. *The Fiscal Survey of the States*, April 2004, ix.

10. CONTEMPORARY POLICY CONCERNS

1. Edmund S. Muskie, *Journeys* (Garden City NY: Doubleday, 1972), 80.

2. Richard Saltonstall Jr., *Maine Pilgrimage* (Boston: Little, Brown, 1974), 148.

3. Duane Lockard, *New England State Politics* (Princeton NJ: Princeton University Press, 1959), chap. 5.

4. These developments are discussed in Pease and Richard, *Maine*, 121–22.

5. Arthur Lerman Associates, *Evaluation of the Enforcement of Four Maine Environmental Statutes* (Augusta: Arthur Lerman Associates, August 1981), chap. 5.

6. Much of the following analysis relies on Orlando Delogue, "The Law and Maine Environment: Toward a New Ethic," in *Changing Maine*, ed. Barringer, 331–46.

7. Cheryl Harrington, "Maine Energy Policy: More Like the Nation," in *Changing Maine*," ed. Barringer, 348.

8. General information for this section is drawn from the governor's Web site and that of the Maine Department of Community and Economic Development.

9. *Kennebec Journal*, December 22, 2002.

10. *Bangor Daily News*, August 27, 2005.

11. Figures in this paragraph are drawn from Lisa Pohlmann, "Being Poor in Maine: Working Hard, Falling Behind," in *Changing Maine*, ed. Barringer, 51–69.

12. Jym St. Pierre, "Next Steps for Maine's Creative Economy," *Times Record*, August 25, 2005.

13. See David Vail, "Tourism in Maine's Expanding Service Economy," in *Changing Maine*, ed. Barringer, 429–49.

14. Market Decisions, *The People of Maine: A Psychographic Study*, vol. 2 (South Portland ME: Market Decisions, 1989).

15. See Measures of Growth 2001, Maine Development Foundation.

16. Mark Peters, "Home Prices Upset Town's Balance," *Maine Sunday Telegram*, December 18, 2005.

17. See Robert C. Wood, *Suburbia, Its People and Their Politics* (Boston MA: Houghton Mifflin, 1958) and Frederick Wirt, Benjamin Walter, Francine F. Rabinovitz, and Deborah R. Hensler, *On the City's Rim: Politics and Policy in Suburbia* (Lexington MA: D. C. Heath, 1972).

18. See Joel Garreau, *Edge City* (New York NY: Doubleday, 1991).

19. Charles Colgan, "Maine's Changing Economy: The Rise of Urban Maine," in *Changing Maine*, ed. Barringer, 37.

20. See John M. Levy, *Contemporary Urban Planning* (Upper Saddle River NJ: Prentice Hall, Inc., 1997), 159–63; and Andres Duany, et al., *Suburban Nation: The Rise of Sprawl and the Decline of the American Dream* (New York NY: North Point Press, 2000).

21. Executive Department, Maine State Planning Office, "The Cost of Sprawl," (May 1997), 5.

22. Executive Department, Maine State Planning Office, "The Cost of Sprawl," (May 1997), 5. Also see Robert W. Burchell, *Costs of Sprawl—Revisited* (Washington DC: National Academy Press, 1998), and Gregory D. Squires, ed., *Urban Sprawl: Cause, Consequences, and Policy Responses* (Washington DC: Urban Institute, 2002).

23. Misty Edgecomb, "Moosehead Plan's Impact Weighed," *Bangor Daily News*, April 7, 2005.

24. "Moosehead Lake Planning," *Bangor Daily News*, May 4, 2005.

25. Misty Edgecomb, "LURC Gives 'Lake Concept Plan' a Boost," *Bangor Daily News*, May 5, 2005.

26. Karen Woodsum, "Wilderness Heritage at Stake in Maine," *Bangor Daily News*, July 27, 2005.

27. *Piscataquis Observer*, April 6, 2005.

28. Misty Edgecomb, "Critics Pan Plum Creek Development," *Bangor Daily News*, July 26, 2005.

29. Scott K. Fish, "Soapbox: What Factors Should We Consider in Evaluating Plum Creeks' Proposal?" *Bangor Metro*, October 2005, 50–51.

30. "Plum Creek Foes Cite Sprawl," *Bangor Daily News*, July 27, 2005.

31. Diana Bowley, "Greenville Hears Plan for Tax Revenue Sharing," *Bangor Daily News*, August 17, 2005.

32. Bob Duchusue, "Plum Creek's Fine Print Revealing," *Bangor Daily News*, July 16/17, 2005.

33. "Economist Touts Proposal by Plum Creek," *Bangor Daily News*, August 10, 2005.

34. "Economist Touts Proposal by Plum Creek," *Bangor Daily News*.

35. "Economist Touts Proposal by Plum Creek," *Bangor Daily News*.

36. "Economist Touts Proposal by Plum Creek," *Bangor Daily News*.

37. Patrick K. McGowan, "Strong Principles for Maine Woods," *Bangor Daily News*, August 8, 2005.

38. Kevin Miller, "Plum Creek May Alter Moosehead Area Plans," *Bangor Daily News*, December 22, 2005.

39. This section depends heavily on the analysis of Elizabeth Kilbreth, "Health Policy in Maine: Recurring Themes, Persistent Leadership," in *Changing Maine*, ed. Barringer, 89–111.

40. The Fiscal Survey of the States: July 2005, 7.

41. Scott Serota, "The Individual Market: A Delicate Balance," *Health Affairs—* Web Exclusive, October 23, 2002, 377.

42. Serota, "The Individual Market," *Health Affairs*.

43. *Report to the Legislature, Dirigo Health*, Commission to Study Maine's Hospitals, February 2005.

44. *2003 Maine Community Report*, Anthem, 4.

45. Annual Report 2005, Maine Health Access Foundation, 4.

46. "MaineCare and Its Role in Maine Healthcare System," *Kaiser Commission on Medicaid and the Uninsured*, January 2005, 33.

47. "Review of Aggregate Measurable Costs Savings Determined by Dirigo Health for the First Assessment Year," Department of Professional and Financial Regulation, Bureau of Insurance, Docket No. INS-05-700.

48. A. J. Higgins, "Dirigo Panel Weighs Future Participation; Funding at Issue," *Bangor Daily News*, August 10, 2006, 1.

49. "Making Maine the Healthiest State," Maine's State Health Plan, 2007, 116. See also Pam Belluck, "As Health Plan Falters, Maine Explores Changes," *New York Times*, April 30, 2007.

50. See *Accepting the Challenge: Maine Conference on Aspirations Proceedings*, April 27, 1987; Wayne Reilly, "Student Aspirations Key to Economic Future," *Bangor Daily News*, Saturday–Sunday, June 4–5, 1988.

51. Karlene K. Hale, "Bither Urges Better Job Training," *Morning Sentinel*, August 10, 1988. Also see Terrence J. MacTaggart, "Higher Education in Maine," in *Changing Maine*, ed. Barringer 133–49; and Frances Lindemann, "Higher Education for All Maine People," *Report of the Maine Center for Economic Policy* (Augusta ME, 2002).

52. Karlene K. Hale, "Bither Urges Better Job Training."

53. See *Accepting the Challenge*, Reilly, "Student Aspirations."

54. Wayne Reilly, "Maine Schools Battle Dropout Problem," *Bangor Daily News*, June 6, 1988.

55. MacTaggart, "Higher Education for All," 149. Also see *Measuring Up 2002, State-by-State Report Card for Higher Education* (San Jose CA: The National Center for Public Policy and Higher Education, 2002).

56. "Social Development," in *Maine*, ed. Pease and Richard, 68; and "Maine Transformed," in *Changing Maine*, ed. Barringer, xxxiii.

57. Ruth Ellen Cohen, "Schools ARE on Target to Meet Goals," *Bangor Daily News*, September 23, 2005.

58. David Silvernail, "K-12 Education in Maine: Steering from a Distance," in *Changing Maine*, ed. Barringer, 125–26.

59. Silvernail, "K-12 Education in Maine," 125–26.

60. Ruth E. Cohen, "Schools on Target," *Bangor Daily News*, September 23, 2005.

61. *Task Force on Maine's Learning Technology Endowment* (Augusta ME: Maine Legislature, Office of Policy and Government Analysis, 2001).

62. Silvernail, "K-12 Education in Maine," 127–28.

63. David Silvernail and D. M. Lane, *The Impact of Maine's One-to-One Program on Middle School Teachers and Students* (Gorham ME: Maine Educational Association Policy Research Institute, USM, February 2004).

64. Walter Griffin, "Maine Number 2 in Student Web Access," *Bangor Daily News*, May 5, 2005.

65. Kevin Bushweller, *Technology Counts 2005*, Washington DC: 2005.

66. "Achieving Prosperity for All Maine Citizens," *Report by the Governor's Task Force to Create Seamless Pre-kindergarten through Sixteen Grade Education Systems*, Augusta, Maine, 2005.

67. Ruth Ellen Cohen, "Panel Proposes State Education Changes," *Bangor Daily News*, October 28, 2005.

68. Cohen, "Panel Proposes State Education Changes."

11. MAINE IN THE FEDERAL SYSTEM

1. See Elazar, *American Federalism*, 14–25.

2. One of the best books on the political history of Maine in the nineteenth century is Louis C. Hatch, ed., *Maine: A History* (New York: American Historical Society, 1919). Chapter 22 describes the Maine congressional delegation of the 1890s.

3. See William C. Lewis Jr., ed., *Margaret Chase Smith: Declaration of Conscience* (New York: Doubleday, 1972).

4. See David Nevin, *Muskie of Maine* (Brattleboro VT: Book Press, 1972).

5. Material for these paragraphs has been drawn largely from state newspaper files.

6. Statistics in this section have been drawn from *State Policy Data Book, '89* (McConnellsburg PA: Brizius and Foster, 1989), and Kendra A. Hovey and Harold A. Hovey, *CQ's State Fact Finder, 2005: Rankings Across America* (CQ Press: A Division of Congressional Quarterly, Inc., Washington DC, 2005).

7. Bret Shulte, "Covering All the Bases," *U.S. News & World Report*, July 4–11, 2005, 20–21.

8. Claude E. Robinson, "Maine—Political Barometer," *Political Science Quarterly* 47 (June 1932): 161–84.

9. 107 S.Ct. 2211.

10. S. J. Warren Co. v. Maine Board of Environmental Protection 126 S.Ct. 1843 (2006).

11. 102 S.Ct. 49.

12. 113 S.Ct. 1562.

13. 119 S.Ct. 2240.

14. 117 S.Ct. 1590.

15. 100 S.Ct. 2502.

16. 104 S.Ct. 1735.

17. 106 S.Ct. 477.

18. Mark Starr, "Neighbors, Not Friends: A New England Feud," *Newsweek*, June 5, 1989, 27.

19. New Hampshire v. Maine 121 S.Ct. 1808 (2001).

20. Kenneth M. Curtis and John C. Carroll, *Canadian-American Relations: The Promise and the Challenge* (Lexington MA: Lexington Books, 1983), chap. 7.

21. Roger F. Swanson, *Intergovernmental Perspectives on the Canada-U.S. Relationship* (New York: New York University Press, 1978), chap. 6.

22. Wilson Ring, "Border Security No Obstacle When the Fire Bells Sound," *Maine Sunday Telegram*, March 10, 2002.

12. LOCAL GOVERNMENT

1. Kenneth T. Palmer, "Governing Maine: Tensions in the System," in *Changing Maine*, ed. Barringer, 185.

2. Dr. Edward Dow, "The Smothering of Democracy," *Bangor Daily News*, August 17, 1976.

3. Andrew E. Nuquest, *Town Government in Vermont* (Burlington VT: Government Research Center, University of Vermont, 1964), 3–4; Daniel R. Grant and Lloyd B. Omdahl, *State and Local Government in America* (Boston: Allyn and Bacon, 1987), 370–73; Lane W. Lancaster, *Government in Rural America* (Princeton NJ: D. Van Nostrand, 1937).

4. Kenneth L. Roberts, *Local Government in Maine* (Augusta: Maine Municipal Association, 1979).

5. Seven towns disincorporated in the 1980s, becoming plantations or unorganized townships. See Tom Weber, "Deciding a Town's Future," *Bangor Daily News*, Saturday–Sunday, March 19–20, 1988.

6. James Haag, *A Study of Plantation Government in Maine* (Orono: Bureau of Public Administration, University of Maine, 1973).

7. Haag, *Study of Plantation Government in Maine*, 16.

8. See U.S. Census Bureau, 2000 Census (www.census.gov/population/cen2000).

9. David Y. Miller, *The Regional Governing of Metropolitan America* (Boulder CO: Westview Press, 2002), 63–65.

10. Miller, *The Regional Governing of Metropolitan America*.

11. For an excellent empirical study of town meetings, see Frank M. Bryan, *Real Democracy: The New England Town Meeting and How It Works* (Chicago: University of Chicago Press, 2004); Joseph F. Zimmerman, "The New England Town Meeting: Pure Democracy in Action?" in *The Municipal Yearbook* (Washington DC: International City Management Association, 1984), 102–6; and Jane J. Mansbridge, *Beyond Adversary Democracy* (New York NY: Basic Books, 1980).

12. A helpful manual prepared to assist moderators is *Maine Moderator's Manual* (Augusta: Maine Municipal Association, 2005).

13. See G. Thomas Taylor and Kenneth T. Palmer, "Maine," in Dale Krane et al., eds., *Home Rule in America: A Fifty State Handbook* (Washington DC: CQ Press, 2001) 184–86.

14. Thomas Jefferson, quoted in James Haag, *Forms of Municipal Government in the United States and Maine* (Orono: Bureau of Public Administration, University of Maine, 1970), 25–27.

15. James Bryce, *The American Commonwealth*, 2d ed. (London: Macmillan, 1881), 1:591.

16. Zimmerman, "New England Town Meeting," 104–5. Also see Joseph Zimmerman, *The New England Town Meeting* (Westwood CT: Praeger, 1999).

17. Bryan, *Real Democracy*, 280.

18. Bryan, *Real Democracy*, 81.

19. Bryan, *Real Democracy*, 233.

20. Roberts, *Local Government*, 28–30.

21. International City Management Association, *The Municipal Yearbook 1987* (Washington DC: International City Management Association, 2004).

22. Haag, *Forms of Municipal Government*, 21–23; and Taylor and Palmer, "Maine," in *Home Rule in America*, ed. Krane et al., 184–86.

23. For a historical perspective, see Richard S. Childs, *The First Years of the Council-Manager Plan of Municipal Government* (New York: National Municipal League, 1965); Richard J. Stillman, *The Rise of the City Manager: A Public Professional in Local Government* (Albuquerque NM: University of New Mexico Press, 1974), chap. 4; Harold Stone, Don K. Price, and Kathryn H. Stone, *City Manager in the United States* (Chicago: Public Administration Service, 1940).

24. See James Svara, "Dichotomy and Duality: Reconceptualizing the Relationship Between Policy and Administration in Council-Manager Cities," in G. Frederickson, ed., *Ideal And Practice in Council Manager Government* (Washington DC: IMCA, 1994) and see Daniel W. Martin, "The Fading Legacy of Woodrow Wilson," *Public Administration Review* 48 (March–April 1988): 631–35. See also Richard J. Stillman, "Woodrow Wilson and the Study of Administration: A New Look at an Old Essay," *American Political Science Review* 67 (June 1973): 582–88.

25. For a more complete discussion, see Frederickson, *Ideal and Practice in Council Manager Government*; and Deil S. Wright, "The City Manager as a Developmental Administrator," chap. 6 in *Comparative Urban Research*, edited by Robert T. Daland (Beverly Hills CA: Sage Publications, 1969), 203–48. Also see Ronald O. Loveridge, *City Managers in Legislative Politics* (Indianapolis IN: Bobbs-Merrill, 1971).

26. Chuin-Wei Yap, "Residents Approve Shift of Power in Waterville," *Morning Sentinel*, November 9, 2005, and Final Report Explanation and Comparison of Proposed Changes, The Charter Commission of the City of Waterville, 2005.

27. See Haag, *Forms of Municipal Government*, 30–35; and C. Wheeland, "Mayoral Leadership in the Context of Variations in City Structure" in H. George Frederickson, ed., *The Future of Local Government Administration* (Washington DC: IMCA, 2002).

28. Charles Colgan, "Maine's Changing Economy" in *Changing Maine*, ed. Barringer, 34–35.

29. Colgan, "Maine's Changing Economy" in *Changing Maine*, ed. Barringer.

30. Oliver P. Williams and Charles R. Adrian, *Four Cities* (Philadelphia: University of Pennsylvania Press, 1963), 23–32; Oliver Williams, "A Topology for Comparative Local Government," *Midwest Journal of Political Science* 5 (May 1961): 150–64.

31. Clarence N. Stone, Robert K. Whelan, and William J. Murin, "Village Politics," *Urban Policy and Politics in a Bureaucratic Age* (Englewood Cliffs NJ: Prentice Hall, 1986), 78.

32. Michael Zuckerman, *Peaceable Kingdoms* (New York: Alfred A. Knopf, 1970), 169–71.

33. Roscoe C. Martin, *Grass Roots* (University AL: University of Alabama Press, 1957), 40–41.

34. Kenneth T. Palmer, "Governing Maine," in *Changing Maine*, ed. Barringer, 187.

35. Palmer, "Governing Maine," 187–88.

36. Philip Trostel, "Administrationland," *Bangor Daily News*, March 30, 2005.

37. For more detail, see G. Thomas Taylor and David Sullivan, "Local Fiscal Conditions and Management: Results of a Survey of City and Town Managers," paper presented to the Western Social Science Association, Denver, CO, April 1988.

38. "Remaking the Penobscot," *Bangor Daily News*, March 3, 2005.

39. See Robert Dahl, *Who Governs* (New Haven CT: Yale University Press, 1961); Floyd Hunter, *Community Power Structure* (Chapel Hill NC: University of North Carolina Press, 1953).

40. William C. Osborn, *The Paper Plantation: Ralph Nader's Report on the Pulp and Paper Industry in Maine* (New York: Grossman Publishers, 1974).

13. SUBSTATE REGIONALISM AND STATE-LOCAL RELATIONS

1. H. S. Gilbertson, *The County: They "Dark Continent" of American Politics* (New York: National Short Ballot Organization, 1917), 23.

2. John C. Bollens, John R. Bayes, and Kathryn L. Utter, *American County Government* (Beverly Hills CA: Sage Publications, 1969); Hebert S. Duncombe, *Modern County Government* (Washington DC: National Association of Counties, 1977).

3. Edward F. Dow, "County Government Should Go," *Bangor Daily News*, August 20, 1976.

4. Duncombe, *Modern County Government*, 21.

5. Beverly A. Cigler, "Administration in the Modern American County," in *Future of Local Government Administration* ed. Frederickson; Bollens et al.,

American County Government, 98; Duncombe, *Modern County Government*, chap. 2.

6. John B. Forster, "Substate Regionalism in Maine" (Master's thesis, University of Maine, Orono, 1976).

7. Forster, "Substate Regionalism in Maine," chap. 4.

8. See also "Counties," *Intergovernmental Perspective* 17 (Winter 1991): 5–48.

9. Ralph R. Widner, "Foreword," in Duncombe, *Modern County Government*, v.

10. For an extensive account of Maine county government, see Edward F. Dow, *County Government in Maine: Proposals for Reorganization* (Augusta: Maine Legislative Research Committee, October 1952); Maine Intergovernmental Relations Committee, *County Government*, publication no. 103–9, Augusta, 1967.

11. Maine Municipal Association, Bureau of Public Administration, and Greater Portland Council of Governments, *Maine County Government: The Charter Alternative: A Working Paper*, 1981, 4.

12. Maine Municipal Association, *Maine County Government*, 3.

13. "County Government Study," *Legislative Bulletin* (Maine Municipal Association) 12 (January 12, 1990): 1–2.

14. Taylor and Palmer, "Maine," in *Home Rule in America*, 184–88.

15. See Gilbertson, *The County*; M.R.S.A. Title 30, sec. 202.

16. David Piszcz, "More Counties Hiring Administrators," *Republican Journal*, May 2, 2005.

17. Dawn Gagnon, "Bangor City Council Votes to Join Regional Dispatch," *Bangor Daily News*, June 24, 2004.

18. Doug Kessel: "County and State Police Sign Agreement," *Bangor Daily News*, June 24, 2004.

19. Kessel, "County and State Police Sign Agreement," *Bangor Daily News*, June 24, 2004.

20. Mary A. Clancy, "Ambulance Authority OK'd: Washington County Donates $40,000 to Establish Regional Services," *Bangor Daily News*, February 6, 2001.

21. Executive Order No. 6 was issued pursuant to Title 30, Chapter 239, Sections 4501–3 of M.R.S.A.

22. Maine Legislature, Office of Policy and Legal Analysis, "An Overview of Maine's Regional Councils" (unpublished draft, December 1987) 2–6.

23. Deborah Ellingwood, Interview with Dean Bennett, Director of PVCOG, July 28, 2005.

24. Executive Order 6FY 83–84 (November 15, 1983), "State Policy on Regional Councils."

25. 30 M.R.S.A. (1981–86); for a discussion of COGs' evolution nationally, see

Nelson Wikstrom, "Studying Regional Councils: The Quest for Developmental Theory," *Southern Review of Public Administration* 4 (June 1980): 81–98.

26. For a summary of the Portland area's evolution as a council of governments, see James F. Horan and G. Thomas Taylor Jr., *Experiments in Metropolitan Government* (New York: Praeger, 1977), chap. 7.

27. Interview with Dean Bennett, director of PVCOG, July 28, 2005.

28. Evan D. Richert, "Taking a Second Look at Delivering Local Services," *Bangor Daily News*, September 24, 2002.

29. State Planning Office, "Proposal to Reduce the Cost of Government Through Reform of Governmental Relations," 1998.

30. Kenneth T. Palmer, "Governing Maine," in *Changing Maine*, ed. Barringer, 188.

31. Palmer, "Governing Maine," in *Changing Maine*, ed. Barringer, 189.

32. Dawn Gagnon, "PVCOG to Apply for State Regionalization Grant," *Bangor Daily News*, January 13, 2005.

33. Gagnon, "PVCOG to Apply for State Regionalization Grant."

34. Nok-Noi, "Regionalism Grants Awarded to 121 Groups," *Bangor Daily News*, March 16, 2005.

35. Mark Peters, "Baldacci Yields on Regional Services," *Portland Press Herald*, July 31, 2005.

36. *A More Responsive Government: The Final Report to the Governor of the Task Force on Regional and District Organizations* (Augusta: State of Maine Planning Office, 1978).

37. Forster, "Substate Regionalism in Maine," chap. 2.; Edward F. Dow, "Plantations Have Powers Similar to Towns," *Bangor Daily News*, Augusta 19, 1976); also see origins of special districts nationwide in Nancy Burns, *The Formation of American Local Governments: Private Values in Public Institutions* (New York NY: Oxford University Press, 1994).

38. Kenneth T. Roberts, *Local Government in Maine* (Augusta: Maine Municipal Association, 1979), 67–70.

39. Scott Bollens, "Examining the Link between State Policy and the Creation of Local Special Districts," *State and Local Government Review* (Fall 1986): 117–24; John C. Bollens, *Special District Government in the U.S.* (Berkeley and Los Angeles: University of California Press, 1957).

40. See Jo Josephson, "New Regionalism," *Maine Townsman* 53 (August 1991): 12–19.

41. For a favorable review of the application of public choice theory to special districts, see Robert B. Hawkins Jr., *Self Government by District, Myth and Reality* (Stanford CA: Hoover Institution Press, Stanford University, 1976), 47 and 120.

42. Robert B. Hawkins Jr., "Special Districts and Urban Services," in *The Delivery*

of Urban Services, edited by Elinor Ostrom, (Beverly Hills CA: Sage Publications, 1976), 171–87.

43. David Y. Miller, *The Regional Governing of Metropolitan America* (Boulder CO: Westfield Press, 2002), 20–21 and chap. 5.

44. Howard A Dawson and Floyd W. Reeves, *Report of the National Commission on School District Reorganization: Your School District* (Washington DC: Department of Rural Education, National Education Association, 1948), 26–27.

45. Miller, *The Regional Governing of Metropolitan America*, 20–21; Bollens, *Special District Government*, 198.

46. John W. Skeehan, "School District Reorganization in Maine" (Nashville TN: Vanderbilt University, Unpublished EdD dissertation, 1981).

47. For a discussion of the landmark S.A.D. legislation, see Stephen K. Bailey, Richard Frost, Paul E. Marsh, and Robert C. Wood, *Schoolmen and Politics: A Study of State Aid to Education in the Northeast* (Syracuse NY: Syracuse University Press, 1962), 73–81.

48. Associated Press, "Governor to Unveil Plan for School Consolidation," *Bangor Daily News*, January 19, 2004.

49. Associated Press, "Governor to Unveil Plan for School Consolidation."

50. Associated Press, "Governor to Unveil Plan for School Consolidation."

51. Silvernail, "K-12 Education in Maine," 129.

52. *Report of the School Administration Unit Task Force* (Augusta ME: Maine State Board of Education, December 2003).

53. R. Sherwood, *Projected Public School Enrollments* (Augusta ME: Maine State Planning Office, 2001).

54. Ruth-Ellen Cohen, "Report: Consolidated Schools Cheaper," *Bangor Daily News*, July 15, 2005.

55. Cohen, "Report: Consolidated Schools Cheaper."

56. "Losing 251 School Districts," *Bangor Daily News*, December 2, 2005.

57. For more specifics see, Phillip J. Cooper, *Governing by Contracts* (Washington DC: CQ Press, 2002).

58. For more analysis of this survey, see G. Thomas Taylor and David Sullivan, "Local Fiscal Conditions and Management: Results of a Survey of City and Town Manager," paper presented at the Western Social Science Association, Denver, CO, April 1988.

59. "1996 Summer of Interlocal Agreements. Report of Findings," (Maine Development Foundation, Augusta ME, May 1997).

60. See Geoff Herman, "Interlocal Cooperation: Options Which Are Available?" *Maine Townsman* 53 (August 1991): 5–10.

61. Aimee Dolloff, "909 Acres Purchased in Conservation Effort," *Bangor Daily News*, May 26, 2005.

62. *A More Responsive Government*, 35–42.

63. Mark Peters, "Baldacci Yields on Regional Services," *Portland Press Herald*, July 31, 2005.

14. CONCLUDING OBSERVATIONS

1. Phyllis Austin, "Who Runs Maine?" *Maine Times*, July 22, 1988, 8.

Index

In the Politics and Governments of the American States series

Alabama Government and Politics
By James D. Thomas and William H. Stewart

Alaska Politics and Government
By Gerald A. McBeath and Thomas A. Morehouse

Arizona Politics and Government: The Quest for Autonomy, Democracy, and Development
By David R. Berman

Arkansas Politics and Government, second edition
By Diane D. Blair and Jay Barth

Colorado Politics and Government: Governing the Centennial State
By Thomas E. Cronin and Robert D. Loevy

Delaware Politics and Government
By William W. Boyer and Edward C. Ratledge

Hawai'i Politics and Government: An American State in a Pacific World
By Richard C. Pratt with Zachary Smith

Illinois Politics and Government: The Expanding Metropolitan Frontier
By Samuel K. Gove and James D. Nowlan

Kansas Politics and Government: The Clash of Political Cultures
By H. Edward Flentje and Joseph A. Aistrup

Kentucky Politics and Government: Do We Stand United?
By Penny M. Miller

Maine Politics and Government, second edition
By Kenneth T. Palmer, G. Thomas Taylor, Marcus A. LiBrizzi, and Jean E. Lavigne

Michigan Politics and Government: Facing Change in a Complex State
By William P. Browne and Kenneth VerBurg

Minnesota Politics and Government
By Daniel J. Elazar, Virginia Gray, and Wyman Spano

Mississippi Government and Politics: Modernizers versus Traditionalists
By Dale Krane and Stephen D. Shaffer

Nebraska Government and Politics
Edited by Robert D. Miewald

Nevada Politics and Government: Conservatism in an Open Society
By Don W. Driggs and Leonard E. Goodall

New Jersey Politics and Government: Suburban Politics Comes of Age, second edition
By Barbara G. Salmore and Stephen A. Salmore

New York Politics and Government: Competition and Compassion
By Sarah F. Liebschutz, with Robert W. Bailey, Jeffrey M. Stonecash,
Jane Shapiro Zacek, and Joseph F. Zimmerman

North Carolina Government and Politics
By Jack D. Fleer

Oklahoma Politics and Policies: Governing the Sooner State
By David R. Morgan, Robert E. England, and George G. Humphreys

Oregon Politics and Government: Progressives versus Conservative Populists
By Richard A. Clucas, Mark Henkels, and Brent S. Steel

Rhode Island Politics and Government
By Maureen Moakley and Elmer Cornwell

South Carolina Politics and Government
By Cole Blease Graham Jr. and William V. Moore

West Virginia Politics and Government
By Richard A. Brisbin Jr., Robert Jay Dilger, Allan S. Hammock,
and Christopher Z. Mooney

West Virginia Politics and Government, second edition
By Richard A. Brisbin Jr., Robert Jay Dilger, Allan S. Hammock,
and L. Christopher Plein

Wisconsin Politics and Government: America's Laboratory of Democracy
By James K. Conant

To order or obtain more information on these or other University of Nebraska Press
titles, visit www.nebraskapress.unl.edu.